# The Philosophy of
# SOCRATES

Modern Studies in Philosophy is a series of anthologies presenting contemporary interpretations and evaluations of the works of major philosophers. The editors have selected articles designed to show the systematic structure of the thought of these philosophers, and to reveal the relevance of their views to the problems of current interest. These volumes are intended to be contributions to contemporary debates as well as to the history of philosophy; they not only trace the origins of many problems important to modern philosophy, but also introduce major philosophers as interlocutors in current discussions.

Modern Studies in Philosophy is prepared under the general editorship of Amelie Oksenberg Rorty, Livingston College, Rutgers University.

Gregory Vlastos is Stuart Professor of Philosophy at Princeton University. He had previously taught philosophy at Queen's University in Kingston, Ontario, and at Cornell University.

# MODERN STUDIES IN PHILOSOPHY

AMELIE OKSENBERG RORTY, GENERAL EDITOR

# The Philosophy of SOCRATES

## A Collection of Critical Essays

### EDITED BY GREGORY VLASTOS

UNIVERSITY OF NOTRE DAME PRESS
Notre Dame, Indiana 46556

University of Notre Dame Press edition published 1980
First published by Anchor Books, 1971
Published by arrangement with Doubleday and Company
Copyright © 1971 by Gregory Vlastos

**Library of Congress Cataloging in Publication Data**

Vlastos, Gregory, comp.
    The philosophy of Socrates.

    Reprint of the ed. published by Anchor Books,
Garden City, N.Y., in series:  Modern studies in
philosophy.
    Bibliography: p.
    Includes index.
    CONTENTS: Vlastos, G.  Introduction: the
paradox of Socrates.—Lacey, A. R.  Our knowledge
of Socrates.—Dover, K. J.  Socrates in the
Clouds. [etc.]
    1.  Socrates—Addresses, essays, lectures.
I.  Title.
[B317.V55  1980]          183'2          80–308
ISBN 0-268-01540-6
ISBN 0-268-01537-6 pbk.

Manufactured in the United States of America

# CONTENTS

# PREFACE

I am proud to present here five new studies of the philosophy of Socrates by Professors R. E. Allen, M. F. Burnyeat, A. R. Lacey, George Nakhnikian, and A. D. Woozley; and to reprint previously published essays by Professors S. Marc Cohen, Kenneth J. Dover, Richard Robinson, Gerasimos Santas, and James J. Walsh. I am grateful to each of these authors for his collaboration; and to the following publishers for permission to reproduce previously published material: the *Journal of the History of Philosophy* and the *Review of Metaphysics;* also to the Columbia University Press, the Oxford University Press, and Routledge and Kegan Paul.

For works which regrettably could not be included in this volume, the reader is referred to the bibliography at the end. Though some are old, a reassuringly large number fall within the last two decades, attesting the continuing vitality of Socratic studies, which seem to be pursued more intensively today in the English-speaking world than at any previous period of philosophical and classical scholarship.

I wish to make special acknowledgment of the help of Paul H. Drymalski, my editor at Anchor Books, and of his assistant Ronnie Shushan, for her generous cooperation. I am also grateful to Robert Van Gulick, Princeton, '70, who prepared the index and helped in many other ways.

My wife died suddenly while this book was in press. I dedicate my essay to her memory. I do so because of what our love meant to my work. The best insight in this essay—that Socrates' ultimate failure is a failure in love—grew out of what I learned about love from her.

Gregory Vlastos

Princeton, April 1970

# 1. INTRODUCTION: THE PARADOX
## OF SOCRATES

GREGORY VLASTOS

The Socrates of this book is the Platonic Socrates, or, to be more precise, the Socrates of Plato's early dialogues. That this figure is a faithful and imaginative recreation of the historical Socrates is the conclusion of some very reputable scholars, though not of all. It is the conclusion I would be prepared to defend myself. To try to do this in detail would be out of place in this Introduction. All I can do here is to indicate the main consideration which has led me to this conclusion.

There is one, and only one, serious alternative to Plato's Socrates, and that is Xenophon's.[1] The two are irreconcilable at certain points, and these are crucial.

Xenophon's is a Socrates without irony and without paradox. Take these away from Plato's Socrates, and there is nothing left.

This Introduction is adapted from an address to a meeting of the Humanities Association of Canada at Ottawa on June 13, 1957, published in the *Queen's Quarterly* (Kingston, Ontario), Winter 1958. It is reprinted here (with slight changes) with the permission of the editors. I offer no apologies for the style and form of the presentation. For more scholarly treatment of the same topics, though not necessarily of the same theses, the reader need only turn to the rest of this volume. If he should like to see how I try to ground interpretations of Socrates on a close reading of Plato's text, he may consult papers of mine listed in the bibliography at the end of this volume.

[1] Why the Aristophanic portrait, though composed much earlier than either Plato's or Xenophon's, offers no basis for correcting Plato's, will be clear to anyone who goes through Kenneth Dover's masterly study, "Socrates in the *Clouds*," in this volume. As for the Aristotelian references to Socrates (on which see Section V of A. R. Lacey's "Our Knowledge of Socrates" in this volume; for more detailed treatment see Th. Deman, *Le Temoignage d'Aristote sur Socrate* [Paris, 1942]), they tally completely with the portrait of Socrates in Plato's early dialogues, supporting the latter at every point on which it differs from the Aristophanic or the Xenophonean portraits or from both.

Xenophon's Socrates is so persuasive that, "whenever he argued," Xenophon declares, "he gained a greater measure of assent from his hearers than any man I have ever known" (*Memorabilia* 4.6.16). Plato's Socrates is not persuasive at all. He wins every argument, but never manages to win over an opponent. He has to fight every inch of the way for any assent he gets, and gets it, so to speak, at the point of a dagger.

Xenophon's Socrates discourses on theology and theodicy, argues for the existence of a divine mind that has created man and ordered the world for his benefit. Plato's refuses to argue over anything other than man and human affairs.

Plato's Socrates maintains that it is never right to repay evil with evil. He says this in studied defiance of the contrary view, axiomatic in Greek morality from Hesiod down, and fixes here the boundary-line between those who can agree with him on fundamentals and those who can't. Xenophon's Socrates has never heard of the boundary-line. He stands on the wrong side, the popular side, parrots the common opinion that the good man will "excel in rendering benefits to his friends and injuries to his enemies" (*Memorabilia* 2.6.35).

What does this prove? If Plato and Xenophon cannot both be right, why must Plato be right? That his Socrates is incomparably the more interesting of the two figures, in fact the only Socrates worth talking about, proves nothing. We cannot build history on wish-fulfillment. Fortunately there is another consideration that proves a great deal. It is that Plato accounts, while Xenophon does not, for facts affirmed by both and also attested by others. For example: that Critias and Alcibiades had been companions of Socrates; or again: that Socrates was indicted and condemned on the charge of not believing in the gods of the state and of corrupting its youth. Xenophon's portrait will not square with either of these. Not with the first, for his Socrates could not have attracted men like Critias and Alcibiades, haughty aristocrats both of them, and as brilliant intellectually as they were morally unprincipled. Xenophon's Socrates, pious reciter of moral commonplaces, would have elicited nothing but a sneer from Critias and a yawn from Alcibiades, while Plato's Socrates is just the man who could have gotten under their skin. As for the second, Plato, and he alone, gives us a Socrates who could have plausibly been indicted for subversion of faith and morals. Xenophon's account of Socrates, apologetic from beginning to end, refutes itself: had the facts been as he tells them, the indictment would not have been made in the first place.

How far can we then trust Plato? From the fact that he was right on some things it does not follow, certainly, that he was right in all his information on Socrates, or even on all its essential points. But we do have a check.[2] Plato's *Apology* has for its *mise en scène* an all-too-public occasion. The jury alone numbered 501 Athenians. And since the town was so gregarious and Socrates a notorious public character, there would have been many more in the audience. So when Plato was writing the *Apology*, he knew that hundreds of those who might read the speech he puts into the mouth of Socrates had heard the historic original. And since his purpose in writing it was to clear his master's name and to indict his judges, it would have been most inept to make Socrates talk out of character. How could Plato be saying to his fellow citizens, 'This is the man you murdered. Look at him. Listen to him,'[3] and point to a figment of his own imagining? This is my chief reason for accepting the *Apology* as a reliable recreation of the thought and character of the man Plato knew so well. Here, as before, I speak of *recreation*, not reportage. The *Apology* was probably written several years after the event. This, and Plato's genius, assures us that it was not journalism, but art. Though the emotion with which Plato had listened when life and death hung on his master's words must have branded those words into

[2] In a fuller discussion I would have added other checks, notably Aristotle's testimony.

[3] Here and throughout this introduction I use single quotation marks to indicate an *imaginary* quotation, reserving regular quotation marks for citations from the texts.

his mind, still, that emotion recollected in tranquillity, those remembrances recast in the imagination, would make a new speech out of the old materials, so that those who read it would recognize instantly the man they had known without having to scan their own memory and ask, 'Did he open with that remark? Did he really use that example?' or any such question. This is all I claim for the veracity of the *Apology*. And if this is conceded, the problem of our sources is solved in principle. For we may then use the *Apology* as a touchstone of the like veracity of the thought and character of Socrates depicted in Plato's other early dialogues. And when we do that, what do we find?

We find a man who is all paradox. Other philosophers have talked *about* paradox. Socrates did not. The paradox in Socrates is Socrates. But unlike later paradoxes, Scandinavian, German, and latterly even Gallic, this Hellenic paradox is not meant to defeat, but to incite, the human reason. At least a part of it can be made quite lucid, and this is what I shall attempt in the main part of this essay. For this purpose I must point out the roles whose apparently incongruous junction produces paradox:

In the *Apology* (29D–E) Socrates gives this account of his lifework:

> So long as I breathe and have the strength to do it, I will not cease philosophizing, exhorting you, indicting whichever of you I happen to meet, telling him in my customary way:
> Esteemed friend, citizen of Athens, the greatest city in the world, so outstanding in both intelligence and power, aren't you ashamed to care so much to make all the money you can, and to advance your reputation and prestige—while for truth and wisdom and the improvement of your soul you have no care or worry?

This is the Socrates Heinrich Maier had in mind when he spoke of "the Socratic gospel."[4] If this makes us think

[4] *Sokrates* (Tuebingen, 1913), pp. 296 ff.

of the Christian gospel, the evocation is not inappropriate at this point. Socrates could have taken over verbatim the great question of our gospels, "What shall it profit a man, if he gain the whole world, and lose his own soul?"

The only gloss I need add here is a caution that one should not be misled by the other-worldly associations with which the word "soul" is loaded in our own tradition and which were nearly as heavy in the Greek. If there is anything new in the way Socrates uses the word "soul" it is that he quietly narrows down its meaning to something whose supernatural origin or destiny, if any, is indeterminate, and whose physical or metaphysical structure, if any, is also indeterminate, so that both theological and anti-theological, mystical and physicalistic doctrines of the soul become inconsequential. His is a gospel without dogma. You may hold any one of a great variety of beliefs about the soul, or none of them, without either gaining or losing any essential part of what Socrates wants you to think about and care for when he urges you to "care for your soul." In particular you don't have to believe in the immortality of the soul. Socrates himself does believe in it,[5] but for this faith he has no argument. In the *Apology* he muses on how pleasant it would be *if* it were true, the soul carrying along to Hades all its intellectual equipment, so it could carry on Socratic arguments with no more fear of interruption. Such a life, he says, would make him "unspeakably happy." But he does not say this is a good reason for believing in it, or that there is some other good reason. He says nothing to exclude the alternative he mentions: total extinction of consciousness; death could mean just this, and if it did, there would be nothing in it to frighten a good man, or dissuade him from the "care of the soul." The soul is as worth caring for if it were to last just twenty-four more hours, as if it were to outlast eternity. If you have just one more day to live, and can expect nothing but a blank after that, Socrates feels that you would still have all the reason you need for improving your soul; you

[5] The question is left open in the *Apology*. But see *Cr.* 54 B–C.

have yourself to live with that one day, so why live with
a worse self, if you could live with a better one instead?

How then is the soul improved?—Morally, by right action; intellectually, by right thinking; the two being
strictly complementary, so that you can't have one without the other and, if you do have either you will be sure
to have the other. This, of course, is his famous doctrine,
that 'virtue is knowledge,' which means two things:

First, that there can be no virtue without knowledge.
This is what gives such intensity to Socrates' arguments,
such urgency to his quests for definition. He makes you
feel that the failure to sustain a thesis or find a definition
is not just an intellectual defeat, but a moral disaster. At
the end of the *Euthyphro* that gentleman is as good as
told that his failure to make good his confident claim to
know "exactly" (5A, 15D) what piety is, means not just
that he is intellectually hard up, but that he is morally
bankrupt. I am stating what Socrates believes in as extreme a form as Plato allows us to see it. One of the many
things for which we may be grateful to Plato is that, as
Boswell said of his own treatment of Johnson, he "did
not make a cat out of his tiger." Unlike Xenophon's cat,
Plato's tiger stands for the savage doctrine that if you
cannot pass the stiff Socratic tests for knowledge you
cannot be a good man.

No less extreme is the mate to this doctrine, that if you
do have this kind of knowledge, you cannot fail to *be*
good and *act* as a good man should, in the face of any
emotional stress or strain. The things which break the
resolution of others, which seduce or panic men to act
in an unguarded moment contrary to their best insights
—"rage, pleasure, pain, love, fear" (*Prt.* 352B)—any one
of them, or all of them in combination, will have no
power over the man who has Socratic knowledge. He
will walk through life invulnerable, sheathed in knowledge as in a magic armor which no blow from the external world can crack or even dent. No saint has ever
claimed more for the power of faith over the passions
than does Socrates for the power of knowledge.

So here is one side of Socrates. He has an evangel to proclaim, a great truth to teach: Our soul is the only thing in us worth saving, and there is only one way to save it: to acquire knowledge.

What would you expect of such a man? To propagate his message, to disseminate the knowledge which is itself the elixir of life. Is this what he does? How *could* he, if, as he says repeatedly in the dialogues, he does not have that knowledge? Plato makes him say this not only in the informality of private conversations but also in that most formal speech of all, the *Apology.* If he is wiser than others, Socrates there declares (21D), it is only because he does not *think* he has the knowledge which others think they have but haven't.[6]

Could this be true? If it were, then on his own teaching, he too would be one of the damned. But no man ever breathed greater assurance that his feet were planted firmly on the path of right. He never voices a doubt of the moral rightness of any of his acts or decisions, never betrays a sense of sin. He goes to his death confident that "no evil thing can happen to a good man" (*Apology* 41D)—that "good man" is himself. Can this be the same man who believes that no one can be good without knowledge, and that he has no knowledge?

But there is more to the paradox. It is not merely that Socrates *says* things—as in his disclaimer of moral knowledge—which contradict the role of a preacher and teacher of the care of the soul, but that he *acts* in ways which do not seem to fit this role. Socrates' characteristic activity is the *elenchus,* literally, "the refutation." You say *A,* and he shows you that *A* implies *B,* and *B* implies *C,* and then he asks, 'But didn't you say *D* before? And doesn't *C* contradict *D?*' And there he leaves you with your shipwrecked argument, without so much as telling you what part of it, if any, might yet be salvaged. His tactics seem unfriendly from the start. Instead

---

[6] And see especially *Grg.* 506A, 508E–509A.

of trying to pilot you around the rocks, he picks one
under water a long way ahead where you would never
suspect it and then makes sure you get all the wind you
need to run full-sail into it and smash your keel upon it.
This sort of thing happens so often in Plato's Socratic
dialogues and is so perplexing, that one can't help won-
dering whether the historical Socrates could have been
really like that. I have had to ask myself more than once
whether this pitiless critic, this heartless intellectual, this
man who throws away his chances to preach a gospel
so he may push an argument instead, is not, after all,
only a Platonic projection, and tells us more about the
youthful Plato than about the aged Socrates. As often as
this doubt has reared its head in my mind, I have
chopped it down by going back to the *Apology*. Here,
where Socrates' evangelistic mission is stated so emphati-
cally, it is most distinctly implied that his customary
conduct did not fit the evangelist's role. I am thinking, of
course, of that story[7] about the supposed oracle of Delphi that no one was wiser than Socrates; this supposedly
started Socrates on his search for someone wiser than
himself, trying everyone who had the reputation for wisdom, first the statesmen, then the poets, then, scraping
the bottom of the barrel, even the artisans, only to find
that the wisdom of all these people, from top to bottom,
was worse than zero, a minus quantity. What to make
of this whole story is itself a puzzle for the scholar, and
I will not try to crack it here. But whatever the Pythian
priestess may or may not have said in the first place, and
whatever Socrates may or may not have thought about
whatever she did say, the one thing which is certain is
this: the story frames a portrait of Socrates whose day-in,
day-out role was known to his fellow-citizens as that of
a destructive critic, whose behavior looked from the outside like that of a man who saw nothing in his interlocutors but balloons of pretended knowledge and was bent
on nothing else but to puncture them. So the *Apology*

[7] *Ap.* 20E–21A.

confirms the conduct which presents our paradox. It tells of a Socrates who says the care of the soul is the most important thing in the world, and that his mission in life is to get others to see this. And yet it also as good as says that if you were going down the Agora and saw a crowd around Socrates you could take three to one bets that Socrates would not be saying anything about the improvement of the soul, nor acting as though he cared a straw for the improvement of his interlocutor's soul, but would be simply arguing with him, forcing him into one corner after another, until it became plain to all the bystanders, if not the man himself, that his initial claim to know this or that was ridiculously false.

Here then is our paradox. But it is no use looking for the answer until we have taken into account still another side to Socrates: the role of the *searcher*. "Don't think," he says to the great sophist Protagoras, "that I have any other interest in arguing with you, but that of clearing up my own problems as they arise" (*Prt.* 348C). Or again, when that nasty intellectual, Critias, accuses him of just trying to refute him instead of advancing the argument, Socrates replies:

> And what if I am? How can you think that I have any other interest in refuting you, but what I should have in *searching myself*, fearing lest I might fool myself, thinking I know something, when I don't know (*Chrm.* 166C–D)?

Moments of self-revelation like these are rare in the dialogues. Socrates is not a character out of Chekhov introspecting moodily on the public stage. He is a man whose face is a mask, whose every word is deliberate, and seems calculated to conceal more than to reveal. One gets so used to this artful exterior, that one is left unprepared for moments like these, and is apt to discount them as irony. I speak for myself. This is the way I used to take them. And so long as I did, I could find no way through the paradox of which I have been speaking. But then it

occurred to me that in the statements I have just cited
Socrates means to be taken at his word, and in this one
too:

> Critias, you act as though I professed to know the answers
> to the questions I ask you, and could give them to you if
> I wished. It isn't so. I inquire with you . . . because I
> don't myself have knowledge (*Chrm.* 165D).

Can he really mean this? He can, if in such passages
he is using "knowledge" in a sense in which the claim to
know something implies the conviction that any further
investigation of its truth would be superfluous. This is the
sense in which the word "knowledge" is used in formal
contexts by earlier philosophers, and nothing gives us a
better sense of the dogmatic certainty implied by their
use of it than the fact that one of them, Parmenides,
presented his doctrine in the guise of a divine revelation.
In doing this Parmenides did not mean in the least that
the truth of his philosophy must be taken on faith. He
presented his system as a purely rational deductive argument which made no appeal to anything except the understanding. What he meant rather is that the conclusions of this argument have the same certainty as that
which the devotees of mystic cults would attach to the
poems of Orpheus or of some other divinely inspired
lore. This, I suggest, is the conception of wisdom and
knowledge Socrates has in mind in those contexts where
he disclaims it. When he renounces "knowledge" he is
telling us that the question of the truth of anything *he*
believes can always be sensibly re-opened; that any conviction he has stands ready to be re-examined in the
company of any sincere person who will raise the question and join him in the investigation.
Consider his great proposition that it is never right to
harm the enemy. Would you not think that if there is
anything Socrates feels he *knows*, this is it; else how
could he have taken his stand on it, declaring that for
those who believe it and those who do not "there can

be no common mind, but they can only despise each other when they confront each other's counsels" (*Crt.* 49D)? But even this he is prepared to re-examine. He continues to Crito:

> So consider very carefully whether you too are on my side and share my conviction, so we can start from this: that neither doing nor returning wrong nor defending oneself against evil by returning the evil is ever right? Or do you dissent and part company with me here? For myself this is what I have long believed and still do. But if you think differently, go ahead, explain, show me (49D–E).

You would think this hardly the time and place to re-open this issue, but Socrates is quite willing. And I suggest that he is always willing; that he goes into every discussion in just this frame of mind. Previous reflection has led him to many conclusions, and he does not put them out of his mind when jumping into a new argument. There they all are, and not in vague or jumbled up form, but in a clear map, on which he constantly relies to figure out, many moves in advance, the direction in which he would like to press an argument. But clear as they are, they are not finally decided; everyone of them is open to review in the present argument, where the very same kind of process which led to the original conclusion *could* unsettle what an earlier argument may have settled prematurely, on incomplete survey of relevant premises, or by faulty deductions. Nor is it only a matter of re-examining previously reached conclusions; it is no less a matter of hoping for new insights which may crop up right in this next argument and give the answer to some hitherto unanswered problem. And if this is the case, Socrates is not just the fighter he appears to be on the surface, intent on vindicating predetermined results by winning just one more victory in an ordeal by combat. He is the investigator, testing his own ideas in the course of testing those of his interlocutor, watching the argument with genuine curiosity to see whether it

will really come out where it should if the results of
previous arguments were sound, and scanning the land-
scape as he goes along, looking for some new feature
he failed to notice before.

Does this show a way out of our paradox? I think it
does. It puts in a new light the roles that seemed so hard
to reconcile before. Socrates the *preacher* turns out to
be a man who wants others to find out his gospel so far
as possible by themselves and for themselves. Socrates
the *teacher* now appears as the man who has not just
certain conclusions to impart to others, but a *method of
investigation*—the method by which he reached these
results in the first place, and which is even more important than the results, for it is the means of testing, revising, and going beyond them. Socrates the *critic* is much
more than a mere critic, for he exhibits his method by
putting it to work; even if not a single positive result
were to come out of it in this or that argument, the
method itself would have been demonstrated, and those
who saw how it works could put it to work for themselves to reach more positive conclusions. Even Socrates
the *professed* agnostic becomes more intelligible. His 'I
don't know' is a conscientious objection to the notion
that the conclusions of any discussion are secure against
further testing by further discussion. Seen in this way,
Socrates no longer seems a bundle of incompatible roles
precariously tied together by irony. He seems one man,
unified in his diverse activities by the fact that in all of
them he remains the searcher, always pursuing his own
search and seeking fellow-seekers.

May I offer a particular illustration, for I would not
like to leave this solution hanging in generality. I take
the *Euthyphro*, though almost any one of Plato's early
dialogues would do. On your first reading of this dialogue
you come to the end with a sense of disappointment that
after all this winding and unwinding of argument no
positive result seems to be reached, and Socrates is ready,
as he says, "to begin all over again" with the original

question, "What is piety?" As you watch Euthyphro hurry off, this is what you feel like telling Socrates: 'I don't believe you really care for that man's soul, for if you did, how could you have let him go with his head still stuffed with his superstitions? You know that the pollution he fears has nothing to do with the only piety you think worth talking about, the kind that will improve what *you* call the soul. Why then not tell him this, and show him the difference between religion and magic?'

But if you go back and re-read the dialogue more carefully, you can figure out Socrates' reply:

"That is what I did try to show him. But I wanted him to find it out for himself. For this purpose it would have been no use telling him his notion of piety was all wrong, which would not even have been true. It was *not* all wrong, but a jumble of right and wrong beliefs, and my job was to help him see that he could not hold both sets at once. If he could see this, he would become his own critic, his own teacher, even his own preacher, for if this man could see the implications of some things he already believes, I would not have to preach to him that he should care for his soul as it should be cared for. He would be doing his own preaching to himself."

Socrates might then add that though he failed in this objective, the fault was not entirely his own. For sheer sluggishness of intellect it would be hard to beat this complacent fanatic whom Plato ironically calls *Euthyphro*, "Straight-thinker." How straight he thinks on matters of religion we may judge by his response when Socrates shows him that, on his view, religion is a business-relationship between men and gods, a barter of divine favors for human offerings. Faced with this consequence our Mr. Straight-thinker sees nothing positively wrong with it: "Yes, you may call it (piety) a commercial art, if you like" (14E). Yet even with such unpromising material on his hands, Socrates tries hard, and makes good headway, coming at one point within a stone's throw of success: He gets Euthyphro to admit that piety cannot be defined as "that which is pleasing to the gods,"

i.e., as obedience to any demand the gods might happen
to make on men; the demand must itself be *just,* and piety must consist of discharging services we *owe* the gods.
Socrates then pushes Euthyphro to say what sort of services these might be. Why do the gods *need* our services,
he presses; what is that "wonderful work" (13E) the
gods can only achieve through our own cooperating efforts? I suppose it was too much to expect Euthyphro
to see the answer once Socrates has led him so far, and
say to himself, in line with Socrates' reasoning, with all
of which he agrees: since the gods are great and powerful past all imagining, they surely don't need our services
to improve *their* estate; and since they are also good and
benevolent, they do desire what is best for us—and what
can this be, but the improvement of our souls? Isn't this
then the object of piety, this the discharge of the highest
obligation we owe the gods? Socrates evidently thought
this was *not* too much to hope that Euthyphro would
have seen for himself on the strength of the Socratic
prodding. When Euthyphro went hopelessly off the track
in a wordy tangent, Socrates remarked:

> Certainly, Euthyphro, you could have answered my main
> question in far fewer words, if you had wished. . . . Just
> now when you were on the very edge of telling me what
> I want to know, you turned aside (14B–C).

Clearly Socrates has *not* been playing a cat-and-mouse
game with Euthyphro in this dialogue, putting questions to him only to pounce on the answers and claw
them to pieces. He has been doing his best to lead
Euthyphro to the point where he could see for himself
the right answer. What he positively refuses to do is to
*tell* Euthyphro this answer, and this, not because he
does not think Euthyphro's soul worth the saving, but
because he believes there is only one way to save it and
that Euthyphro himself must do the job by finding this
one right way, so that he too becomes a searcher.
Whether or not you think Socrates was right in this, I

trust you will agree with me that he was at least consistent.

But *was* Socrates right? On some fundamental points I think him wrong.

I do not think the Socratic way is the only way to save a man's soul. What Socrates called "knowledge" he thought both necessary and sufficient for moral goodness. I think it neither. Not necessary, for the bravest men I ever met would surely have flunked the Socratic examination on courage. Why this should be so would take long to unravel, and I have no confidence I could do it successfully. But I don't need to for the point at issue. For this I need only stick to the fact: that a man can have great courage, yet make a fool of himself when he opens his mouth to explain what it is that he has. I am not saying that it would not be a fine thing if he could talk better, and know more. I am not depreciating Socratic knowledge. I am only saying it is not necessary for what Socrates did think it necessary. And I would also say that it is not sufficient. For this I need no better example than that famous saying of his, in the *Apology*, (29A–B) that the fear of death is the pretense of wisdom. 'Why do we fear death?—Because we think we know it is a great evil. But do we *know* this?—No. We don't know anything about death. For all we know to the contrary, it might be a great good.' So argues Socrates, and implies confidently that if you saw all this, your fear of death would vanish. Knowledge—in this case, knowledge of your ignorance of what death is and what, if anything, comes after it—would dissipate your fear. You couldn't fear death or anything else unless you knew it to be evil. But why couldn't you? 'Because it would be absurd,' Socrates would say. But could it not be absurd, and exist just the same? Aunt Rosie is afraid of mice, but she knows quite well that a mouse can do her no great harm. She knows she runs a far graver risk to life and limb when she drives her car down Main Street, but she is not a bit afraid of that, while she is terrified of mice. This is absurd, but it happens; and her knowing that it is absurd does not prevent it from happening either, but only adds shame and guilt to fear. This is not evidence of a high order; it is just a *fact* that does not square with Socrates' theory.

But Socratic knowledge has all too little interest in facts. That is the main trouble with it. Socrates' model for knowledge was what we would call deductive knowledge now-a-days. The knowledge he sought, and with such marked success, is that which consists in arranging whatever information one has in a luminous, perspicuous pattern, so one can see at a glance where run the bright lines of implication and where the dark ones of contradiction. But of the other way of knowing, the empirical way, Socrates had little understanding, and he paid for his ignorance by conceit of knowledge, failing to understand the limitations of his knowledge of fact generally, and of the fact of knowledge in particular. Had he so much as felt the need of investigating knowledge itself as a fact in human nature, to determine just exactly what, as a matter of fact, happens to a man when he has or hasn't knowledge, Socrates might have come to see that even his own dauntless courage in the face of death he owed not to knowledge but to something else, more akin to religious faith.

But to explain Socrates' failure merely in this way would be itself to concede more to Socrates' theory than the facts allow, for it would be to explain it as only a failure of knowledge. I will put all my cards on the table and say that behind this lay a failure of love. In saying this I am not taking over-seriously the prickly exterior and the pugilist's postures. I have already argued that he does care for the souls of his fellows. But the care is limited and conditional. If men's souls are to be saved, they must be saved his way. And when he sees they cannot, he watches them go down the road to perdition with regret but without anguish. Jesus wept for Jerusalem. Socrates warns Athens, scolds, exhorts it, condemns it. But he has no tears for it. One wonders if Plato, who raged against Athens, did not love it more in his rage and hate than ever did Socrates in his sad and good-tempered rebukes. One feels there is a last zone of frigidity in the soul of the great erotic; had he loved his fellows more, he could hardly have laid on them the burdens of his "despotic logic,"[8] impossible to be borne.

Having said all this, let me now add that grave as these complaints are, they do not undermine his greatness. Let me try to say why, in spite of this or a longer bill of particulars which might be drawn against him, he is still great.

Let me start where I just left off: his character. To be different in some way or other from everyone else one need not be a great man; one need only be a man. But to find in this difference the material for a personal creation wherewith to enrich the common life of humanity —this is a difficult achievement for anyone, and was exceptionally so for Socrates, for his initial endowment was so discouraging: physical ugliness. This he had to live with among a people who adored beauty. Socrates solved the problem classical antiquity would have judged insoluble. In the world of the fine arts—plastic, graphic, auditory—classical antiquity just took it for granted that if the product is to be fine the materials must be beautiful to begin with. Socrates proved this was not so in the medium of personal life. He showed how there at least art could fashion beauty out of ugliness. He did this by stylizing his deformity, making an abstract mask out of it, and so detaching himself from that, while he could never put it off, he could always laugh at it as from a great distance with his mind. And as a good artist does not drop a theme once he gets hold of it, but puts it to new and surprising uses, so Socrates with this theme of ugliness as a comic mask. He made his words common and vulgar, like his face. He

---

[8] I borrow here from Nietzsche, who called Socrates "this despotic logician" (*Birth of Tragedy*, Section XIV; translation by Francis Golffing, New York, 1956, p. 90).

said he could not make fine speeches, or even understand the fine ones others made. His memory, he said, was short, he could only take things in a sentence or two at a time; nor could his wits move fast, so everything must be explained to him in painfully slow, dragging steps. His manners, too, he said, were poor; he must be forgiven if he could not be as polite in argument as other men. With this cumulative renunciation of ornaments of culture and graces of mind he built his character. Its surface traits, uncouth, ludicrous to the casual eye, were so severely functional, so perfectly adapted to the work he had to do, that men with the keenest eye for beauty, men like Alcibiades and Plato, found more of it in Socrates than in anyone they had ever known. The test of art is: Will it last? And for this kind of art: Will it last in adversity? Socrates' art passed this test. The self behind the mask was never shown up as just another mask. He was the same before his judges as he had been in the market-place. When he took the poison from the hands of the executioner there was "no change of colour or expression on his face" (*Phd.* 117B).

Second, Socrates was great as a reformer of morality: not a social reformer, but a reformer of the conscience which in the very long run has power to make or break social institutions. A poet like Aristophanes sensed this, without really understanding it; so did Callicles in the *Gorgias* (481C), when he asked Socrates:

> If you're serious, and what you say is really true, won't human life have to be turned completely upside down?

I trust that even some of the incidental illustrations I have used here will document the truth of this rhetorical question. Think of the answer to 'What is piety?' Socrates is fishing for in the *Euthyphro*. How could Athenian piety remain the same, or how could ours for that matter, if Socrates is right on this, if man's obligation to the gods is one he would have to his own self, even if there were no gods: to improve his own soul? Again, how many practices or sentiments in Socrates' world or ours would remain intact if his conviction that it is never right to return evil for evil were taken seriously as really true?

There is another change Socrates wrought in the texture of the moral conscience, one which is scarcely mentioned in the books about him. I cannot hope to remedy this deficiency here. But I can at least remind you that Greek morality still remained to a surprising extent a class-morality. The conviction that high-grade moral virtue was possible only for a man who was well born or, at least, moderately well off, ran wide and deep. The disinheritance of a majority of the urban population—not only the slaves, but the free-born manual workers—from the life of virtue is a reasoned belief in Aristotle. Even that radical remolder of the social fabric, Plato, did not reject the dogma; he only sublimated it. Socrates did reject it. He expunged it from the universe of moral discourse when he made the improvement of the soul as mandatory, and as possible, for the manual worker as for the gentleman of leisure, when he redefined all the virtues, and virtue itself, in such a way as to make of them, not class attributes, but human qualities.

But even this is not his greatest contribution. If my solution of the paradox of Socrates is correct, then certainly Socrates himself would have attached far more importance to his method of moral inquiry than to any of its results. If we could get past the palaver of his mock-humility and make him say in simple honesty what he thought was his greatest achievement he would certainly have put that method far above anything else. I cannot now argue further for this point which is as crucial to my estimate of Socrates' greatness as it was to the resolution of the paradox. I can only point out that if what I am now contending were not true, that paradox would not have been there. Had he valued the results of his method above the method itself, he would have been just a preacher and teacher of moral truths, not also the professed agnostic, the tireless critic, examiner and re-examiner of himself and of others; in other words, he would not have been the Socrates of the Platonic dialogues and of this book.]

Why rank that method among the great achievements of humanity? Because it makes moral inquiry a common human enterprise, open to every man. Its practice calls for no adherence to a philosophical system, or mastery of a specialized technique, or acquisition of a technical vocabulary. It calls for common sense and common speech. And this is as it should be, for how man should live is every man's business, and the role of the specialist and the expert should be only to offer guidance and criticism, to inform and clarify the judgment of the layman, leaving the final decision up to him. But while the Socratic method makes moral inquiry open to everyone, it makes it easy for no one. It calls not only for the highest degree of mental alertness of which anyone is capable, but also for moral qualities of a high order: sincerity, humility, courage. Socrates expects you to say what you really believe about the way *man* should live; which implies, among other things, about the way *you* should live. His method will not work if the opinion you give him is just *an* opinion; it must be *your* opinion: the one you stand ready to live by, so that if that opinion should be refuted, your own life or a part of it will be indicted or discredited, shown up to be a muddle, premised on a confusion or a contradiction. To get into the argument when you realize that this is the price you have to pay for it—that in the course of it your ego may experience the unpleasant sensation of a bloody nose—takes courage. To search for moral truth that may prove your own life wrong takes humility that is not afraid of humiliation. These are the qualities Socrates himself brings to the argument, and it is not entirely clear that he realizes how essential they are to protect it against the possibility that its dialectic, however rigorous, would merely grind out, as it could with impeccable logic, wild conclusions from irresponsible premises.

But is there not still a residual risk, you may ask, in making the Socratic method the arbiter of moral truth,

inviting thereby every man to take, on its terms, a place
in the supreme court which judges questions of morality?
Certainly there is a risk, and a grave one. For though the
method has some built-in protection against moral irre-
sponsibility—the one I have just mentioned—it offers no
guarantee whatever that it will always lead to truth. On
this Socrates himself, if the foregoing interpretation of
his agnosticism was correct, is absolutely clear. His 'I
don't know' honestly means 'I could be mistaken in results reached by this method.' And if Socrates could be
mistaken, how much more so Tom, Dick, and Harry.
Why then open it to them? Socrates' answer is clear:
Because each of them is a man, and "the unexamined
life is not worth living by man" (*Apology* 38A). I could
not go so far as he did at this point. I believe that many
kinds of life are worth living by man. But I do believe
that the best of all is the one in which every man does
his own examining. I have dissented earlier from Socrates' assumption that his is the only way by which any
man's soul can be saved. But I can still give whole-
hearted assent to Socrates' vision of man as a mature,
responsible being, claiming to the fullest extent his freedom to make his own choice between right and wrong,
not only in action, but in judgment. I do not see how
man can reach the full stature of his manhood unless he
claims the right to make his own personal judgments on
morality; and if he is to claim this right, he must accept
the implied chance of misjudgment as a calculated risk.
This is the price he must pay for being free. I am using
now very un-Socratic language, and I will compound
the offense by adding that this vision of human freedom,
of which the Socratic method is an expression, could not
be appropriately described as knowledge, and that the
best name for it is faith. That the man who had this faith
to a supreme degree should have mistaken it for knowledge, is yet another part of the paradox of Socrates.

# 2. OUR KNOWLEDGE OF SOCRATES

A. R. LACEY

I

Two of the reasonably certain facts about Socrates are
that he was executed by the state in 399 B.C. at the age
of seventy and that he did not write anything.[1] Our picture of him is therefore entirely dependent on others:
on those of his own generation who lived and thought
alongside him; on those of the next generation who knew
him in their early years but wrote about him largely if
not entirely after his death, writing from memory or borrowing from each other or elaborating a creation of their
own; and on those born after his death, but who had
access to vastly more secondhand material than we have
ourselves and were perhaps free from at least some of
the polemical motives that beset their predecessors. The
need to decide among these various and conflicting
sources immediately confronts us with a problem: do we
judge our conception of Socrates by what we find in the
sources or do we judge the sources by what we think we
already know about Socrates? It is the incoherence that
results from uncritically doing the former, together with
the constant temptation to engage prematurely in the
latter, that creates the Socratic problem as we have it.

One thing at least seems clear: if two sources disagree,
or one source in different places, at least one must be

This is a previously unpublished essay, written especially for
this volume.

[1] Plutarch in DK Vol. I, pp. 104–5; cf. Diog. Laert. 1.16. The
isolated passage of Epictetus (2.1.32), implying that he not only
wrote but wrote voluminously, can hardly stand against the silence
of the rest of antiquity, and must surely refer by a misunderstanding to the writings *about* Socrates. Cf. phrases like οἱ τοῦ Σωκράτους
λόγοι (Arist., *Pol.* 1265A11).

wrong. Even here, though, the disagreement may be only apparent, or may refer to different times in Socrates' life. But can we assume that when they agree they must be right? Surely what Plato and Xenophon both say, or what Aristotle confirms one of them in saying, must be right? Unfortunately no. We have no guarantee that the confirmer is not relying on the confirmed for his information, whether on the passage in question or on another, or that both of them are not relying on some common and perhaps vanished source. Sometimes, in fact, it may even be that disagreement puts us in a stronger position, since, though at least one source must be wrong, it is the more likely that one is right in that the situation does not fall under some generally accepted convention governing Socratic discourses.

But if borrowing is established, does this render the borrower's testimony worthless? If Xenophon, for instance, copies something from Plato, at least it helps us to see what he wanted to bring out, and may confirm Plato as a source to the extent that Xenophon was aiming at historical accuracy and thought the passage plausible (though we must avoid begging the question by using Xenophon to confirm Plato while denying that Xenophon had any independent knowledge: cf. Magalhaes-Vilhena's strictures on Burnet and Taylor at *Le Problème de Socrate*, p. 218). In the case of Aristotle, since all his information must be borrowed, the question is simply how far he uses sources already known to us. But even when he does, or even if he is only making an inference, we must not forget that, despite his foibles as a historian, Aristotle is applying a first-rate critical intelligence to a vast mass of knowledge drawn from all sorts of sources, and his borrowings or inferences are performed in the light of this. We must take account of not only *what* he borrowed but the fact *that* he borrowed as he did.

What we are primarily interested in about Socrates is his philosophy, and then the personality that accompanied it. But philosophies and personalities have a cer-

tain indefiniteness about them that sometimes makes it
hard to tell when two sources are consistent and when
they are not. Detailed biographical facts often are, or
seem, easier to come to grips with. Did Socrates marry the
daughter or grand-daughter of Aristides as well as Xan-
thippe?[2] Was he chairman of the Council or just an ordinary member when he refused to vote in favour of an
illegal procedure at the trial of the Arginusae generals?[3]
Such questions are of minor interest in themselves, but can
sometimes be used to throw light on the practices and
relationships of our sources. The latter, for instance, has
been used to show that Xenophon cannot be taking all
his information about Socrates from Plato, but yet was
using Plato, because the same piece of information appears once correctly (*Hell.* 1.7.14–15), but elsewhere
(*Mem.* I 1.18, IV 4.2) in a form suggesting confusion
derived from a passage in Plato.[4] Although such passages
tell us something of the relationships between our
sources, they must be used with caution when it comes
to judging the practices of our sources themselves. Just
as these biographical details are of minor interest to us,
so they may also have been to ancient writers who were
primarily concerned with the philosophy or general personality of Socrates. Thus, accuracy concerning these details would be of less account.

Add to these difficulties the lack of a tradition of objective historical writing at the time and it is not surprising that some scholars[5] have thrown up their hands and
taken "Socrates" to be a mere literary creation by a
group of writers at the beginning of the fourth century,
the real man, if there ever was one, being lost in the

[2] For the evidence see T. Deman, *Le Témoignage d'Aristote sur
Socrate*, p. 38.
[3] See Burnet's note to Plato, *Apol.* 32B6.
[4] E. de Strycker, "Les témoignages historiques sur Socrate," in
*Mélanges Grégoire* (1950), § II. Cf. L. Robin, *La Pensée hel-
lénique*, pp. 114–15 (written in 1910).
[5] E. Dupréel, *La Légende socratique et les Sources de Platon*
(1922), O. Gigon, *Sokrates. Sein Bild in Dichtung und Geschichte*
(1947), A.-H. Chroust, *Socrates, Man and Myth* (1957).

mists of time. However, the "myth" theory is now generally rejected, at least in its extremer forms. The evidence, inadequate though it is, is too widespread[6] to allow such an agnosticism without insisting on a degree of rigour we are unwilling to use elsewhere (an unwillingness sometimes inconsistently used to throw out our knowledge of Socrates in particular: see de Vogel's review of Gigon in *Mnemosyne*, 1951).

II

Let us start with the evidence in works written in Socrates' own lifetime. This has an advantage in that these works are most likely to be first-hand accounts, written from a fresh memory and for an audience familiar with Socrates himself and before any tradition could have arisen of the "Socratic discourse" as a literary genre that could take liberties with history. It has the disadvantage, apart from its scantiness, of stemming almost entirely from non-philosophers or those out of sympathy with Socrates.

The most important single source is the satire by Aristophanes in his comedy the *Clouds,* produced in 423 and followed by a second edition some years later where the poet tells us (ll. 518 ff.) that the first edition was not successful and where certain features, notably the debate of the Just and Unjust Arguments and the final burning of Socrates' school, were either added or radically revised.[7]

How far can a comedian go? Whether Aristophanes' real target was Socrates himself, the subversive tendencies of the Sophistic movement, the apparent absurdities of Ionian "science," or just "long-haired intellectuals"

[6] Cf. E. de Strycker's article (n. 4 above).

[7] Our main evidence is an ancient summary known as Hypothesis I. See K. J. Dover's edition, pp. lxxx ff.; but even if the burning was new ( $\Sigma^{VE}$ 543), ἥμεıπται in Hyp. I does not seem definitely to exclude *a* debate in the first version. The Arguments are referred to several times in the play.

in general (and the contrasts we find so obvious between
these various elements may not have been at all so obvious to their contemporaries), his selection of Socrates
as his chief butt must surely mean that Socrates was
known to a fairly wide audience, and vaguely associated
with the "modern" tendencies. But it need mean little
more than this. A playwright may well write for more
than one audience. Provided his plays have enough in
them to hold the attention of the audience's lowest de-
nominator there is no reason why the poet should not
indulge his fancy in all manner of sophistications to be
appreciated only by the few. Consider, for instance, the
complexities of plot, language, and thought in a writer
like Shakespeare, especially in view of the supposed
spanking pace of Elizabethan productions. This double
role of the play means that there is nothing to be sur-
prised at if shrewd hits at points in Socrates whose existence is confirmed by Plato or other writers occur side
by side with gross and palpable distortions and inconsistencies, of a kind rendered not only probable but even
desirable if the poet wants to fuse multifarious elements
in the social scene into a single target.

When Socrates appears as head of the "Reflectory"
(Starkie), replacing Zeus by Air and Vortex, is this evidence for that early "scientific" period in Socrates' life
that *Phaedo* 96A ff. seems to imply and *Apol.* 19C–D and
*Mem.* I 1.11 and IV 7 to contradict? It could only be so
for a period not long before 423, the date of the *Clouds*,
and certainly not for one in Socrates' youth, say around
450, nor even one which ended in the mid-430s, as Burnet thinks.[8] The picture cannot be all that stale.[9] But

[8] A. K. Rogers (*The Socratic Problem,* p. 146, n. 16) points out
that in the *Protagoras,* with a dramatic date probably earlier than
the *Clouds,* Socrates seems to live in an ordinary private house.
See 310A ff., though strictly it is not conclusive. In the *Clouds,*
Socrates lives as well as works in the Reflectory (175 ff.).

[9] Though I see no reason to follow Hackforth (*The Composition of Plato's Apology,* p. 156) in constructing complicated hypotheses to explain why Aristophanes does not portray Socrates as
buttonholing people in the street. Aristophanes has already pre-

all the other evidence for a scientific theory implies that it is early, and so is not confirmed by the *Clouds*. In fact, the pabulum of the "Reflectory" is clearly a mere jumble of current ideas, in which consistency is not to be expected. The airy-fairiness of Socrates with his head in the clouds to escape the base concerns of the ground is not, for instance, on the face of it very consistent with his minute attention to the parts and behaviour of insects. It is indeed hardly surprising that a person of Socrates' intellectual curiosity should have acquired a working knowledge of the intellectual preoccupations of his day. But the doxographical tradition contains not the slightest trace of any scientific theory attributable to Socrates, and it seems equally unlikely that a man of his presumed ability should have made no contribution to the subject had he persisted in it so far as to become head of a school, or that any contribution he did make should have sunk without trace. As for his long association with Archelaus, it may well be, as Hackforth says (p. 153), that "what kept him was his teacher's lectures on ethics and politics."[10]

But this indifference on the poet's part to historical accuracy also makes it improbable that he was scrupulous to exonerate Socrates personally from the effects of the general milieu Socrates is taken to represent, in the way H. Erbse (*Hermes*, 1954) has tried to argue (cf. also T. Gelzer in *Mus. Helv.*, 1956). It is true that Aristophanes appears on friendly terms with Socrates in Plato's *Symposium*,[11] but he could hardly have expected the bulk of his audience not to see Socrates in an unfavourable light in the play. We must not suppose that Aristophanes looked at things as we do (cf. Dover's in-

---

empted Socrates to be head of the Reflectory and cannot put him in two places at once. He does appear outside the Reflectory at 362; cf. R. Philippson in *Rhein. Mus.*, 1932, p. 35.

[10] See A1, 3, 4 in DK on Archelaus.

[11] Xenophon's *Symposium* contains a certain Lycon, but it is not clear whether this is the same as Socrates' accuser in 399. See Ollier in the Budé edition, p. 28, n. 1.

troduction to the *Clouds*, p. lii ff.; p. 82 in this volume).

Leaving these general considerations, then, can we extract anything from the points Aristophanes may have
inserted for his more knowledgeable hearers?

R. Philippson (*Rhein. Mus.*, 1932) and W. Schmid
(*Philologus*, 1948) see in the *Clouds* not only the question and answer method but also the doctrine of division
that looms large in Plato's dialectic. The former is obviously well suited for comic parody, which lessens Aristophanes' value as evidence, though if Socrates did use
it this might help to explain his appearance in the play.[12]
Much of the evidence brought for the latter is rather
forced. The *Clouds* says nothing of repeated division or a
method of division,[13] with the possible exception of 742:
ὀρθῶς διαιρῶν καὶ σκοπῶν ("rightly dividing and investigating"). Philippson's attempt, followed by Schmid, to
see here a distinction between Socrates' division of things
and Protagoras' and Prodicus' distinction of words lays
an incredible weight on the word πράγματα (741), if this
is supposed to embody some doctrine of substantialised
concepts; even Aristophanes' most sophisticated listeners
would be hard put to get the point, and Heraclitus B1
(referred to by Dover in his discussion on p. xliii [p. 62
in this volume]) talks of dividing words and things (ἔπεα
and ἔργα) quite indifferently. It is not clear whether 742
refers to a right manner of dividing or to dividing being
a right thing to do, but the former seems the more natural interpretation. It remains true that, as Dover puts it
(*ibid.*), "to break down a problem into its components

[12] Is *Clouds* 137 ("You have just aborted a thought in the making") evidence for Socrates' comparing himself to a midwife? That
only a few would have seen the point is no evidence against this,
though I agree with Dover (p. xliii; p. 61 in this volume) that it
could be a common and obvious metaphor without significance,
and see no grounds for Taylor's (*Varia Socratica*, p. 148) reference to fifth-century Attic as "a language so chary of its
metaphors."

[13] J. S. Morison (*Phronesis*, 1963) sees division in Antiphon and
the περὶ τέχνης as well as in the *Clouds*. The present objection
applies to these works as well.

is a necessary stage towards its solution," and so nothing remarkable; but the passage shows a certain explicit concentration on method which we do not find in what remains of the cosmologists, and this motif, though probably not its scientific application, *may* be an echo of Socrates—but we must not exaggerate the passage.

References to Socrates' ethical doctrines have been seen at *Birds* 603-5 (414 B.C.: Stark in *Rhein. Mus.*, 1953, pp. 86–89) and in Euripides' *Hippolytus* (428 B.C.: Snell in *Philologus*, 1948). The birds ask how, in replacing the gods, they can give health to men, and are told that men can get this by acting rightly, for "there is simply no man who is of healthy mind while acting wrongly." The logic is not perfect, but good enough for comedy, and the reference Stark sees to a Socratic "no-one knowingly does wrong" gives pungency to an otherwise flat passage. This is just the sort of point Aristophanes could have thrown out in a piece of quickfire repartee, to be taken by the more knowledgeable of the audience and missed by the rest, no doubt the great majority. Snell thinks that Euripides' Phaedra (*Hippol.* 380 ff.) is opposing an intellectualistic view of wrong-doing which is Socratic rather than Protagorean in form, and refers also to fragments of Euripides written about 410.[14] The evidence is slender, though the position is possible, but Euripides does not of course mention Socrates, and so all such evidence can only confirm what we know already from other sources (though it might in theory affect the chronology of Socrates' thought).[15]

[14] Snell also thinks Socrates was himself stimulated by Euripides' *Medea* (431 B.C.). But Pohlenz (*Die griech. Trag.*[2], pp. 112–13) points out that, according to "die feste Tradition der Sokratiker," Socrates was already talking philosophy to Alcibiades before 431 (which, he adds, is further evidence against Socrates being a "scientist" in the 420s). Cf. also N. E. Collinge's illuminating article "Medea versus Socrates" in the *Durham University Journal*, 1950.

[15] Snell also follows Diller (*Gnomon*, 1939, p. 118) and Kapp in seeing a favourable reference to Socrates' political views in the "Old Oligarch," 2.19. Rogers (*The Socratic Problem*, p. 73) sees Aristophanes' *silence* as evidence against Socrates' having anti-

Before leaving Socrates' contemporaries we must mention the *Dissoi Logoi* (Double Arguments),[16] a work written near the time of Socrates' death (it mentions the Athenian defeat in 404 as a recent event [1.8]) and developing a series of antinomies, using arguments clearly culled from the contemporary scene. A number of similarities to the works of Plato and Xenophon have been seen in it, sometimes extending to points of detail. Among the main similarities are these: (i) the arguments for the thesis that just equals unjust (3.2–12) resemble Xenophon's *Mem.* IV 2.14–18, as well as Plato's *Rep.* 331C, 382C–D; (ii) the "Forms" terminology in 4.5 ff.; (iii) the arguments in 6 about the teachability of virtue resemble those of the *Protagoras* and *Meno;* (iv) the arguments in 7 against political selection by lot recall arguments attributed to Socrates by Xenophon (*Mem.* I 2.9) and Aristotle (*Rhet.* 1393B3–8);[17] (v) the importance of knowledge for efficient conduct (8); (vi) 1.12–14 has been seen as a crude attempt at Socratic dialogue.

Of these arguments (vi) (for which see Ramage) is at most a possible testimony to Socratic "induction"; (v) hardly goes beyond what any fee-taking sophist might be expected to say, though it does refer to the question and answer method. It only says that he who knows will be *able* to do and teach aright (8.2), and the point that there is one science of opposites, which Tay-

democratic opinions; this would not, of course, bear on Socrates' views after the second edition of the *Clouds,* whenever that was (see below on *Dissoi Logoi* 7), and it is not obvious that Aristophanes would have wanted to satirise oligarchic arguments. Critias, B28, has a slightly Socratic ring, though it need not be very significant. Cf. also Epicharmus, frag. 78 Kaibel, where, however, πονηρός need not have a moral sense.

16 Translated in *Mind,* April, 1968. See A. E. Taylor, *Varia Socratica,* chap. 3, W. Kranz in *Hermes,* 1937, esp. 230 ff., E. S. Ramage in *Am. Jnl. of Philol.,* 1961, and for a more sceptical approach H. Gomperz, *Sophistik und Rhetorik,* pp. 150–59, A. Levi in *Am. Jnl. of Philol.,* 1940, pp. 302 ff.

17 Aristotle talks of τὰ Σωκρατικά, which *could* refer merely to a disciple.

lor (p. 125, n. 4) calls Socratic, could as well be Heracli-
tean (B23, 111). The second would require a long discussion and I can only say here that I think Form
language preceded and gave rise to the theory of Forms
itself, which requires, among other things, a metaphysical interest in certain problems, not merely the use of
certain language. Note how in early and naturalistic Platonic dialogues Form language causes no trouble to the
man in the street (*Euthyp.* 5D, 6D–E, *Prot.* 330C, *Hip.
Ma.* 287C–D, *Gorg.* 467E–8A, 497E). The present passage is probably no more significant than the English
phrase "There is much truth in what you say." The first,
third, and fourth probably do show that these arguments
were going the rounds during Socrates' lifetime and were
not inventions of Plato or Xenophon. Some of them may
indeed go back to Socrates himself, though Taylor (118)
allows that arguments used by Socrates need not have
been invented by him.[18] I conclude that the *Dissoi Logoi* contains little conclusive evidence but enough of interest not to be neglected by Socratic scholars.

III

Turning to the fourth century we at once meet our
two main sources, Plato and Xenophon.[19] It is usual, and

[18] Cf. the way the teachability of virtue is introduced in the
*Meno* as though it were a stock subject of debate, as indeed one
would expect in the age of the Sophists. There is no reason to think
that Socrates alone held the negative position. Cf. also Gomperz,
pp. 156–58.

[19] Space forbids a discussion of the other Socratic writers, despite
Gigon's (*Sokrates*, p. 28) insistence that the paucity of their remains does not imply their unreliability. It does imply that we can
do little but use them as an occasional check on our main sources.
They would be important if they radically *differed* from those main
sources, which they do not seem to do, though Antisthenes, like
Plato, had a philosophy of his own to develop. Where they do
differ they often interpret Socrates in a traditionalist way, as though
failing to understand innovations which our other sources suggest
that Socrates made. Cf., e.g., what looks like a mixture of Socratic
and Homeric ideas in Antisthenes' *Odysseus*—hardly attributable

in general I think inevitable, to give preference to (the early) Plato. Plato is a philosopher and Xenophon is not, and it is easier to extract philosophy from a source that contains too much of it than from one that contains too little. But neither can be ignored, and we can hardly do better than start from Schleiermacher's[20] often quoted remark and ask, "What *can* Socrates have been, in spite of what Xenophon tells us of him, without contradicting those traits of character and those maxims of conduct which Xenophon definitely exhibits as Socratic, and what *must* he have been to have given Plato cause and justification for introducing him in the way he does in his dialogues?"

Plato and Xenophon have much in common. They both knew Socrates personally (Xenophon [*Mem.* III 6.1] mentions Plato *en passant* in a way suggesting considerable intimacy with Socrates. Plato, like Aristotle, never mentions Xenophon). Two of their writings share a common name (*Apology* and *Symposium*). They both upon occasion abandon Socrates for another mouthpiece, whether Socrates keeps a significant role (Diotima, Parmenides; Ischomachus) or has little or no role at all (Aspasia, Timaeus, the Eleatic Visitor, the Athenian; Cyrus). But how far is the "Socratic discourse," which they and others wrote, a literary genre with conventions of its own which, if ignored, can distort historical interpretation? Can they attribute to Socrates what the reader well knows he never held or did? A. E. Taylor (*Socrates,* p. 32, n. 2) chides those who use Plato as a main source for our knowledge of the Sophists but reject him as a source for Socrates. The point is fair enough, but it ignores two things: first, that Plato says far more about Socrates than about anyone else, and his picture may not always be consistent; and second, that

---

to dramatic realism, or why the reference to the good man being immune to harm? Dionys. Hal. (see G. C. Field, *Plato and his Contemporaries,* p. 216) tells us that all the non-Platonic Socratic dialogues were ἠθικοί.

[20] *Sämtl. Werke* III 2, pp. 297–98. Written in 1815. Transl. mine.

Socrates may have a special role to play, this fact being known and accepted by readers. In any case, the ancients were notoriously lax, to our mind, in matters of quotation and attribution, and though these points are different, they are related. When Polycrates wrote his indictment of Socrates he had no hesitation in making the real prosecutor, Anytus, his mouthpiece, and gave no indication that this was a fiction, for later generations accepted it as historical, though the speech refers to the rebuilding of the Long Walls five years after Socrates' trial.[21] For the attitude to quotation, note the way Niceratus, introduced as an expert on Homer, makes no objection when Socrates misquotes Homer to him at Xenophon's *Symposium* 8.32.

But we cannot just point to a "special role" and leave it at that. There are presumably limits even to ancient tolerance, and, more important, there are the questions of how such a convention grew up in the first place,[22] and why Socrates was chosen, and why abandoned—which returns us to Schleiermacher's question.

On the whole Xenophon has been badly treated in the pages of Socratic historians. "Few scholars show at their best in dealing with Xenophon," says G. C. Field (*Plato and his Contemporaries*, p. 140). But it must be added that Xenophon does not show at his best in writing the *Memorabilia*. It is a dreary and moralising work, with the avowed aim (I 3.1) of showing how "useful" Socrates was to his associates as a moral guide, both by precept and by example. Its first two chapters form a separate entity, which may be referred to as the *Defence*[23] and which starts by quoting and answering the

[21] R. Hackforth, *The Composition of Plato's Apology*, p. 5. For the contents of Polycrates' attack see Chroust, chap. 4.

[22] Works like Xenophon's *Hiero*, whatever its date, bring in characters long since dead and so are hardly evidence of a convention allowing liberties to be taken with Socrates.

[23] This term is sometimes used, as by Chroust, for the *Apology*. The indictment is also quoted at *Apol.* 10 and, with differences, Plato's *Apol.* 24B. Taylor (*Var. Soc.*, p. 6) thinks Xenophon, being

indictment of 399 but is largely concerned with answering an anonymous "accuser," who seems to be Polycrates. The rest is a set of dialogues which exonerate Socrates from the least suspicion of intellectual or moral subversiveness. However, this does not completely deny its historical value, provided we realise the situation.

To assess this value let us look briefly at Xenophon's other Socratic writings. The *Economicus*, where Socrates discourses on how to run a farm, is generally agreed to be unhistorical, since everything else we know about Socrates, including what we learn from Xenophon himself, makes him a townsman, whereas Xenophon himself did run a farm (during his long exile at Scillus). The work is mainly of interest in showing that Xenophon is willing to use Socrates in this way in what looks otherwise simply like an unusually long section from the *Memorabilia*, though it is here that Xenophon, like Plato in his *Symposium*, makes Socrates appeal to another authority for his main contribution.

The *Apology* is a rather strange work. Its aim is to explain the proud bearing of Socrates at his trial, which Xenophon thinks other writers have not explained, and the explanation it gives is simply that Socrates wished to avoid the ills of old age and so sought a kind of euthanasia. That this was Socrates' main motive seems implausible (the Socrates of Plato's *Crito* would be an utter humbug in his rejection of the appeal to family responsibilities if Plato knew this was the real Socrates' motive, and if he did not know, how should Xenophon?). The most that seems plausible (cf. Plato's *Apol.* 37E ff.) is that *part* of his motive was to avoid a release conditional upon being muzzled, a release which he might regard as a betrayal of his philosophy as well as personally intolerable. Could Xenophon have confused these motives,[24] or was he even desperate for an excuse to write

---

absent in Asia during the trial, would be more likely to consult the official record.

[24] I.e., heard the second motive ascribed to Socrates by an oral source, possibly garbled, taken it in the sense of the first, and then

his own account of what purported to be a historical occasion which others had already described, including eye-witnesses if Plato wrote first?[25]

The date of the *Apology*, as of Xenophon's other works, is uncertain. Its failure to answer Polycrates is hardly relevant, though the implication at § 31 that Anytus has been dead for at least some time suggests it was not written immediately after the trial, even if the Anytus who held office in 388–87 was a different one (as Ollier thinks: Budé edition, p. 89). If Xenophon read Plato it is perhaps odd that he made no use of the free meals at the town hall proposal. In any case, with regard to what Socrates actually said, Xenophon can only be a secondary source and Plato should be given preference unless there is positive reason to do otherwise. But Xenophon probably does represent a genuine tradition as to what Socrates said, differing from Plato's account on such matters as the reasons for accepting death, the role of the "demon," and the oracle episode. Whatever Socrates did say, it must have been such as to make some of those who had voted for his innocence vote for his death on the second vote, if Diogenes Laertius' report (2.42) is correct.[26]

Xenophon's *Symposium* is undoubtedly one of his better works, despite the clumsiness of the sentences linking its episodes. Xenophon and Plato choose quite different characters and occasions, and there is no reason to seek a historical origin in either case; a symposium is a

concluded, whether or not he had read Plato, that no-one had attributed *this* motive to Socrates.

[25] Note incidentally his reference in § 1 to the question of historical accuracy, an unlikely remark if he thought of Socratic discourses as a mere literary genre. Both here and in the related last chapter of *Mem.* he cites Hermogenes as his source, though these are the only times he cites a source at all. There seems no good reason to reject the *Apology* as spurious.

[26] Cf. Hackforth, pp. 135–38. But I cannot agree that "a mere reproduction [by Plato] of Socrates' actual speech [would] have fallen flat" (p. 48). The Greeks had no newspapers or tape-recorders.

natural enough form for a Socratic discourse to take. Xenophon speaks of himself as present at the occasion, but this is clearly a literary device, one which he uses several times elsewhere, including the *Economicus*.[27] However, there are many similarities between the two *Symposiums* which suggest they are not entirely independent.[28] Most scholars now seem to accept, rightly, I think, that Plato's came first, which leaves us with the questions of why Xenophon wrote his and what historical value it has.[29] Its opening sentence, saying that great men should be portrayed at play *as well as* at work, suggests that at least part of the *Memorabilia* had already been written (thus confirming a relatively late date for the *Symposium*), and that Xenophon may have the same apologetic motive.

Plato's *Symposium*, for all its merits, has a certain formality, even stiltedness, of structure. Xenophon's has a freer dramatic flow and portrays Socrates not only in the opinions he utters but in his contribution to the course of the banquet itself.[30] Ollier's opinion that Xenophon was trying to portray a Socrates altogether

[27] Only once (*Mem.* I 3) does Xenophon appear in conversation with Socrates, and then in an undistinguished role, which hardly fits Robin's suggestion (*La Pensée hell.*, p. 97) that he sought Socrates' company out of vanity, whatever his motives in writing the *Anabasis*. A further stylistic trick is his use of resumptive particles at the beginning of his works. This does not imply he intended them as parts of a single work. Cf. the opening of Plato's own *Symposium*.

[28] See, e.g., the list in H. G. Dakyns' trans. of Xenophon, Vol. III, Pt. I, pp. lix ff.

[29] See Ollier, *Notice* to Budé edition, Erbse in *Gymnasium*, 1966, von Fritz in *Rhein. Mus.*, 1935, Dover in *Phronesis*, 1965 (who ignores [top of p. 14] the possibility that "Pausanias" in Xenophon's *Symp.* 8.32 is a non-Platonic literary creation; cf. H. Maier, *Sokrates*, p. 17, n.). The contrary view is argued in Wimmel's complex article in *Gymnasium*, 1957. Note for instance the way Plato brings in the Silenus image with a flourish, as something new (215A), which would be clumsy if Xenophon's casual reference (4.19) and neat play (5.7) had already appeared.

[30] Von Fritz brings out the dramatic skill of the treatment of Socrates and Antisthenes.

more human and plausible than Plato's is persuasive. In any case, it is clear that Xenophon's *Symposium* is certainly not just a pale and uninspired copy of Plato's. Even where he *may* have borrowed structural features, such as the round-the-table contributions or the interruptions from outside, he has made them his own and written a piece that has a body and life of its own. It seems then that Xenophon did indeed know of Plato's writings,[31] but had both the desire and the resources to build an independent and contrasting image of Socrates (which is not to say that he borrowed none of his knowledge from Plato). He may indeed have used other Socratic writers as well (von Fritz sees a debt to Aeschines). This would be natural enough if his own acquaintance with Socrates was limited. But that he only used these other writers to supplement a picture whose basis lay in his own experience, and that he was not creating a purely imaginary picture following a literary fashion, is suggested by the very inadequacies of his main Socratic work, the *Memorabilia,* whose earnest dullness suggests an attempt to record and defend, and not a literary inspiration, however protreptic in aim.[32, 33]

[31] The satire on stock dialogue responses at 4.56–59 clearly shows that Xenophon had some dialogues in mind, whether or not Plato's. For what looks like a use of Plato in a non-Socratic context, cf. the argument that the soul must have two parts to desire good and bad things (*Cyrop.* 6.1.41; cf. *Rep.* 436B ff.)

[32] *Mem.* IV is on the whole more philosophical and sophisticated than the earlier books, and in particular IV 6 (with the end of 5) has been used to show that Xenophon both depends on Plato and is the source of Aristotle's reports on Socrates' method in passages like *Met.* 1078B17 ff. (See, e.g., Maier, *Sokrates,* pp. 57–62, 96 ff.) The references to distinguishing things by their kinds, to dialectic, and to hypotheses, have suggested comparisons with the *Phaedo* (100A, 101D–E), *Republic* (437A, 510B, 511B, 532A ff.), and *Statesman* (285–87), and the intervening definitions have been compared with their Platonic analogues.
But there are differences. The context in Xenophon is a practical one, even though knowledge is required as a means. There is no reference to the specialised educational system of the *Republic* or to the elaborate methodological apparatus and systematic procedure of the *Phaedo* and *Statesman.* The "hypothesis" of 6.13 is sim-

One of the most puzzling discrepancies between Plato and Xenophon is the extent to which Socrates put forward positive views of his own. Plato's early dialogues end in apparent bewilderment, and when Socrates does

---

ply the underlying premise or position accepted by both sides, in Xenophon's example the function of the good citizen. The definition of courage at 6.11 differs from *Laches* 194E11 and *Republic* 429C–30B. Similarly 6.4 defines piety while the *Euthyphro* ends in bewilderment.

Xenophon may have misunderstood Plato, but this hardly accounts for his omitting all reference to the theory of Forms. If he thought that Plato had distorted Socrates out of all recognition and so was trying to restore the true Socrates, why did he *not* omit technical phrases which could so easily give his readers the wrong impression (especially if he took them from a dialogue like the *Statesman* where Socrates is not even the speaker)? If he thought that Socrates did indeed use this sort of language but did not mean by it what Plato makes him mean, this would explain why he might borrow from Plato (see next note), but would presuppose that he also had other sources, and so would preclude his being a superfluous witness. In fact he would be a very important witness, though no doubt to be used with care owing to his limited philosophical ability. It seems plausible that what Xenophon understood by "distinguishing things by their kinds" was simply making the proper distinctions and seeing things as they are. That Xenophon uses such phrases is *some* evidence that Socrates talked in that kind of way (cf. "rightly dividing" at *Clouds* 742), whatever he may have meant by it. But what Xenophon also portrays Socrates as doing here is defining the virtues in terms of knowledge and holding (indeed taking for granted) that he who knows what is right will do it. If we agree that Xenophon was not simply copying from Plato then these are significant points.

I have not discussed whether Xenophon is simply copying from Antisthenes, etc. I cannot see why he should be *simply* doing this, but if he was, then the agreement between such mutually hostile sources as Antisthenes and Plato would itself be some evidence of a Socratic origin. Cf. Maier, p. 148.

[33] *Meno* 75D is a likely source, especially for the need for agreed premises. One of the main lessons a reader of Plato would learn is the difference between the definition of a term and a list of things it applies to (e.g., *Meno* 72A ff., *Theaet.* 146D ff.). Note how *Mem.* I 1.16 completely fudges this distinction. IV 6 is not much better. But this does not necessarily mean that the distinction is a Platonic invention, though perhaps it suggests that Plato made more of it than Socrates or other writers did. Plato's very repetition of it suggests it was a lesson that took a long time to sink in, and Xenophon's was no doubt a hard head to sink into.

start putting forward positive views they are of a kind now generally regarded as Platonic rather than Socratic. Apart from the fact that Aristotle distinguishes between Plato and Socrates, the early dialogues differ from the later (those after and including the *Meno* and *Gorgias*) by more than mere omissions; and it would be odd that Plato should keep Socrates' views in reserve for so long and come to reveal views of his own even later still.[34] Xenophon, on the other hand, makes Socrates give dogmatic expression to "improving" sentiments. It has been disputed whether this is due to Xenophon's own purposes and deficiencies or whether it represents a more faithful picture of Socrates than the more negative and probing mind we see in the early works of Plato (N. Gulley, *CQ*, 1952, pp. 74–75).

Xenophon himself portrays Socrates as using the question and answer method (see especially *Mem.* IV 2), while Plato seems to attribute it to the historical Socrates at *Crito* 50C. But Xenophon goes even further at *Mem.* IV 4.9–10,[35] where Hippias bursts out against Socrates' habit of "laughing at others and asking questions and probing everyone, while never consenting to defend a position yourself or reveal your own opinion about anything"—an impression one hardly gets from the rest of Xenophon![36] On the other hand, Plato's *Apology*

[34] For the Burnet/Taylor view that Plato's portrait of Socrates is substantially accurate throughout see J. Burnet, *Greek Philosophy, Thales to Plato* and A. E. Taylor, *Varia Socratica* and *Socrates*, as well as their editions of various dialogues. For criticisms of it see, e.g., W. D. Ross in *Proc. of the Class. Assoc.*, 1933, L. Robin in *Rev. des Et. gr.*, 1916 (reprinted in *La Pensée hell.*, pp. 138–76). J. W. Miller (in *Rev. of Met.*, 1953) supports the Burnet/Taylor view by studying the dramatic dates of the dialogues, but though he makes some interesting points he does not answer the objections (and his own discussion of Recollection unduly ignores the *Euthyphro*).

[35] Mentioned but dismissed by Gulley (p. 75, n. 1), who seems to ignore that Plato's insistence on Socrates' agnosticism also comes in the *Apology* (20C ff.).

[36] Deman (*Témoignage*, p. 69), commenting on Aristotle's reference to Socratic irony at *Nic. Eth.* 1127B22 ff., refers to *Mem.* I 2.36 for something similar. Cf. in Plato *Theaet.* 150C.

33B, though hard to translate in detail, suggests that Socrates would answer as well as ask (cf., with Burnet, *Prot.*
348A6). Another passage in Xenophon (*Mem.* IV 2.40,
coming at the end of the long inquisition of Euthydemus) suggests that Socrates used such inquisitions only
as a preliminary and then "talked straight." This might
seem to reconcile the two pictures, but it only does so
superficially and inadequately. The maieutic or midwife's
method which Plato pictures in Socrates, and attributes
to him at *Theaet.* 149A ff., certainly involves first purging
the learner of the false conceit of knowledge; but it also
involves that the learner himself must produce his own
brain-children and not have them just handed to him on
a plate. *Mem.* IV 2 is one of Xenophon's more sophisticated chapters, and may indeed rely to some extent on
Plato,[37] but this merely heightens the contrast with the
dull didacticism of what Xenophon seems to envisage as
coming next.

There is, I think, a further argument against the idea
that Socrates proceeded in this didactic way, and that is
the diversity of the people he influenced. It is easier to
see how he could have impressed at the same time Plato
and Xenophon, Antisthenes and Aristippus, and sent
them off to write such different philosophies, if we suppose that he did *not* put forward much in the way of
positive views himself, or at any rate not in a direct and
explicit form. The children of one midwife can have a
far richer diversity among themselves than the children
of one mother. Xenophon's more didactic passages are
perhaps to be explained as his putting into explicit form
what he took to be the natural implications of Socrates'
teaching, though we can assume that Socrates made it
plain enough that he was "against sin."

[37] The relativism in it is not inconsistent with the Platonic Socrates' view, as is sometimes thought (Rogers, p. 176), for this says
that ordinary goods are not unconditionally good. This is not upset
by Xenophon's addition of σοφία to the list of relative goods at 2.33,
though that suggests that Xenophon is not just copying from Plato.
There are various kinds of σοφία. Similarly with εὐδαιμονία in
2.34–35.

IV

Plato himself, as we have seen, is naturally regarded as our main source for Socrates, though only in his earliest dialogues. This does not, however, mean that nothing in the later dialogues can be used. The change in Socrates' role in the dialogues is a gradual one and the fact that he is sometimes abandoned shows that Plato thought of himself as in some sense following Socrates for the rest of the time. In fact, if we look at the occasions where Socrates is decisively abandoned we find that they consist of a set-piece funeral oration (*Menexenus*), an essay in cosmology (*Timaeus*), studies in logic and dialectic, albeit with a political application (*Sophist* and *Statesman*), and the second-best political constitution (*Laws*). Socrates as champion of the Forms is criticised by Parmenides, who later gives way to the Eleatic Visitor (no doubt simply for reasons of dramatic chronology), and Socrates attributes the mystical climax of the *Symposium* to a priestess, a fact against rather than for a mystical conception of the historical Socrates of the kind suggested by Rogers. It is clear from this that Plato did not make a definite decision to abandon him. He appears in the late *Philebus*, presumably because of its ethical nature, and there is possibly even a hint (*Statesman* 258A; cf. F. M. Cornford, *Plato's Theory of Knowledge*, pp. 168–69) that he was already planned for the leading role in the unwritten *Philosopher*. The appearance of logic and dialectic in the *Philebus* suggests that his subordination in the *Sophist* and *Statesman* was due not to these but to the criticism and modification of the theory of Forms, which by this time was associated with his name. But this does not mean that Plato thought of the theory as historically belonging to Socrates. To us monism is a defining characteristic of the Eleatics, but the Eleatic Visitor is willing enough to criticise it, because Plato chooses an Eleatic simply as representing the logical outlook. Similarly, he chooses Socrates as embodying the philosophical spirit and not because he held particular doctrines.

The comparison of Socrates to a midwife in the *Theaetetus* (149A ff.) is so apt for what seems to emerge as our general picture of Socrates that one feels tempted to say that if Plato had not written it we would have had to invent it. In fact the *Theaetetus*, despite its late date and un-Socratic subject matter, still has much of the spirit of the Socratic dialogue in its negative nature and in Socrates' insistence that Theaetetus produce the hypotheses for discussion. Similarly, the passage in the *Meno* (84D ff.) where Socrates extracts a geometrical theorem from a slave is set in a context of trying to prove the theory of Recollection which, like an interest in mathematics, is unlikely to have belonged to Socrates himself. But the general procedure by which Socrates tries to make his interlocutor come up with the answer for himself[38] can still be eminently Socratic. Contrast the procedure of Plato himself, with or without Socrates, in works such as the *Republic* or *Laws*, or even the *Sophist* or *Phaedo*.[39]

[38] The charge that Socrates relies unduly on leading questions is misguided. The dialogue has to be kept reasonably short, but the point is that once the slave gets the answer he is convinced of it. If Socrates made a slip and got the answer wrong himself the slave could in theory correct him. Contrast the way the slave is simply *told* what "diagonal" means at 85B.

[39] A further reminiscence of the genuine Socratic maieutic method can perhaps be seen in Xenophon's *Economicus* 15.10 and the ensuing discussion. Socrates is there reporting Ischomachus, but the fact that Xenophon was unwilling to make Socrates actually own a farm, and so replaces him, does not preclude Xenophon's still using some of the lessons he learned from Socrates. But it is of course possible, especially if the *Economicus* is a late work, that this is a lesson he learned via Plato. Of course even in the most genuinely Socratic writings one must be careful about how much can be attributed to Socrates. The dialogues are clearly not verbatim reports. For instance much of the argumentation in the *Protagoras* may represent real Socratic arguments, but we surely cannot attribute to Socrates the slippery business around 350C, which is presumably required in some way by Plato's dramatic context.

Unlike Xenophon Plato does not speak in his own person.[40] The dialogues are either presented simply as such, or else are introduced by one of the speakers, or else are set within another dialogue which may or may not be introduced by one of its speakers. Socrates is confronted with a fair number of the Sophists (Protagoras, Gorgias, Hippias, Prodicus, Thrasymachus, Critias, Euthydemus), mostly in quite early dialogues (including *Rep.* I as early in spirit if not in composition); whereas Xenophon mentions few Sophists apart from Antiphon and Hippias (his Euthydemus is presumably different from Plato's), but pays more attention to people like Aristippus and Antisthenes, generally numbered among Socrates' followers, though Xenophon does not entirely treat them as such. But their choice of interlocutors does perhaps fit Xenophon's desire to show Socrates as "useful" and Plato's desire to show him as educative[41] but also critical if not revolutionary.

There are two places outside the *Apology* where Plato seems to be speaking of the real Socrates: Alcibiades' speech in the *Symposium* (215A ff.) and Socrates' "autobiography" in the *Phaedo* (96A ff.). Both come from dialogues outside the first period, but it is the latter which has led to most controversy. However, of the three main things which it attributes to Socrates (an early scientific period, an interest in teleological explanation, and the theory of Forms with an associated philosophical method), we have already seen that there is no good evidence to attribute the first (in any significant sense) or the last to Socrates. There is little positive reason therefore to attribute the second to him either, though

[40] Except, of course, in the *Epistles,* or such of them as are genuine. He mentions himself as present at Socrates' trial and offering to contribute to a fine (*Apol.* 34A, 38B), and as absent through illness from the execution (*Phaedo* 59B). Incidentally, the appearance of Plato's own name at 38B is as near a guarantee as we can have that Socrates did propose a fine of thirty minae, whatever Xenophon (*Apol.* 23) may say.

[41] *Apol.* 19D9 is not inconsistent with this if one considers what παιδεύειν means there.

it might seem to be rather vaguely confirmed by Xenophon (*Mem.* I 4, IV 3).[42] It is tempting to think that the
autobiography is really Plato's.[43] But *Epistle* 7 and the
dialogues in general, though perhaps not inconsistent
with this, suggest rather that Plato had a *later* scientific
period and an early political impulse, and there is no real
reason to treat the autobiography as any less fictional
than the rest of the *Phaedo*.

If we use Plato as a source we must obviously ensure
that he does not contradict himself in what he tells us.
The relations in this respect between the *Phaedo* passage we have just been discussing and the *Apology* have
been treated by, among others, Hackforth (*The Composition of Plato's Apology*, pp. 160 ff.). The *Protagoras*
(351B ff.) appears to attribute to Socrates a hedonism
notably absent from, and indeed contradicted in, the
*Gorgias* (492D–500A), *Republic* (583B–8A), and *Philebus* (31B–55C). This has been hotly discussed (for some
references see Gregory Vlastos' *Introduction* to the Liberal Arts translation of the *Protagoras*, p. xl, n. 50, N.
Gulley in *CR*, 1962, pp. 38–40), but here I shall only
mention the need to compare the *Protagoras* with other
*early* dialogues. N. Gulley, in *Phronesis*, 1965 (cf. his
book *The Philosophy of Socrates* [1968]), contrasts the
form the Socratic paradox takes in the *Protagoras* and
in the *Gorgias*, attributing the former to Socrates and the
latter to Plato.


v

Finally we come to Aristotle,[44] our only substantial

[42] Perhaps Xenophon's teleological arguments were not as trite
then as they have since become. Cf. his rather cogent arguments
against Anaxagoras in *Mem*. IV 7.
[43] The discovery of Anaxagoras through his writings rather than
through personal contact suits this view well, especially if the
copies were secondhand or remainders going cheap (cf. L. R. Shero
in *Class. Wkly*, 1941–42, pp. 219–20).
[44] For Aristotle see T. Deman's extremely useful collection and
commentary, *Le Témoignage d'Aristote sur Socrate* (1942), and for

later source. Barring pure invention, whatever Aristotle tells us about Socrates must come from further sources, and his value to us depends on what these sources were, and on how reliably, and so with what purpose, he used them. If he had only the sources that we also have ourselves his value would be only that of a highly intelligent modern colleague; his opinion would be just one among others. But this does not follow if it turns out simply that everything he tells us can be traced to some otherwise available source. Such a conclusion might be disappointing but it would still be valuable for us if Aristotle chose his material from sources far exceeding those available to us now. It would show which sources he thought reliable on the point in question, and would suggest that the lost ones were either not among these or did not contradict those we have.

That his sources did vastly exceed our own no one would doubt, and though it is only natural that he should make much use of Plato's writings, there are many things he tells us—such as that Plato, not Socrates, "separated" the Forms, or that Plato's earliest teacher was Cratylus—which it is hard to see how he can have got from the dialogues.[45] Specific evidence for his use of other sources is scanty. Nothing compels us to believe that he had read Xenophon, though some passages suggest a resemblance, such as *Eud. Eth.* 1235A35–B2 with *Mem.* I 2.54. But neither need we think that he did not read Xenophon, or that he must have used him if he did. In particular we must beware of assuming that whatever Aristotle says must have some *one* source, as though he were incapable of surveying several sources and exercising his own judgement on them.

---

discussion of some post-Aristotelian evidence see G. C. Field, *Plato and his Contemporaries,* Appendix III. I am particularly indebted to the editor of the present volume for suggestions about this section.

[45] *Met.* 987B1–6, 1086A37–B5, 1078B30–32, 987A32. See n. 34 above for literature. To say that Aristotle does not get something *from* the dialogues is not to say that he does not infer it at least partly *on the basis of* them.

We know little of what life was actually like in the
Academy, of how much contact, formal and informal,
there was between Plato and his colleagues, and of how
much interest there was in historical questions and historical accuracy. This makes it very hard to say how far
Aristotle could have benefited from oral tradition and
general atmosphere; comparisons with a modern university may well be misleading here, and the question of a
"special role" for Socrates may appear again.

One sign that Aristotle did intend to distinguish Socrates from Plato is the so-called Fitzgerald canon, that
Aristotle is referring to the Platonic Socrates when and
only when he puts the definite article before the name
"Socrates" (as Greek allows).[46] It is worth noting that

---

[46] First proposed by W. Fitzgerald, *Selections from the Nic. Eth.
of Aristotle* (1850), p. 163, this canon has been attacked by Taylor
(*Var. Soc.*, pp. 40–51) and defended by W. D. Ross (edition of
Aristotle's *Metaphysics*, pp. xxxix–xli), who is followed by Deman.
Ross dismisses Taylor's references as exceptional and often relies
on emendation, though mostly with the paleographical plausibility
he claims. Deman's (pp. 102–3) ingenious explanation of *Nic. Eth.*
1116B4 (that it represents an interim point in Socrates' thought,
not its final position) requires the premise that the *Nic. Eth.*, as a
*redaction plus achevée* than Aristotle's other ethical writings, would
be more concerned with historical accuracy than they are. In fact
the other roles of the article confuse the issue and in any case suggest that Aristotle is not using the criterion as an explicit device
for clarity. Clearly the criterion is an unsafe one to judge individual
passages by, though cumulatively it reinforces the view that Aristotle thought of Socrates as a historical person and not a mere
literary fiction. The absence of the article does not, of course, mean
that Aristotle is not relying on Plato or other written sources, but at
most that he then thinks of them as real evidence for Socrates,
while in the other cases he either thinks they are not or is simply
not interested. Incidentally much the same applies to the use of
"Socrates" as a dummy name in examples, where the article is rare
but cannot always be easily explained, and to the use of tenses in
verbs describing Socrates ("says," "said," "used to say," etc.).
This latter criterion corresponds fairly well, though not exactly,
with the article one, though the imperfect could refer to several
dialogue occurrences and the admittedly dubious *Mag. Mor.* has
"used to say . . . said" at 1198A10–13 and "said . . . says" at
1187A5–8.

none of the passages which on this criterion refer to the real Socrates demands reference to a Platonic dialogue later than the *Meno* or *Euthydemus* (though Deman [p. 107] compares *Magna Moralia* 1187A5–13 with *Rep.* 589C–E). But later dialogues are frequently referred to when the article is used.

Like Plato and Xenophon, however, Aristotle may have had different motives at different times in what he says about Socrates. Sometimes he is referring to biographical details or personal characteristics, as in some of the fragments, or passages like *Rhet.* 1390B31, 1398A24. Most of the other references come either in the *Metaphysics* or in the ethical writings, and there are certain differences between these two groups. The references in the *Metaphysics* (to which we can add *De Partibus* 642A24–31) seem to have a more serious historical intent, and it is here mainly that we discover the difference that Aristotle saw between Socrates and Plato. The more numerous references in the ethical works are also more casual and brought in for the purposes of the argument at hand rather than from historical interest (except for 1182A15–23 and perhaps 1200B25–9, both in the dubious *Magna Moralia*).

When he is most clearly historical, Aristotle insists on three features of Socrates: That he concerned himself with ethics, that in this sphere he sought definitions of universals, and that he did not "separate" these universals as Plato did.[47] Aristotle adds (1078B27) that one can attribute two things to Socrates, inductive (or analogical?) arguments and general definition. It is not clear whether he means that Socrates was original in using these or simply (with Ross, *Aristotle's Metaphysics*, II, p. 422) that he was the first to recognise their importance

---

[47] The Burnet/Taylor view that the Forms were only "separated" by the "Friends of the Forms" of *Soph.* 248A has been amply refuted in the literature cited in n. 34 above, as well as in Deman, pp. 80–82, and Rogers, pp. 141–42. That Aristotle approves of Socrates' refusal to separate the Forms (1086B4) is not conclusive; but why should he emphasise the point so much when his main target is clearly Plato and not the "Friends of the Forms"?

and use them systematically. It is certainly odd that no
one should have argued analogically before, but though
the originality 1078B17 attributes to Socrates lies in seeking general definitions *in ethics,* Aristotle seems to think
that those, namely Democritus and the Pythagoreans,
who had sought definitions in science or elsewhere had
done so in a very inchoate way. *De Partibus* 642A24–31
seems to hint that the need for definitions became more
urgent when interest switched, with Socrates, from science to ethics.

The explicit description of Socrates as "concerning
himself with ethics and not at all with nature in general"
(987B1) excludes any significant scientific period from
Socrates' life, though no doubt it need not be taken to
exclude the layman's knowledge we have already allowed him. It is not so obvious that it excludes metaphysical interests as opposed to scientific ones, but when
Aristotle tells us in the *De Partibus* passage that interest
in definitions increased in Socrates' time he adds that
the study of nature was replaced by practical questions
in ethics and politics, and makes no mention of the sort
of metaphysics we find in Plato's middle and later dialogues and in Aristotle himself.

Aristotle also supports in one or two passages the picture of an agnostic and questioning Socrates that pre-
dominates in the early Plato. I have already mentioned
(n. 36) the reference to Socrates' "irony" at *Nic. Eth.*
1127B22 ff. In the *Sophistic Refutations* (183B6–8) Aristotle makes Socrates' agnosticism the reason why he took
the part of questioner but not that of answerer. Aristotle
is talking of general roles in a debate, and since the rest
of our evidence makes it most unlikely that Socrates engaged in formal debates with an organised structure, the
truth is probably what we have already seen at the end
of § III.[48]

[48] I cannot do more here than mention the use of Aristotle made
by N. Gulley, *The Philosophy of Socrates,* in his distinction of a
Socratic from a Platonic version of the "no one does wrong willingly" paradox, referred to in § IV above.

## VI

My conclusion is an unexciting one. There is no royal road to a knowledge of Socrates, any more than there is justification for throwing up our hands and treating him as a myth. The early Plato is rightly regarded as our main source, but no source can be trusted or ignored entirely, and no source can be assumed to be equally reliable throughout. We simply have to go about it the hard way and examine the available evidence *ad hoc* for the particular problem that we happen to be concerned with.

# 3. SOCRATES IN THE *CLOUDS*

KENNETH J. DOVER

Socrates was seventy at the time of his trial in 399 B.C.,[1] and therefore forty-five when Aristophanes conceived and composed the original version[2] of the *Clouds*. He was physically hard,[3] and we should certainly not imagine that he had more fat and less muscle than other Athenians;[4] in the autumn of 424 he fought as a hoplite at Delion and took part in the gruelling retreat.[5] It is probable that his hair was greying noticeably;[6] the allegation that he was bald (which can be traced back to a story told by Hegesandros of Delphi [second century B.C.], *ap.* Ath. 507A ff.) may be only an inference from *Clouds* 147 about Socrates in old age (cf. scholion), and even if it were better founded than that it would not mean that he was already bald in his forties. His eyes were prominent, his nose upturned, and lips thick—features customarily attributed by the Athenians to satyrs and silenoi.[7]

This essay is a part of the Introduction to the *Clouds* of Aristophanes, edited with Introduction and Commentary by Kenneth J. Dover (Clarendon Press, Oxford, 1968). It is reprinted (with slight changes made by the author) by permission of the publishers and the author.

[1] Pl. *Ap.* 17D; Apollodoros 34; Demetrios of Phaleron fr. 10 [Wehrli]; Favorinus *ap.* Diog. Laert. ii. 39.

[2] The version which we possess is revised by the poet.

[3] It is therefore wrong, in staging the play, to portray Socrates as a white-bearded 'professor', but some editors seem to have visualized him so; Blaydes on 887 refers to Strepsiades and Socrates as 'the two old men'.

[4] He is sometimes visualized by modern writers as fat.

[5] Cf. below, p. 60.

[6] Aischines i. 49 contrasts his own numerous grey hairs, at forty-five, with Misgolas' lack of them at the same age.

[7] Pl. *Smp.* 215B, *Tht.* 143E, Xen. *Smp.* 4.19, 5.7. Satyrs are sometimes depicted on vases as having a very high hair-line, and this may be the origin of the idea that Socrates was bald.

Since there is no reference to his physiognomy in
*Clouds,* it may be that he was ugly only by the high
aesthetic standards of the aristocratic company which he
keeps in the pages of Plato and Xenophon, and that he
would not have seemed particularly ugly to the man in
the street. The actor who took the part of Socrates in
the play may have worn a portrait-mask. Aelian, in telling the story of how Socrates answered the question
whispered among the foreigners in the audience, 'Who
*is* this man Socrates?', by silently standing up (*Var. Hist.*
ii. 13), assumes (but does not know) that a portrait-
mask was worn; but the story loses little or none of its
point if there was no portrait-mask.[8] If Socrates was
really ugly, and his ugliness was of the conventional sa-
tyric type, a portrait of him would have been hard to
distinguish from a characteristic comic mask designed
for a fictitious character.[9]

Socrates in *Clouds* is the head of a school; Chairephon, who seems in 104, 144 ff., 830 f., 1465 to be treated
as his equal, is classed in 502 ff. among his students, and
has no part in the teaching of Strepsiades or Pheidippides. The students, unlike the boys who journey to and
from conventional schools every day (964 f.), live in; the
student who shows Strepsiades round speaks of 'us' as
'having nothing for dinner last night' (175), and we are
clearly meant to imagine (1131 ff.) that when Strepsiades comes to collect Pheidippides he has not seen him
for some time.

Socrates and his students are pale from their indoor
life (103, 119 f., 198 f., 1112, 1171), and Chairephon in
particular is 'half-dead' (504). They are unkempt and
dirty (836 f.), they wear no sandals (103, 362), their

[8] Webster, *Greek Theatre Production* (London, 1956), 60, says
that Socrates stood up 'so that the audience could see his likeness
to the actor'. It seems to me that Aelian may have thought that
Socrates stood up for precisely the opposite reason, to imply 'Do I
look like the sort of man who's playing the fool on stage?'

[9] Cf. especially the Lyme Hall relief (Webster, *op. cit.*, pl. 16);
and on the general question of portrait masks cf. Dover in *Kōmōi-
dotragēmata* (Groningen, 1967), 16 ff.

premises and furniture are verminous (694 ff., cf. 144 ff.),
and since they do nothing which the man in the street
(or the field) regards as work (316, 334) it is not surprising that they are poor (175) and rely for a living on
stealing other people's clothes (179, 497, 856 ff.). Anyone
who enrolls in the school must be prepared (414 ff.) to
endure cold and hunger, and to abstain from wine and
athletic exercise. The activities of the school are 'mysteries' which must not be divulged (140 ff., 824), and the
new student is 'initiated' by a rite (250 ff.).

The work of the school comprises research and teaching. The principal field of research is astronomy and me-
teorology (171 f., 193 f., 201, 225 ff., cf. 95 ff.), which, of
course, involves practical observation and the use of apparatus; natural history (144 ff., 156 ff.), which involves
experiments; geology (188 ff.), geometry (177 f., 202 f.)
and geography (206 ff.).

Socrates teaches for payment (98, 245 f., 1146 ff.), and
he teaches forensic rhetoric, by means of which a man
in the wrong can persuade his hearers that he is in the
right. That is why Strepsiades seeks out Socrates, and
that is what Pheidippides learns.

Metric (638 ff.) and grammar (658 ff.) are propaedeutic; metric, for Socrates, is the analysis and classification of existing verse-forms, but grammar involves
also the rationalization of current usage. There is no direct indication that natural science is propaedeutic to
oratory.

Socrates has two different ways of teaching. His 'ex-
pository' method, answering the student's direct or implied questions and filling the void of ignorance with
information, proceeds by analogy and illustration
(314 ff., 340 ff., 342 ff., 385 ff.) or clears the ground for
exposition by demonstrating that some of the beliefs
hitherto held by the student are irreconcilable with other
beliefs or assumptions (369 ff., 398 ff.). His 'tutorial'
method is, first, to assess by questions the character of the
student (478 ff.); second, to set him problems (757 ff.,

775 ff., cf. 489 f.), exhort him to reduce each problem to its constituent elements (741 f.), and criticize the solutions which he offers.

Socrates holds a mixed collection of physical, cosmological, and meteorological doctrines (95 ff., 227 ff., 376 ff., 404 ff.), and in particular he rejects the gods of cult and myth (247 f., 366 ff.), putting in their place sometimes the operation of physical laws (e.g., 379 f.), at other times his own deities—the Clouds alone (365) or a trio, Chaos, Clouds, and Tongue (423 f.). There is no consistency in the portrayal of Socrates' 'atheism'; we find him invoking Aer and Aither (264 ff.) and swearing by Breath, Chaos, and Aer (626). The Greek tendency to personification of natural phenomena and abstractions ensures that a man who is regarded as rejecting the traditional gods is assumed to worship gods of his own choice, not to reject worship as such.

Wrong,[10] who embodies the spirit of Socrates' teaching, has evidently put behind him the unworldly discomforts proper to the pursuit of science, and values both the power of oratory, as a weapon to be wielded in one's own interest, and the pleasures available to those who have learned to demolish by destructive argument the precepts of traditional morality. Pheidippides graduates from Socrates' school as a replica of Wrong, with a cool determination to do as he pleases and an equally cool dexterity in invalidating, or at least parrying, the protests of tradition. His taste in poetry is for Euripides, who (we are given to understand) shows a comparable readiness to reject established values.

Such is Aristophanes' portrayal of the behaviour, interests and teaching of Socrates. He uses similar language with reference to Socrates on other occasions: *Birds* 1554 ('unwashed') and *Frogs* 1491 ff. ('chatter', 'nonsense', 'idle'). In *Birds* 1564 Chairephon 'the bat' is described as 'coming up from below' as the pale, bloodless souls

---

[10] This character is commonly called 'The Unjust Argument', 'Dishonest Logic', etc.

came to Odysseus at the entrance to the underworld.[11] In fr. 291 (from *Dramata*) Aristophanes apparently referred to Chairephon as a thief.

If it was Aristophanes' purpose to caricature the genus 'intellectual'[12] as a whole, the evidence suggests that it is a fair caricature in essentials, with the addition of one or two elements which go a stage beyond caricature and one or two more which relate to the individual Socrates rather than to the genus. It is also a caricature which combines features of distinct species of the genus.

The one philosopher who was immortalized in folklore was Thales. Strepsiades exclaims in 180, in admiration for the ingenuity of Socrates, 'Why do we go on admiring old Thales?', and in *Birds* 1009 Peisetairos comments on Meton: 'The man's a Thales!' Now Thales was remembered in connexion with the phenomena of the heavens. Hdt. i. 74.2 tells us that he was believed to have foretold the solar eclipse of 585, and Pl. *Tht.* 174A relates an anecdote of popular type: that Thales was so engrossed in the sky that he failed to see the well before his feet, and fell down it. This being the popular idea of an intellectual, it is to be expected that caricature of one in Aristophanes' time would give a prominent place to astronomy, from which it is naturally difficult to separate cosmology, physics, and geology. This would have happened even if intellectual interests had all turned in a different direction (popular conceptions of the intellectual are usually a generation out of date), and in fact, despite great diversification and enlargement (*v. infr.*), astronomy and related scientific subjects remained prominent. The works of Anaxagoras were known at Athens, even if more by vague repute than from careful study

[11] On Socrates in the *Birds* see R. Stark, *Rhein. Mus.* xcvi (1953), 77 ff.—who, however, sees allusions in some passages where the humour in no way requires allusion.

[12] Since Plato we have been accustomed to distinguish between the sophist and the philosopher, and therefore lack a word to cover both. The distinction was not made in the language of Aristophanes' time, nor was the word σοφιστής so narrowly confined as later; cf. 331 n.

(cf. Pl. *Phd.* 97B, *Ap.* 26D, Xen. *Mem.* iv. 7.6., Isok. xv. 235); Kratinos (fr. 155) ridiculed Hippon for a cosmological doctrine which recurs in *Clouds* 95 ff.;[13] several of the doctrines which Aristophanes puts into the mouth of Socrates can be identified as those of the contemporary philosopher Diogenes of Apollonia (e.g., 226 ff.); Hippias of Elis taught astronomy (Pl. *Hp. Ma.* 285B, *Prt.* 315C).

During the second half of the fifth century the men who in an earlier generation might have confined themselves to expounding abstract doctrines in didactic poetry intervened more directly and effectively in society by teaching oratory. Persuasive speaking, in assembly and law courts, was felt to be the key to worldly success, the way to wealth and influence and power. The example of Perikles, who was both uniquely influential at Athens and a uniquely persuasive speaker, stimulated an interest in the technique of political and forensic success; the sophists professed to refine and to impart this technique (Pl. *Phdr.* 266D ff.). In so doing they made a departure of very great importance from the earlier philosophical tradition. Concentration on persuasion diverted them from what is (scientifically speaking) probable to what can be made to seem probable (*Phdr.* 272D–E). Protagoras taught his pupils to 'praise and blame the same thing', and this necessarily involves 'making wrong appear right' (Arist. *Rhet.* 1402A23, Eudoxos fr. 4). The 'Tetralogies' ascribed to Antiphon are a fifth-century exercise in presenting both sides of a case with equal conviction and ingenuity. Pl. *Euthd.* 272A represents Euthydemos as able to refute any argument 'whether it is false or true'. Lys. viii. 11, 'and I thought that they were simply philosophising about the case and "putting the case for the opposite"', is an interesting reflection of the plain man's view of philosophy: and Isok. xv. 15 faces the accusation 'that I can make wrong appear right'.

[13] The scholiast comments that this fact shows that Aristophanes did not write the *Clouds* 'out of personal hostility to Socrates'.

Certain branches of study are more relevant to oratory than others, and it is not surprising that the sophists, notably Prodikos and Protagoras, devoted much attention to semantics (Pl. *Cra.* 384B, *Euthd.* 277E, *Cra.* 391C, Arist. *Soph. El.* 173B17); Hippias, too, taught phonetics, metre, and music (Pl. *Hp. Ma.* 285D), the relevance of which to oratory is at best marginal. Astronomy and physics have no relevance; that they were taught by the same men as oratory was a legacy from the past,[14] and that they were believed to be relevant by teacher and pupil alike must be ascribed partly to the fact that the idea of intellectual specialization had not yet taken recognizable shape, partly to the total intellectual inadequacy of education as it had been hitherto understood. Traditional education imparted techniques, but there was no stage at which it satisfied intellectual curiosity or encouraged independence of thought; the sophists occupied, with an indiscriminate variety of subjects, the void which Greek society had created for them.

Devotion to the technique of persuasion was incompatible with a firm belief in objective values; rational thought about the universe inevitably and immediately brought mythology and popular religious assumptions into discredit. No matter how dutifully an intellectual followed the observances of conventional piety, it was hard for him, when he opened his mouth, to escape or rebut suspicion that he was offending the gods by scepticism or by a doctrine which dethroned them from their traditional seat at the controls of the universe, and that he was subverting that complex of attitudes, values, and behaviour which the Greeks subsumed under the term *nomos*. This, of course, is precisely what he was doing, for custom and rational thought are seldom reconcilable. Greek intellectuals had never hesitated to regard most of their fellow men as afflicted with blind stupidity (cf.

---

[14] It would be interesting to know the grounds on which Aristotle (fr. 65 = 15 [Ross]) regarded Empedokles as the 'inventor' of rhetoric.

Herakleitos B1,[15] B5, Hekataios fr. 1A, Xenophanes
B14–16, and Empedokles B2, B11)[16] and those of Aristophanes' time were not timid in their criticisms of un-
thinking tradition. For this they suffered, not only in
reputation but in the courts: notably Anaxagoras (Diog.
Laert. ii. 12, Plu. *Per.* 32.2), Socrates himself, and possibly Protagoras–to whom we owe classic formulations
of agnosticism (B4) and of relativism (B1)–though the
evidence for his prosecution is not good (A12), and the
fact that Eupolis (fr. 146B) referred to him on the comic
stage as *halitērios* is more important for our present purpose.[17] Pl. *Lg.* 967A (cf. Plu. *Nic.* 23.4 f.) makes the
point that what the ordinary Greek found hard to stom-
ach was the idea that celestial phenomena could be explained in terms of scientific laws and not as the
separately motivated actions of supernatural personalities.

Sophists did not teach for nothing, and Plato refers
often, sometimes in general terms, sometimes with the
specification of a sum, to the fees which they charged;
Prodikos (*Cra.* 384B, 'the fifty-drachma lecture-course';
*Ap.* 19E, *Hp. Ma.* 282E); Euenos of Paros (*Ap.* 20B,
'five mnai'); Gorgias (*Ap.* 19E, *Hp. Ma.* 282B); Hippias
(*Ap.* 19E, *Hp. Ma.* 282D); Protagoras (*Cra.* 391B, *Hp.
Ma.* 282D). In Plato's *Protagoras* the sophists are assem-
bled in the house of Kallias, a man of exceptional wealth,
who was reputed to have spent heavily on fees to sophists (Pl. *Cra.* 291B).[18] It does not seem to have been an
invariable rule that pupils should 'live in', for Pl. *Prt.*
318A implies that a young man under instruction from
Protagoras would return home every day, but Plato also
represents Protagoras as bringing with him to Athens for-

[15] Cf. Guthrie, *A History of Greek Philosophy* (Cambridge,
1962), i. 410 ff.

[16] References to the presocratic philosophers are numbered as in
Diels-Kranz, *Fragmente der Vorsokratiker.*

[17] Cf. *Clouds* 830 n. on Diagoras of Melos (in K. J. Dover,
*Aristophanes' Clouds* [Oxford, 1968]).

[18] For a later period, cf. Dem. xxxv. 42 on Lakritos.

eigners 'from all the cities through which he passes' (315B).

Sophists who earned these fees did not need to save money on haircuts and sandals, and they are not represented by their contemporaries as ascetics. It was in the fourth century that nakedness, vermin, dirt, and an indifference to what they ate and to the appearance of the women with whom they had intercourse became trade marks of certain kinds of philosopher. Antisthenes seems to have led the way (Xen. *Smp.* 4.34 ff.), and the 'Pythagorean' was a stock figure of fourth-century comedy.[19] Very little can be said for certain about the real Pythagoras, but it is probable that by Aristophanes' time the Pythagoreans had a reputation for asceticism, and fakirs of various kinds may have been one of those phenomena of which we catch only a fleeting glimpse in fifth-century literature.

It will be apparent from this summary that most of the elements in Aristophanes' portrayal of Socrates can be identified either as general characteristics of the sophists or as conspicuous characteristics of some contemporary intellectuals. Two elements peculiar to the play must now be mentioned.

One is the experiment reported in 148 ff. We have very little evidence for experimentation in fifth-century science, but it should not be underrated; note especially Hp. *Aer.* 8 and Empedokles B100.[20] This is a case where it is appropriate to remind ourselves that comic caricature must be caricature of something, and when we recall the scale of artistic experiment which characterized the fifth century it seems prudent to accept the implications of 148 ff., including the fact that Strepsiades says,

[19] The passages are collected by Diels-Kranz, i. 478 ff. Cf. also the 'Pythagorean' of Theokr. 14.5 f.

[20] On the whole question of experiment cf. G. E. R. Lloyd, *Proc. Camb. Phil. Soc.* cxc (1964), 50 ff.; remember also that Meton was a contemporary of Aristophanes, and that at least one famous experiment had been enshrined in legend (the Egyptian king's attempt to discover the original language of mankind) by the time that Hdt. ii. 2 was written.

on hearing that Socrates had asked Chairephon how far a flea jumped, not 'And did Chairephon know?' but 'How then did he measure it?'—not, perhaps, the question which a real Strepsiades would have asked, but revealing in its implication. There was probably much more scientific experiment in the fifth century than a cursory acquaintance with the fragments of the Presocratics might suggest. Against our general impression that there was little interest in particular species of animal (though there was certainly readiness to generalize about the animal kingdom as a whole, especially with reference to reproduction), we must set the fact that Alkmaion is alleged to have believed that goats breathe through their ears (A7), Anaxagoras (A115) and Diogenes (A31) held theories about the respiratory system of fishes, and Demokritos had something to say about the movement of caterpillars (B126) and how a spider spins its web (A150). We must also remember that in 331 ff. Aristophanes treats doctors on the same footing as seers, musicians, and philosophers. In Epikrates fr. 11 Plato and his pupils are represented as studying the classification of vegetables; we do not have to believe that Plato did this, but we must recognize taxonomy as a fourth-century intellectual activity which a comic poet could incorporate in philosophy.

The second element is the extensive treatment of entry to the school as initiation into mysteries. There is nothing in our evidence for the sophists to suggest that they used the language or procedures of mysteries and initiation, and from earlier times the nearest approach to this is the 'secrets' of the Pythagoreans (Arist. fr. 192 = 132 [Ross]; Pythagoras A7);[21] but the analogy between initiation and admission to a course of instruction is an obvious one—Plato's Socrates exploits it humorously in *Euthd.* 277D and more seriously in *Smp.* 209E—and the reasonable explanation is that Aristophanes is not caricaturing here but presenting a metaphor in concrete form,

---

[21] Cf. Guthrie, *op. cit.,* i. 175 ff.

again in accordance with the broad and reckless sweep
of 331 ff.

In the portrait of Socrates there are certain distinctive
features which recur in the individual Socrates whom
we know from Plato and Xenophon.

In Pl. *Smp.* 221B Alkibiades says, with reference to
Socrates' cool bearing on the retreat from Delion, 'I
thought, Aristophanes, as you put it, that he went on his
way there as he does here, "swaggering and glancing
sideways"' (an abbreviation and adaptation of *Clouds*
362).

Plato also represents Alkibiades (*Smp.* 220B) as describing the astonishment which Socrates evoked at the
siege of Poteidaia by going barefoot and thinly clad in
the coldest weather. Xenophon comments (*Mem.* i. 2.
1, 3.5 ff., 6.2) on his indifference to cold, heat, hunger,
and discomfort in general. Philosophical pallor is a contradictory ingredient within Aristophanes' portrait;[22] living indoors is not conducive to endurance out of doors,
but either can be treated separately as a consequence
of alienation from ordinary life. As for philosophical
squalor, it seems unlikely that a man whose company
was cultivated by Alkibiades and Kritias actually smelt
worse than his contemporaries and carried more vermin,
but there are indications that washing—as one might expect in a place where the water-supply fell short of what
we should regard as adequate and the sanitary conditions far short of what we could even tolerate—was regarded by the Greeks as a luxury rather than a necessity
and was associated with great occasions (*Peace* 868, Pl.
*Smp.* 174A).[23] Possibly Socrates *was* rather dirty, and
possibly his dirtiness was treated as a manly and high-
minded indifference to discomfort.[24]

Many points of contact between *Clouds* and the ex-

[22] Cf. the 'Pythagorean' of Theokr. 14.5 f., and Gow ad loc.
[23] Cf. *Clouds* 837.
[24] The Scholion on *Clouds* 835 observes that what is there intended to show the Socratics in a ridiculous light could also be
taken as reflecting creditably on their manliness.

tant corpus of Socratic dialogues have been considered, and many have been thought to show that Aristophanes knew and expected his audience to recognize characteristic peculiarities of Socrates' methods and manners. The test case is 137, where the student tells Strepsiades that by knocking at the door so noisily he has 'caused the miscarriage (*exēmblōkas*) of a discovery'.[25] The metaphor reminds us of the famous passage in *Theaetetus* where Plato makes Socrates speak of his technique as 'midwife' to the birth of ideas from the minds of others; the term *exambloun* is used there (150E) of those who have left Socrates' company too soon. If this is a genuine point of contact, some remarkable conclusions follow. The first is that Aristophanes is so well acquainted with Socrates' terminology that he can allude to it in a single word, without any enlargement—without even ending the line within the same field of metaphor. The second is that, if this is so, the play should be full of similar allusions; yet, as we read on, we find that the words and phrases which sound like allusions (479 f. 'apply devices' [*mēkhanās*], 489 f. 'snatch it up [*hypharpasei*] at once') are not attested in Plato. In other words, comparison with Plato does not work as a criterion of the authenticity of terminology ascribed to Socrates in *Clouds*. The third conclusion is that a Socratic metaphor so important and well known that one word in the *Clouds* sufficed to make a humorous allusion was wholly neglected by Plato in his earlier representations of Socrates (including *Ap.*) and exploited, at a comparatively late date, in one dialogue alone.[26] These conclusions so lack plausibility that they tempt us to seek another explanation of 'caused a miscarriage', and the obvious explanation is that since words meaning 'give birth' were so freely used in a metaphorical sense the interruption of an intellectual exercise

---

[25] Cf. W. Schmid, *Philologus*, xcvii (1948), 219 f., and Taylor, *Varia Socratica* (Oxford, 1911), 148 ff.

[26] In Pl. *Smp.* the subject, Eros, not the 'midwife' conceit, is the reason for the detailed subsumption of philosophical study under 'generation (*tokos*) in beauty'.

by a shock and a loud noise was appropriately described
as 'miscarriage'. Strepsiades, whose life has been spent in
close acquaintance with sheep and goats (45, 71 f.),
creatures which are sensitive to sudden fright when preg-
nant, is naturally interested.

Again, that Socrates tells Strepsiades (742) to solve a
problem 'by right division' has no bearing[27] on the 'division' or 'classification' which is introduced by Plato in
*Phdr.* 266B, assumes great importance in *Sph.* and *Plt.*,
and is part-object of Epikrates' caricature of Plato. To
break down a problem into its components is a necessary
stage towards its solution, and 'divide' (*dihairein*) was
used before Aristophanes both of physical division
(Hdt.) and (Herakl. B1) of dividing a topic into items;
Plato also uses it (*La.* 197D) of Prodikos's semantic distinctions. What Xenophon (*Mem.* iv. 5.12) calls 'classify
(*dialegein*) generically' is seen, if we examine the context carefully, to be quite different from Platonic
'division'.

Socrates' tutorial method, as portrayed in the *Clouds*,
could pass as a bare caricature of the dialectical skill
with which, in Plato, he secures the co-operation of
others in a quest for metaphysical proofs.[28] Yet it is hard
to believe that the sophists taught solely by continuous
exposition, and that they never set their pupils problems
and exercises or never listened seriously to the answers
and suggestions which they received. Any teacher of any
subject must on occasion, however inadequately, act as
'midwife', and the enlargement on this metaphor in *Tht.*
is likely to mean not that Socrates was the only person
to attempt such a technique or to have such an experience, but that, given his belief that awareness of one's
own ignorance is the foundation of wisdom (*Ap.*
21B ff.), he did not claim to contribute to our knowledge
of reality *except* as midwife.

The Scholion on *Clouds* 703 acutely observes that the

27 Ctr. Schmid, *loc. cit.*, 221.
28 Cf. *Clouds* 703. R. Philippson, *Rhein. Mus.* lxxxi (1932),
30 ff., presses the resemblance very hard.

advice given to Strepsiades to drop a line of inquiry
which has led to an impasse and take a fresh starting-
point (cf. 743 ff.) is Socratic; so indeed it is, especially
in short early dialogues such as *Lysis;* but it is also characteristic of any active intellect, and the sophists would
not have taken many fees if they had done nothing but
reduce a pupil to a stupefied silence and despair at his
own ignorance.

Thus the characteristics of the individual Socrates
which are common to Aristophanes, Plato, and Xenophon appear to fall entirely within the limits of the
physically obvious.[29] Outside these limits, the disagree-
ments are formidable.

1. Interests. Plato's Socrates absolutely denies that he
has any interest in, or knowledge of, astronomy and geology (*Ap.* 18B ff.); cf. Xen. *Mem.* i. 1.11 ff., iv. 7.6. Indeed, he professes ignorance of all technical and specialized subjects; the manner in which he expresses himself
on the subject of metre (*Rep.* 400B–C), referring uncer-
tainly to words which he has heard from Damon, is
noteworthy.

2. Religion. The Socrates of Plato and Xenophon is
not only a pious man, who participates in the observ-

[29] Some of the arguments by which the list has been extended do
not survive a careful reading of the passages cited in support of
them, e.g., Gelzer, *Mus. Helv.* xiii (1956), 71, on the bed (*skimp-
ous*), 'auf dem man anscheinend bei Sokrates zu Hause sass (Pl.
*Prt.* 310C)'—but Hippokrates sits on Socrates' bed because he has
found Socrates there asleep (it is still dark) and has woken him up;
Schmid, *loc. cit.* 211, thinks (with the scholion) that 'looking sideways' describes the same expression as 'looking up like a bull' (Pl.
*Phd.* 117B), which it obviously does not; he refers also (213, cf.
Taylor, *op. cit.*, 143, 146) to the 'fellow-diners' of Xen. *Mem.* iii.
14.1 ff.—but there is nothing there to suggest that Socrates customarily ate with the same people, and it has no bearing whatever on
the life of the students in the school; on Schmid, *loc. cit.*, 214, cf.
415 n. in my commentary. The remarks of the Xenophontean Socrates on spiders (*Mem.* i. 3.12, iii. 11.6) do not go beyond commonplace observation, and hardly support (*pace* Römer, *Sitz. Bayr.
Akad. Wiss.* 1896, 266, n. 1) Aristophanes' presentation of Socrates
as an entomologist.

ances of the society in which he lives (Xen. *Mem.* i.
1.2 ff., 2.64, 3.1 ff., *Ap.* 24), but displays an unwavering
faith in the reality of the gods (Xen. *Mem.* i. 1.19) and
the providential government of the universe.

3. Teaching. Nothing could be more alien from the
Socrates of Plato and Xenophon than to teach young
men how to achieve worldly success by exploitation of
the arts to which the world yields. He professes total
unfamiliarity with the lawcourts (Pl. *Ap.* 17D) and the
machinery of public life (*ibid.* 32A–B, *Grg.* 473E), and
his hostility to rhetoric is outspoken (*Grg. passim,* cf.
Xen. *Mem.* i. 2.31). So far from taking money for teaching (Pl. *Ap.* 19D ff., Xen. *Mem.* i. 2.60, 6.3), he likens
such a procedure to prostitution (*ibid.* 6.13).

What is the explanation of this fundamental conflict
between Aristophanes on the one side and Plato and
Xenophon on the other? There are three possible explanations.[30]

(i) The first is that Aristophanes portrays, through
caricature, the truth; Plato and Xenophon are writing fiction, putting their own ideas into the mouth of an interesting and stimulating man of their fathers' generation, a
man 'canonized', in the eyes of many reflective and educated Athenians, by a punishment out of all proportion
to any offence which he may have given.

[30] I confine within this footnote one of the curiosities of modern
scholarship, the theory elaborated by H. Erbse, *Hermes,* lxxxii
(1954), 385 ff., that Aristophanes distinguishes between Socrates
and the sophists and absolves Socrates of immoral sophistic teaching. The theory is adequately refuted by (i) simple restatement of
the sequence: Strepsiades entrusts the education of Pheidippides to
Socrates; Pheidippides, duly educated and received from the hands
of Socrates by Strepsiades, assaults his father; Strepsiades, with
divine encouragement, destroys Socrates' house ('nur das Lokal',
pleads Erbse) and pursues him with blows, (ii) by the fact that in
order to explain away passages which are irreconcilable with this
theory it is necessary to pretend that Old Comedy is an art-form
very different from what we know it to be; e.g., Erbse, 411, suggests that the Student who takes Strepsiades in has misunderstood
the teaching of his master—but what of his generic similarity to the
servant of Euripides in *Ach.* and the servant of Agathon in *Thes-
mophoriazusae?*

Arbitration is made difficult by our apparent shortage of witnesses who are not emotionally committed. Socrates became a subject of controversy within a few years of his death, and the works of Plato and Xenophon were necessarily written from the standpoint of parties to the controversy. In the following generation those who interested themselves in Socrates were either the philosophical heirs of Plato or antagonistic to Plato. The following considerations, however, tell somewhat against the hypothesis that Aristophanes was right in suggesting that Socrates professed to teach science and oratory and that he exacted fees for doing so.

(*a*) If Plato and Xenophon are to be regarded as engaged in a conspiracy to conceal the truth, it was a conspiracy of exceptional audacity, trusting to outright denial rather than to suppression; it was also one of exceptional efficiency. There were, after all, other writers of the period who made Socrates the hero of philosophical dialogues. Themistius 34.5 refers to the 'genuine Socratic company (*choros*)', Kebes, Phaidon, Aristippos, and Aischines of Sphettos, who 'remained within the boundaries', *sc.* of inquiry into good and evil in man, household, and city (cf. Euseb. *Prep. Ev.* xv. 62.7 ff.). Sextus Empiricus *Math.* vii. 190.1 refers to the Cyrenaics as rejecting enquiry into scientific causation, and so following (i.e., claiming to follow) the lead of Socrates (cf. Apul. *De Deo Socr.* prol. II, p. 2.11 ff.). Aristotle, who had his emotional commitment to Plato under control and had none to Socrates, gives no sign of entertaining the idea that Socrates was a professional sophist.[31]

(*b*) Allegations which support Aristophanes either lack credentials or are hedged with careful reservations.

References in other comic poets—viz. Telekleides frr. 39, 40 (Socrates a collaborator with Euripides; cf. Aris-

---

[31] If he had entertained it, he would have done so in the lost *Sophistes,* and we could expect to hear something about it in the later literature on Socrates. There are a few biographical data on Socrates in citations from other lost works of Aristotle (e.g., fr. 93 = 58 [Ross]), the implications of which are not really faced by Taylor, 61 f., 66 f.

tophanes fr. 376), Eupolis fr. 352 ('a beggar who wastes his time talking'), Eupolis fr. 361 (Socrates steals an oinochoe at a party), Ameipsias fr. 9 (Socrates shoeless) —simply suggest that the presentation of Socrates in comedy was internally consistent.

Idomeneus (fr. 16) certainly revived the allegation that Socrates taught oratory, and Aristoxenos (fr. 59 [Wehrli]) said that he took money, at least by 'collecting small change thrown to him' as to a beggar. Idomeneus, however, who asserted *inter alia* that Perikles murdered Ephialtes (fr. 8), seems to have belonged to that historiographical tradition which repeated, as if it were the plain truth, the most reckless jokes of comic poets (fr. 14, on Hypereides, smells of comedy) and the allegations of misconduct which politicians brought against their rivals (fr. 12, on the intemperance of Demosthenes, is simply a summary of Aischines i. 171 f.). We may suspect that for Idomeneus *Clouds* was itself the most important evidence for the life of Socrates.[32]

Aristoxenos claimed in his *Life of Socrates* that his father Spintharos knew Socrates personally (fr. 54A); he may have been on the track of the truth when he counteracted the Academic idealization of Socrates by speaking of his vehement anger (frr. 54A, 54B, 56—and reference to the effect of this anger on his face and manner suggests genuine reminiscence) and his considerable sexual appetite (the qualification 'but without crime' [*adikiā:* fr. 55, cf. 54A–B] absolves Aristoxenos from the charge of reckless polemic); but if Aristoxenos was right about 'collecting small change' the origin of the story may lie in something which Socrates once did or said for a joke.

(c) The testimony of Aristippos is not without value. He seems to have been hostile to Plato (Arist. *Rhet.* 1398B29, cf. Demetr. *Eloc.* 288), but this did not entail hostility to Socrates (cf. especially fr. 100A [Mannebach]). He alleged that Socrates received food and wine

[32] Cf. Ephoros fr. 196 on the causes of the Peloponnesian War, and Polybios's criticism (xii. 13.1 ff.) of Timaios fr. 35B.

from wealthy friends (fr. 7): an allegation which could well be true—how Socrates made a living is one of the mysterious things about him—but its edge is blunted by the addition of the detail that Socrates took only a small portion of what he was given.[33] So far from alleging that Socrates took money, Aristippos implied that he did not (frr. 3A, 6). If the evidence of Aristippos and Aristoxenos is the best that could be done by men critical of Plato's version of the Socratic tradition, it is so far from weakening Plato's case that by implication it strengthens it.

( *d* ) What is more important than evidence from philosophical sources is that Lysias, in a speech written for a client prosecuted by Aischines of Sphettos, says (fr. I. 2 [Thalheim]): 'I thought that as my opponent had been a pupil of Socrates and talked so much and so impressively about justice and virtue he would not have attempted or ventured on conduct characteristic of the worst and most dishonest people.' Lysias, of course, was making a point to serve his client's case; yet the line which he decided to pursue was not 'Aischines was taught by Socrates to cheat and make wrong appear right' but 'I trusted Aischines *because* he had learned from Socrates', and what is said here about 'justice and virtue' is fully in harmony with Xenophon's statement ( *Mem.* i. 1.16) of the subjects of Socrates' discourses.

(ii) The second possibility is that Aristophanes caricatures So̎crates as he was in 424/23; Plato and Xenophon portray him as he became in the last twenty years of his life.

All that can be said about this theory is that it is the only recourse of those who believe that because Aristophanes and Plato are both admirable writers they must also both be just, accurate, and truthful. There is no other evidence for or against the theory. Certainly the intellectual autobiography put into Socrates' mouth in

[33] The allegation is part of an anecdote about Aristippos; its source might be Aischines of Sphettos ( cf. fr. 49 [Dittmar]), but is more probably Phainias of Eresos ( cf. fr. 31 [Wehrli]).

Pl. *Phd.* 96A ff. is not evidence for it.[34] Socrates there
says that when he was young he very much wanted to
know the causes (αἰτίαι) of things, and speculated on
physics and biology. Then (97B–C) 'I heard someone
reading from a book which he said was by Anaxagoras,
and relating how Mind was . . . the cause of everything.'
So Socrates read Anaxagoras; but being disappointed to
find that Anaxagoras's explanation was mechanistic and
failed to reveal how Mind operated as the ultimate
cause, he abandoned this line of inquiry (98B–99D). It
is plain that this account of a metaphysical curiosity
which the scientific speculations of others failed to satisfy
is separated by a very wide gulf from Aristophanes' portrayal of a Socrates who professed to teach scientific doctrine in mechanistic terms. In Plato, *Ap.* 19D Socrates
asks all those in the jury 'who have ever at any time up
to now listened to my conversation' to tell their fellow
jurors 'whether anyone among you has ever heard me
say a word on such subjects' (~19B5, C4–6). It is quite
possible for both this and *Phd.* 96A ff. to be true, if we
take them as meaning just what they say; if we read more
into *Phd.* 96A ff. than it says, reconciliation becomes
impossible.

Even if *Phd.* 96A ff. were taken as evidence for Socrates' early interest in science, it would not touch the
question of his teaching oratory for money, which is fundamental to the plot of the *Clouds.*

(iii) The third possibility is that Plato and Xenophon
tell the truth; Aristophanes attaches to Socrates the characteristics which belonged to the sophists in general but
did not belong to Socrates.

This is the view taken by Plato in *Ap.* 23D: 'When
they are asked, by what actions or teaching Socrates
"corrupts the young", they have nothing to say; they
don't know; but so that it may not be apparent that they
are at a loss for an answer, they repeat the accusations
which are so readily made against all philosophers, "what

34 Ctr. Schmid, *loc. cit.,* 215.

is up in the sky and what is below the earth" and "not
believing in gods" and "making wrong appear right".'
Plato treats the formal accusation brought against Socrates in 399 as the culmination of a long process of slan-
der to which the *Clouds* itself made a significant contribution (18B ff., 19C, 26B ff.).

If we adopt this answer, we must go on to ask: was
Aristophanes acting in ignorance? If not, was he actu-
ated by cynical malice, or by an equally cynical decision
to exploit popular prejudice for the purposes of his craft
as a comic poet?

Ignorance can almost certainly be eliminated. Admittedly, to suppose—as if Athens were a village and Attica
a parish—that all adult male citizens knew one another's
business would be naïve, and not only naïve, but contrary to the implications of some passages in Plato and
to the fact that the Athenian orator often introduces a
name in a way which suggests he does not expect the
jury to know the man in question. We should note particularly Pl. *La.* 180C ff., where Lysimachos knows Socrates as a fellow demesman and son of a friend of his
father, but knows so little about him that when he heard
from his son about the edifying and stimulating conversation of a certain Socrates he did not identify the two.[35]
If the *Clouds* had not been written, it would not have
been implausible to suggest that Socrates was at most a
name to Aristophanes. Yet we cannot say both 'Aristophanes knew nothing about Socrates' and 'Aristophanes expected his audience to be familiar with Socrates'.
One of these propositions must be discarded, and there
are difficulties in the way of discarding the second. On
the same occasion as the *Clouds*, Ameipsias won second
prize with a play called *Konnos*. Ath. 218C, speaking of
Protagoras, says: 'Ameipsias in *Konnos*, produced two
years earlier' (*sc.* than Eupolis's *Flatterers*) 'does not
count him (*sc.* Protagoras) in the *choros* of the intel-

[35] Cf. Pl. *Euthyphro* 2B on Meletos, Dem. xix. 244 on Timarchos,
and Dem. xxxix. 7 ff. on the confusion which might result if two
men had the same name, patronymic and demotic.

lectuals.' Whether Athenaios means 'does not speak of
him as being among intellectuals' (cf. Pl. *Prt.* 315B, on
the gathering to listen to the sophists in Kallias's house:
'and there were also some Athenians in the *choros*', and
cf. Themistius above) or 'does not include him in the
chorus ⟨of the play, which is composed⟩ of philosophers' cannot be decided with absolute certainty, but the
former interpretation introduces a most improbable ambiguity into a sentence which is, after all, about a comedy. (Incidentally, I see no good reason to believe that
Ameipsias used the word *phrontistēs* for 'intellectual'.)
Now, Konnos is mentioned by Plato's Socrates (*Euthd.*
272C, 295D, *Mnx.* 235E) as the music teacher from
whom he continued, even late in life, to learn. Furthermore, fr. 9 of Ameipsias begins with words addressed
directly to Socrates and ends with a remark about him.
The assignation of this citation to *Konnos* and the supposition that in that play the chorus represented a gathering
of intellectuals, who at some point in the play were
named individually, do not seem unduly rash. Add to
this that both the *Clouds* and Ameipsias 9 refer to Socrates' physical toughness and that *Clouds* 362 was accepted by Plato as an accurate description of Socrates'
manner in the streets of Athens, and it follows that Socrates' appearance, manner, and way of life were widely
known at Athens in 424/3. If we accept the evidence of
Pl. *Smp.* 219E ff., he must have been talked about after
his remarkable behaviour at Poteidaia, as a man of ex-
traordinary toughness. His bearing on the retreat from
Delion (*Smp.* 220E ff., *La.* 181B) is likely to have spread
his reputation further, but not necessarily for his own
good; human nature being what it is, our reaction to
those who look much braver than we feel in a headlong
retreat is not always generous admiration. At Poteidaia
'the soldiers looked askance at Socrates, feeling that he
despised them' (*Smp.* 220B).

Several years later (later, in fact, than the latest stra-
tum that can be detected in the revision of the *Clouds*),
Aristophanes refers (*Birds* 1281 f.) to current crazes at

Athens: 'they were all Sparta-crazy . . . they wore their hair long, they went hungry and dirty, they socratized, they carried sticks'. Here cultivation of Socratic asceticism is linked with superficial laconism, and it would be hard to believe that Aristophanes used the verb *sōkratein* without assuming that the majority of his audience would know what he was talking about.

However, Socrates was evidently known to Aristophanes in 424/23 as a conspicuous individual and as a subject of some striking anecdotes, something more than a name. Must we then convict Aristophanes of cynicism? Not necessarily; there remains a very important factor which has not been given its due in discussion of this problem.

We *study* Greek literature and philosophy, and in this study we set ourselves very high standards of accuracy. But in order to understand the *Clouds* we must make an imaginative effort to adopt an entirely different position, the position of someone to whom all philosophical and scientific speculation, all disinterested intellectual curiosity, is boring and silly. To such a person distinctions which are of fundamental importance to the intellectual appear insignificant, incomprehensible, and often imperceptible. Nothing is more striking, in all departments of human life, than the extreme subjectivity of the evaluation of differences. For everyone who understands and cares about the difference between Bach and Rachmaninov, the Labour Party and the Communist Party, Oxford and Cambridge, or England and Scotland, there is another to whom the difference is of no interest or consequence. Catholics object when a Protestant tells them that they 'worship' the Virgin Mary; but to an agnostic the dispute seems to be splitting a hair so fine that it is hardly visible. This subjectivity of differences is nowhere more conspicuous than in popular attitudes to the intellectual. Until very recently—nowadays, the illustrator has to choose between library and laboratory as background —a 'professor' in popular literature was a man from

whom one could expect a learned opinion on any subject
from the history of Assyria to the anatomy of the newt.
Aristophanes, as a successful writer of comedies for a
mass audience, did not have to make a great effort to
look at the world from a popular standpoint; he must in
essentials have adopted that standpoint by nature, for
otherwise he would not have been a comic poet. To
judge from the extant citations, the comic poets of the
fifth century were unanimous in their adoption of what
seems to their modern readers a reactionary and philis-
tine *persona*, and in this respect they resemble not so
much modern writers of comedies for the sophisticated
theatre as comedians who cater to a mass audience. The
extent to which artistic devotion, imagination, and craftsmanship could be divorced from genuine intellectual
curiosity was greater among the Greeks than we expect
to find in artists, novelists, or musicians of our own
time.[36] I suggest, then, that although the difference
between Socrates and the Sophists was known to Aristophanes, in the sense that the data which constituted
that difference were available to his organs of perception, he simply did not see it, and if it had been pointed
out to him he would not have regarded it as important.[37]
He drew one basic distinction, between the normal man
and the abnormal man. The normal man works and
fights, and takes as much as he can of song, dance, food,
drink, sex, sleep, and good company. The abnormal man
is essentially parasitic on the normal; he does no real

[36] A. W. Gomme, *More Essays in Greek History and Literature*
(Oxford, 1962), 82 ff., compares Aristophanes to Bernard Shaw,
and although from some points of view they are less alike than
Gomme suggests, from another they are more so. Shaw, who
clothed many frivolous prejudices in the language of rationality,
understood few of the subjects on which he wrote most fluently
and vigorously, but what he did understand better than most other
men was what can be effectively said and done on the stage.

[37] Furthermore, if Socrates conversed and argued as he did, anyone who stayed to hear only part of a conversation might have
gone away with an extraordinarily misleading impression; cf. L. G.
Versenyi, *Socratic Humanism* (New Haven, 1963), p. 155.

work, he undermines the loyalties on which the city's continued existence depends,[88] and he casts a shadow over the ordinary pleasures of life by the unspoken implication that there may be other, secret pleasures accessible to him alone. Aristophanes casts his net very wide in separating the abnormal and parasitic from the normal and essential; in *Clouds* 331 ff. seers, medical writers, and lyric poets are included, under the general heading *Sophistai*, as 'idle', and the parasitic philosopher, as typified by the comic Socrates, has obvious affinities with other parasitic types in comedy: the seer (*Peace* 1043 ff.), the oracle-monger (*Birds* 959 ff.), and the poet (*Birds* 904 ff.).[89]

If Socrates professed no original scientific doctrines, at least he was prepared to talk about them rationally, even if only to pick holes in the doctrines of others (Xen. *Mem.* iv. 7.7), and Plato represents him as devoting his last hour on earth to the exposition of cosmology and geology (*Phd.* 108C ff.). We, as historians of literature and philosophy, can see the difference between the writings of Anaxagoras or Diogenes of Apollonia and the myth which in *Phd.* is wholly subservient to a moral end (114D); but are we to suppose that, if Socrates ever talked as he does in *Phd.*, Aristophanes saw any difference? Again, if Socrates took no fees for teaching the young men who listened to him, these young men came, on Plato's admission (*Ap.* 23C), from the class which had most wealth and leisure; do we suppose that Aristophanes saw any difference between the fees which Kallias paid to Protagoras and the friendship, patronage, and hospitality which Alkibiades made available to Soc-

[88] The extent to which the survival of the city-state depended on the physical toughness of its adult male citizens must never be forgotten. It helps to explain not only the attitude of characters in comedy but Plato's whole approach to the construction of an ideal state.

[89] Cf. Gelzer, *Mus. Helv.* xiii. 76 ff. and A. E. Roggwiller, *Dichter und Dichtung in der attischen Komödie* (Diss. Zurich, 1926), 19 ff.

rates?[40] Or again, if Socrates did not teach his young
men to seek worldly success by means of persuasive oratory, this is, after all, what they did seek, and what some
of them, notably Alkibiades, achieved. Would Aristophanes understand that the 'pupils' were doing what the
'master' had discouraged them from doing?[41]

Perhaps the most revealing single passage in the play
is 358 ff. The Clouds, in saluting Socrates, say 'we would
not listen to any other of the *meteōrosophistai* of the
present time except Prodikos, for his artistry (*sophiā*)
and intelligence (*gnōmē*), and you, because you swag-
ger in the streets . . .' The humorous point of these lines
is the grotesque anticlimax of 'and you . . .' Prodikos
was the most distinguished and respected intellectual of
the day, and achieved in his lifetime (as Einstein did,
uniquely, in this century) something like the 'proverbial'
status of Thales. In *Birds* 688 ff. the birds, giving their
own version of cosmogony, say 'Attend to us . . . so that
when you've heard our account . . . you will know the
truth and not bother about Prodikos any more', as if
Prodikos were the authority which one would otherwise
follow. In fr. 490 (from *Tagenistai*) some very anti-
intellectual character grumbles 'This man's been cor-
rupted by a *book*, or by Prodikos, or by some idle talker

[40] In Ameipsias fr. 9 the second speaker says of Socrates 'But
he, although as hungry, never deigned to flatter'. An impressive
testimonial, at first glance; but what kind of comedy was this, if
the utterance and point ended there? I suspect that the citation
(Diog. Laert. ii. 28, in company with the radically altered 'moraliz-
ing' version of *Clouds* 412 ff.) has been docked of its tail and thus
of its sting.

[41] Alkibiades had already been ridiculed by Aristophanes in 427
(fr. 198.6, from *Banqueters*) and 425 (*Acharnians* 716). It was
common in the first decade of the fourth century to blame Socrates
for the misdeeds of Alkibiades (cf. Xen. *Mem.* i. 2.12 ff., Isok. xi. 5),
and this 'guilt by association' may go back to a time when Alkibiades' behaviour was merely annoying. Aischines i. 173 represents
Socrates as having been executed for his teaching of Kritias. The
meaning of Hypereides fr. 55 'our ancestors punished Socrates *epi
logois* ('for his theories' or 'for what he said') is obscure, since we
do not know the context.

(*ādoleschēs*) or other'! Neither of these two passages expresses hostility on the part of Aristophanes himself towards Prodikos, and it is not difficult to see why this should be so. Prodikos combined intellectual pursuits (perhaps he had not yet committed himself to the rationalist doctrines attributed to him [B5]) with high artistic achievement, and that too in literary genres which were novel enough to be interesting but not so novel as to offend conservative tastes. Xen. *Mem.* ii. I. 21 ff., calling him 'the accomplished (*sophos*) Prodikos', pays him the high compliment of summarizing his allegorical description of Herakles' choice between Virtue and Vice (B1). To Phaidros in Pl. *Smp.* 177B he is 'the excellent Prodikos': and if there is irony in the references to him by Plato's Socrates (*Prt.* 315D, *Tht.* 151B) it is anything but transparent. The statement of Suda π 2365 that he was executed as 'corrupting the young' (~ Scholion on Pl. *Rep.* 600C) is not supported by any early evidence. *Clouds* 358 ff. are intelligible as comedy only if we believe that Aristophanes shared the popular esteem of Prodikos as an artist, and regarded Socrates, by contrast, as a pretentious parasite who inexplicably fascinated some wealthy young men but had nothing coherent to say and produced nothing of any artistic merit. Socrates lacked aesthetic attraction; and he was indifferent to what Aristophanes, in common with most of his audience, regarded as the good things of life. That is why he was chosen as the victim of a comedy which set out to exploit the humorous potentialities of intellectual activity.

One question remains: the nature of the effect at which Aristophanes was aiming. We can at any rate infer, from the mere fact of his writing the play, that he did not regard the pursuit of philosophy as a necessary ingredient of a civilized society, and his portrayal of the effect of Socrates' teaching on the character of Pheidippides is an invitation to violence, or repressive legislation, against such teachers. The inference that it was his

purpose to arouse feeling against the sophists rests on
the existence of the convention that the poet is a teacher
and comedy a weapon. Unfortunately (for those who
like their issues simple) it is improbable that any two
people, or even one poet at two different moments,
treated the convention equally seriously. Plato took it
seriously enough (Lg. 934C–936A exhibit an interesting
sequence of thought: damage by madmen–thoughtless
vilification–ridicule–comedy), but Plato and Aristophanes were not very alike. The abundant anecdotage
about the effects of comedy on individuals ridiculed in
it is of late date and unimpressive pedigree. We can only
observe that the Athenians did not necessarily do what
Aristophanes told them to do (the audience which ac-
claimed *Knights* proceeded to elect Kleon general), and
we must assume that Aristophanes too had observed, before he wrote the *Clouds,* the extent to which a comedy
did or did not influence public opinion. A desire to influence opinion and to combat whatever seems wrong
or foolish is common to comic poets and other people.
But unlike other people, who are free to interpret comedy from any standpoint of their own definition, the
comic poet is affected, in the composition of his plays, by
many forces peculiar to the temperament characteristic
of his own art: willingness to play to the gallery for the
sake of that massive gale of laughter which is the sweet
voice of success; instinctive distrust of appraisals which
are too cool and refined; a craftsman's pleasure in neat-
ness and novelty; a fundamental irreverence which sees
the ludicrous side of everything; a certain insensitivity
to cruelty; and an inability, familiar to many satirists and
caricaturists, to resist the temptation to exploit the possibilities which are revealed after the execution of the
original comic design has begun.

It is tempting to wonder why the *Clouds* came third
out of three when it was performed, but it is best to say
nothing in the absence of the evidence which alone
could suggest a rational answer: the plays presented by

the two other competing dramatists. Perhaps, by the standards of the time, they were better plays; Aristophanes did not think so, but upon this question, as upon others, we are at liberty to refrain from expressing an opinion.

# 4. ELENCHUS

## THE ELENCHUS IN THE EARLY DIALOGUES

The outstanding method in Plato's earlier dialogues is
the Socratic elenchus. 'Elenchus' in the wider sense
means examining a person with regard to a statement he
has made, by putting to him questions calling for further
statements, in the hope that they will determine the
meaning and the truth-value of his first statement. Most
often the truth-value expected is falsehood; and so 'elenchus' in the narrower sense is a form of cross-examination
or refutation. In this sense it is the most striking aspect
of the behaviour of Socrates in Plato's early dialogues.
He is always putting to somebody some general question, usually in the field of ethics. Having received an
answer (let us call it the primary answer), he asks many
more questions. These secondary questions differ from
the primary one in that, whereas that was a matter of
real doubt and difficulty, the answers to all these seem
obvious and inescapable. Socrates usually phrases them
so that the natural answer is yes; and if you say anything
else you are likely to seem irrational or at least queer.
In other words, they are not so much requests for information as demands for an assent that cannot very well
be withheld. They often seem at first irrelevant to the
primary question, and sometimes they seem to fall into
two disconnected groups among themselves. But at last
Socrates says: 'Come now, let us add our admissions
together' (*Prt.* 332D); and the result of doing so turns
out to be the contradictory of the primary answer. Propo-

The three selections by Richard Robinson are Chapters II, III,
and V of his *Plato's Earlier Dialectic*, 2nd edition (Clarendon Press,
Oxford, 1953). They are reprinted by permission of the publishers
and the author.

sitions to which the answerer feels he must agree have entailed the falsehood of his original assertion.

Such is the Socratic elenchus, often referred to also as *exetasis* or scrutiny and as *basanismus* or assay. It is so common in the early dialogues that we may almost say that Socrates never talks to anyone without refuting him. An exception is his conversation with Cephalus in the first book of the *Republic* (the first book of the *Republic* may be regarded as an early dialogue); but there the subject is personal experience and not abstract ethics.

The sureness of the refutation gives the impression that Socrates possesses knowledge about the subject on which he refutes others. This, however, he invariably denies. 'You treat me', he says in the *Charmides* (165B), 'as if I professed to know the matters I ask about, and as if I might agree with you if I wished to. But that is not so. On the contrary, I inquire into the proposition along with you because I do not know. I will tell you whether I agree or not when I have examined it.' (Cf. *Ap.* 23A.) That is always his attitude; and in harmony therewith he always puts the primary question as a request for information and not as if he were examining a candidate. Throughout the early dialogues, whether engaged in elenchus or not, he usually declares himself ignorant of the answers to all the general ethical questions that he raises. There are some extremely confident statements in the *Apology* and the *Crito,* and in the *Euthydemus* (293B) he admits knowing many small matters; but *Meno* 98B seems to be the only place where he actually professes to know something important.

And we must now observe some other curious disclaimers. Not merely does Socrates sometimes deny by implication that it is the answerer who is refuted ('It is the logos that I chiefly examine', he says, *Prt.* 333C); at other times he even denies that it is Socrates who is doing the refuting. He speaks as if the logos were what was doing the refuting, and as if the logos were a person over whom he had no control, refuting not merely the answerer and himself but even the whole company with equal impartiality and inexorability. He denies that he resembles Daedalus, who made statues move; for the logoi run away without his agency, and he would rather they remained (*Euthyph.* 11D). His language implies that he himself did not foresee the course the argument has taken, but was led along by it blindfolded; and that for all he knew the argument might have turned out a proof instead of a disproof of the original thesis. He even implies at times that there is no refutation at all, of anybody or by anybody or anything. There is only a company of persons engaged in determining the truth-value of a proposition, engaged in an impersonal elenchus in the wider sense.

This denial that he is conducting an elenchus is insincere, and constitutes what is known as the Socratic slyness or irony. The arguments could not be so workmanlike and purposeful, the results could not be so invariably negative, by divine inspiration or by mathematical probability. When we examine one of the arguments in detail, and see just what its logical structure is, we become convinced that from the very first of the secondary questions Socrates saw and intended the refutation of the primary answer. There is an elenchus in the narrower sense; and it is Socrates' own work. When he says of an answer 'Well, that is good enough' (*Grg.* 498A), he gives away the fact that, though the answerer has not admitted as much as he expected, he has admitted enough for his downfall. In reality Socrates is always doing what he does openly in *Republic* I 348–49, looking for a way to persuade the answerer that his thesis is false (348A4); and if the answerer refuses to grant him a premiss (348E) he keeps the conversation going somehow (348E–349B) until he has thought of another starting-point which the answerer will admit and which will serve to refute him. The statements that he is 'seeing whether the answer is true' are insincere. So are the earnest requests for instruction by which he obtains the primary answer. So are his occasional invitations to reciprocity in elenchus (e.g., *Grg.* 462A); he makes them only to persuade the other man to submit to questioning; and, when he is taken at his word and made the answerer, his answers soon become speeches. Insincere also is the pose of suffering from bad memory. In the *Meno* (71C) it is a way to entrap Meno into pontificating, so that he can be refuted. In the *Protagoras* (334C–D) it is a way of forcing Protagoras to answer questions; and Plato makes an imprudent admirer of Socrates point out the inaccuracy (336D). Socrates seems prepared to employ any kind of deception in order to get people into this elenchus.

Plato depicts or asserts various effects as following immediately from this ironical elenchus. One of these is the bewilderment of the answerer. Though the word 'elenchus' is scarcely used in the *Meno* (apparently only 75D), the thing itself is very much there; and Plato puts the following description of its effect into the mouth of the victim:

> Socrates, I heard before I met you that you never do anything but puzzle yourself and others too; and now it seems to me that you are bewitching and drugging and completely spellbinding me, so that I have become saturated with puzzlement. In fact, if I may make a little joke, you are absolutely like the broad electric ray of the sea, both in appearance and otherwise. That fish benumbs anyone who comes near and touches it, and that is what you seem to have done to me now; for really I am numb in mind and mouth, and I do not know how to answer you. Yet I have discoursed on virtue thousands of times and to many people; and done it very well too, as I thought at the time. But now I cannot even say what it is. I think it is a wise decision of yours never to leave Athens; for, if you did such things in another city where you were a stranger, you might be arrested as a wizard. (*Mem.* 80A–B.)

Plato notes also that this ironical elenchus often had the effect of making its victims angry with Socrates and ill disposed towards him. He makes Thrasymachus complain of what he calls 'Socrates' usual slyness' (*Rp.* I

337A). Socrates refuses to make any contribution himself; but when any other person makes one he pulls it to pieces. He ought to realize that questioning is easier than answering (336C). Thrasymachus believes that Socrates deliberately tries to make trouble in arguments (341A). However that may be, there is no doubt that the actual result is sometimes the conversion of a pleasant discussion into a quarrel. Even in the *Laches*, where the elenchus is unusually benign in tone, its first effect is to make two old friends quarrel. In the *Apology* Plato makes Socrates attribute his unpopularity to the elenchus (e.g., 21C–D–E, 23A).

Plato also tells us that this elenchus is very amusing to the bystanders (*Sph.* 230C), especially to the young and rich (*Ap.* 23C, cf. 33C), and that young men treat it as a game and imitate it in and out of season (*Rp.* VII 539B). This effect would naturally increase the anger of the victim against Socrates.

### PLATO'S DISCUSSIONS OF THE ELENCHUS

The picture which we have so far obtained of the Socratic elenchus is by no means a favourable one. This elenchus involved persistent hypocrisy; it showed a negative and destructive spirit; it caused pain to its victims; it thereby made them enemies of Socrates; it thereby brought him to trial, according to his own admission in Plato's *Apology;* and so it brought him to his death.

The question thus arises what Plato conceived to be the justification of the elenchus. For what end was it worth while to be so destructive and insincere, and to incur so much enmity?

Plato certainly thought that it could be justified. He did not regard it as a deplorable defect in Socrates' character, to be explained by medical or psychological doctrines but not to be justified. He held that it had a sufficient reason and was a valuable procedure, to be retained in spite of some undesirable consequences. Furthermore, he certainly held that its justification was not merely the amusement provided for the bystanders.

There are three passages in the dialogues that offer something like a general discussion of the purpose of the elenchus; and we shall examine each in turn. Let us take first a passage from Socrates' conversation with Meno's servant (*Men.* 84). The question is how to construct a square double the area of a given square. The solution is yet to come; but the elenctic part, in which Socrates disproves the servant's false suggestions, is over, and Socrates breaks off to discuss the elenchus with Meno.

> Do you notice, Meno, how far he has advanced already in his recollecting? At first he falsely thought he knew which is the line belonging to the eight-foot square, and answered confidently as if he knew, and did not feel at a loss; whereas now, though he knows no more than he did before, he does at least feel at a loss, and no longer thinks he knows.—You are right.—So now he is better off about the thing he did not know?—I think that, too.—Then did we do him any harm in puzzling him and numbing him like the electric ray?—I think not.—At least it seems that we have made him more likely to find out the truth. For now he will be glad to search for it because he knows he does not know it, whereas formerly he might easily have supposed on many occasions that he was talking sense about the double square if he said that it must have a side of double length.—It seems so.—And do you think he would ever have tried to discover the truth, or to learn what he thought he knew though he did not, if he had not fallen into puzzlement and come to believe that he did not know and desired to know?—I do not think so, Socrates.—Then he was benefited by being numbed?—I think so.

Of two ignorant persons, this passage implies, the one who knows that he is ignorant is better off than the one who supposes that he knows; and that is because the one has, and the other has not, a drive within him that may in time lead him to real knowledge. The elenchus changes ignorant men from the state of falsely supposing that they know to the state of recognizing that they do not know; and this is an important step along the road to knowledge, because the recognition that we do not know at once arouses the desire to know, and thus supplies the motive that was lacking before. Philosophy begins in wonder, and the assertion here made is that elenchus supplies the wonder. Though the passage contains no such word as 'curiosity', we can say without fear of 'misinterpretation by abstraction' that Plato in writing the *Meno* believed that curiosity is essential to the acquisition of knowledge, and that elenchus is the way to arouse curiosity. Elenchus is thus a method of teaching, of instilling intellectual knowledge in other persons. It does not, however, actually increase knowledge, but only prepares the ground for it.

Another discussion of the purpose of elenchus occurs in the late *Sophist* (229E–230E), put into the mouth of another than Socrates, and showing how Plato regarded the elenchus at that time of his life.

> Of education one way seems to be rougher, while the other part of it is smoother.—What are these two parts?— One is the time-honoured and traditional method which men used to adopt with their sons when they did something wrong, and still do adopt very often. It consists partly in anger and partly in a gentler sort of exhortation, and the best name for it as a whole is admonition.—Yes.—But some men appear to have reached the conclusion that all ignorance is involuntary, and that no one will ever learn anything if he thinks he is already a wise man in that respect, and that the admonitory form of education involves great labour and achieves little result.—They are right.—So they aim at the removal of this opinion by another means.— What is that?—They question a man on those matters where he thinks he is saying something although he is really saying nothing. And as he is confused they easily convict his opinions, by bringing them together and putting them side by side, and thus showing that they are contrary to each other at the same time in the same respect about the same things. When the man sees this he becomes angry with himself and gentle towards others. Thus he is relieved

of great and overbearing opinions about himself, and this relief is the pleasantest of all to hear and the surest for the patient. For just as the physicians of the body believe that the body cannot benefit from the nourishment it receives until the internal hindrances are removed, so do those who perform this purification believe about the soul. She cannot profit from the knowledge offered to her, until the elenchus is applied and the man is refuted and brought to shame, thus purifying him from opinions that hinder learning and causing him to think he knows only what he does know and no more.—That is the best and most temperate state to be in.—For all these reasons, Theaetetus, we must say that elenchus is the greatest and most sovereign of the purifications; and the man who has not been subjected to it, even if he be the great king himself, must be regarded by us as suffering from the greatest impurities, and as uneducated and base in the respects in which the truly happy man ought to be purest and noblest.

Here the elenchus is explicitly subsumed under the general notion of education, and explicitly preferred to another form of education in words of the highest praise. Its nature is illustrated by a comparison with medical purging, which brings out the doctrine that elenchus is not itself the instilling of knowledge, but an essential preliminary thereto, consisting in the removal of an all but complete bar to knowledge naturally present in man. This bar is the conceit that we already know.

The third passage that contains a discussion of the purpose of the elenchus is the *Apology*, one of Plato's early works. According to this work, Socrates at his trial regarded his habit of elenchus as one of the main counts against him, and set out to justify or at least to explain it. He declared that it arose from the Delphic god's response to Chaerephon, which was that no one was wiser than Socrates. He felt that he had no wisdom; but he also felt that the god could not lie. After a long time of perplexity, it occurred to him to approach a man with a reputation for wisdom and study him at first hand. He found that the man thought he was wise but was not.

Going then to many other men of repute, he always had
the same experience. In one class, the men of skilful
hands, there was some real wisdom; but this led to so
much conceit of other, non-existent wisdom as more
than outweighed it. Socrates concluded that he was
really wiser than the wise because, whereas they knew
nothing, he knew the single fact that he knew nothing.

But why did Socrates continue the elenchus after he
had ascertained these facts to his satisfaction? Because,
he tells us (23A–B), he felt that the god had imposed
upon him the duty of demonstrating to all men that no
man is wise. Later he says that the god has told him to
philosophize and to scrutinize himself and others (28E);
that the purpose of his elenchus and the command of the
god is to shame people into putting first things first, and
that the first thing is the virtue of the soul (29D–E);
that he is to the Athenian people as a gadfly to a noble
but sluggish horse (30E). In his speech after the determination of the penalty he calls his elenchus an examination of men's lives, for that seems to be the meaning
of ἔλεγχον τοῦ βίου (39C); and describes his purpose as
to put men to shame for living wrongly.

The *Apology*, like the *Meno* and the *Sophist*, regards
elenchus as a way of convincing men that they are ignorant of things they thought they knew; but it places
this procedure in a strongly moral and religious setting
of which the other two works show little trace. It tells us
that the elenchus arose out of a divine oracle, and that
Socrates continued it because he felt divinely com-
manded to do so. It represents the ultimate aim of the
elenchus not as intellectual education but as moral improvement. Its purpose is, as it is expressed at the end
of the *Apology*, to make men better men, to give them
more of the highest virtue of a man; and in practising
it Socrates is a moral reformer.

To many persons the Socratic elenchus would seem a
most unsuitable instrument for moral education. They
would argue that such logic-chopping cannot be followed by most persons, does not command respect, and

at best improves only the agility of the mind while leaving the character untouched. Socrates was certainly a unique reformer if he hoped to make men virtuous by logic.

Yet it is clear that Plato consciously intends to depict Socrates as consciously aiming at the moral improvement of his fellows by means of his elenchus. Looking back on the picture from the late *Sophist*, he contrasts the elenchus with another method of altering men which he calls 'admonition'. 'Admonition' includes the more ordinary methods of moral education, such as rebuke and persuasion and harangue and advice. And Plato says that the practitioners of the elenchus deliberately prefer it to 'admonition'.

This is an aspect of the paradoxical intellectualism of the practical philosophy of Plato, and apparently also of the historical Socrates. It hangs together with the proposition that virtue is knowledge. The method of the Platonic Socrates differs from those of all other moral reformers because of his unusually intellectual conception of what virtue is. He believes that you cannot really be virtuous unless you have a philosophical understanding of the definition of virtue. The practice of virtue is identical with the theory of it. The way to become courageous is to find out what courage is. Contrariwise, he who does not know the definition of virtue will not behave in a virtuous manner. When Socrates says early in the *Apology* that he demonstrated to men that they knew nothing, he means that they knew nothing about wisdom and other forms of virtue; for this is the only matter that interests him. And because you cannot be virtuous without knowing what virtue is, there is to him nothing strange or puzzling in representing as vice in his third speech what he represented as ignorance in his first. In order to make men virtuous, you must make them know what virtue is. And in order to make them know what virtue is, you must remove their false opinion that they already know. And in order to remove this false opinion, you must subject them to elenchus. That is the

way in which, according to the Platonic Socrates, the
elenchus comes to be the appropriate instrument for
moral education.

The Socratic elenchus is a very personal affair, in spite
of Socrates' ironical declarations that it is an impersonal
search for the truth. If the ulterior end of the elenchus
is to be attained, it is essential that the answerer himself
be convinced, and quite indifferent whether anyone else
is. In the first place, he must believe his own primary
statement; otherwise the refutation of that statement will
not convict him of thinking he knew when he did not. In
the second place, the answerer must be quite convinced
of the logical validity of the argument; if he thinks that
the contrary of his thesis does not really follow from the
premisses adduced, he will again not be convicted of
ignorance. Lastly, he must genuinely accept the premisses; that is the implication of *Gorgias* 471D and many
other passages. The art of elenchus is to find premisses
believed by the answerer and yet entailing the contrary
of his thesis. Polus fails to refute Socrates because he
cannot find premisses that Socrates accepts. What the
ordinary man believes would entail the contrary of Socrates' thesis; but Socrates does not believe what the ordinary man believes. When the refutation is a reduction
to absurdity, the conclusion must seem absurd to the
answerer himself. Here again Polus fails, for he reduces
Socrates' thesis to results that seem absurd to Polus and
to most men, but not to Socrates. Socrates and Caesippus
fail in the same way to refute Euthydemus and Dionyso-
dorus (*Euthd.* 294, 298).

Plato brings out the personal nature of elenchus in the
*Gorgias*. That dialogue, which contains the root ἐλεγχ-
over fifty times in its eighty pages, represents Socrates as
contrasting his own procedure with that of the law-
courts. Whereas in law-courts you have to convince a
third party, namely the judges, in the Socratic elenchus

you have to convince your opponent himself. Hence the witnesses who are so effective at trials are useless here. The only true witness and authority is the answerer himself; and if he does not admit the fact it is irrelevant how many others do. The result depends not on a majority of votes, but on the single vote of the answerer (471E–472C, 474A, 475E).

Possibly this aspect of the elenchus explains why Socrates sometimes seems to start the argument with premisses that immediately decide the point, and then to hammer out the inference at most unnecessary length (e.g., *Grg.* 474B–479E). The whole essence of the elenchus lies in making visible to the answerer the link between certain of his actual beliefs and the contradictory of his present thesis. This link must be visible to the questioner before the process begins; and so may well be visible to the onlookers too, including ourselves.

In conscious opposition to the ideal of an argument addressed to this man personally, and really convincing him by starting from premisses that he really believes, which receives its clearest statement in the *Gorgias*, Aristotle set up the ideal of the listener who has the sense to recognize the expert and accept on faith what the expert tells him are the principles of the subject. 'The learner ought to believe', he says (*S.E.* 2, 165B3).

By addressing itself always to this person here and now, elenchus takes on particularity and accidentalness, which are defects. In this respect it is inferior to the impersonal and universal and rational march of a science axiomatized according to Aristotle's prescription. Plato might urge, however, that elenchus is the means by which the irrational and accidental individual is brought to the appreciation of universal science, brought out of his individual arbitrariness into the common world of reason.

If the actual Socrates practised elenchus, how did he come to it? Did he first decide to make men virtuous, then cast about for a means of doing so, and then hit upon elenchus? That seems unlikely. More probably he

practised it at first simply because it was his nature to
inquire into things more deeply than other men, and to
be puzzled by difficulties that had not occurred even to
the experts. Only when he had been asking questions
for some time would he perceive that he knew better
than other men in that he knew his ignorance and they
did not know theirs. And only when he had thoroughly
realized this would he give up asking questions for his
old reason (for he would see it to be futile), and ask
them now for the new end of reforming the answerer by
showing him his ignorance. And very likely the new end
would never have occurred to him but for the experience
that his questions did actually have that result.

### CRITICISM OF THE ELENCHUS

The following objection may be made to the method
of elenchus: it only tells you *that* you are wrong, and
does not also tell you *why*. Real conversion makes you
no longer even want to hold your former thesis, because
it shows you the reason why you held it and the ineffi-
ciency of that reason. But Socrates rarely does this; there
are few parallels to that part of the *Gorgias* where, having disproved the view that Pericles and the rest were
good statesmen, he goes on to show us why we thought
they were. And this is why the elenchus so often misses
its avowed aim, the actual convincing of the answerer
(*Grg.* 513C), and why what seems to Socrates a conviction may be described by others thus: 'he was bound and
gagged by you in the discussion' (*Grg.* 482E).

Plato does not take account of this objection anywhere
in his writings. Yet we can indicate with confidence the
sort of answer that his writings suggest, the sort of answer that he would have given if the thought had been
brought to his notice. The aim of the elenchus is not to
switch a man from an opinion that happens to be false
to an opinion that happens to be true. It is not satisfied
by any exchange of one set of opinions for another, even
if the new set is true and consistent whereas the old set

was false and inconsistent. The aim of the elenchus is to wake men out of their dogmatic slumbers into genuine intellectual curiosity. The conviction of one's own ignorance involves and includes some dim realization of the difference between knowledge and all opinions whether false or true. In other words, the notion of the elenchus contains a germ of the Platonic conception of knowledge as absolutely distinct from opinion. The elenchus does not directly give a man any positive knowledge; but it gives him for the first time the idea of real knowledge, without which he can never have any positive knowledge even if he has all the propositions that express it. It is important to separate the realization *that* you are wrong from the realization *why* you are wrong or what the truth is, in order that the mind may dwell on the question what constitutes being wrong or right.

It may be urged that the elenchus would be more successful without the irony. The insincerity of pretending not to be conducting an elenchus must surely lessen the moral effect. It is not possible to make men good by a kind of behaviour that is not itself good. Furthermore, the irony seems to be a main cause of the anger which, as Socrates declares (*Ap.* 21E, &c.), often results from the elenchus; and if elenchus really makes people hate you, surely it is bad teaching and a bad form of intercourse in general. We can hardly suppose that after the victims' anger has cooled they admit their ignorance and start to reform their lives, for the *Apology* implies that most of them have remained angry and unconvinced to the end of their days. The beneficial shame that Alcibiades felt in the presence of Socrates (*Smp.* 216), the pleasantness and utility that Nicias found in being refuted (*La.* 188), must have come from a straightforward and unconcealed elenchus; for Socrates could not refute his intimates many times and still prevent their knowing when he was about to do so.

This objection, like the former one, is not noticed or met in the dialogues. We may conjecture, however, that Plato would have dealt with it differently at different

periods of his life. While he was writing the earlier dialogues he would probably have defended the ironical
form of the elenchus on the ground that it supplied a
necessary shock. For it may be argued that he who an-
nounces beforehand that he is going to prove you ignorant thereby destroys his chance of doing so, because you
will instantly close your mind against him. Especially is
this so on matters of right and wrong and good and bad.
What is required, therefore, is a drastic shock, a practical
demonstration of ignorance accompanied by shame. For
this purpose the victim must be drawn into a parade of
knowledge, and then there must be a violent reversal of
the situation, which can only be accomplished by some
such mummery as Socrates practised.

At a later period of his life, however, Plato would
probably have dealt with the objection by admitting it
and abandoning the irony. The passage in the *Sophist*
(translated above, pp. 84–85) makes no mention of
irony, and asserts that elenchus makes the 'patient' angry
only with himself, but gentle towards others. The sev-
enth *Letter* requires that elenchus shall be conducted in
a friendly manner ( ἐν εὐμενέσιν ἐλέγχοις 344B). The
elenchus which Plato came to approve was a contest in
which both parties openly admitted that the questioner
was trying to refute and the answerer was trying not to
be refuted. It was the formal and open exercise for which
Aristotle wrote rules and hints in his *Topics*.

Three things happen to the elenchus in the middle and
later dialogues. First, as we have just seen, it loses its
irony. Second, it is incorporated into the larger whole of
dialectic, which somewhat changes its character. Though
still negative and destructive in essence, it is harnessed
to the car of construction. Though still moral in its purpose, the ultimate moral end recedes a great deal, and a
large scientific programme occupies the middle view.
Third, while often referred to and recommended, it grad-
ually ceases to be actually depicted in the dialogues.
Refutations take less of the total space. Those that do
occur are less obvious in form; it is not so easy to point

to the separate premisses, to the manner in which each is obtained, and to the place where Socrates puts them together and draws the conclusion. They are less purely negative; there is often positive doctrine that is unnecessary to the proof. In the pure form of elenchus, moreover, there tends to be only one refutation to each thesis. For the refutation professes to be final and absolute, or 'iron and adamantine' as Socrates puts it (*Grg.* 509A); but if you add a second you seem to confess that the first was not so. In the middle dialogues, however, we do find more than one argument for the same conclusion; and this is a distinct change in character. Plato now offers a series of considerations making towards a conclusion, and it is possible to admit of any one that it is not conclusive by itself. He has given up the claim to be incontrovertible, and become in truth more persuasive. Thus elenchus changes into dialectic, the negative into the positive, pedagogy into discovery, morality into science.

RICHARD ROBINSON

## SYLLOGISM IN THE ELENCHUS

Let us now examine the reasoning that Socrates uses in his elenchus. There are all degrees of explicitness and tacitness in reasoning, so that, whatever definition we frame of the difference between reasoned and unreasoned statement, there will be some passages that our definition does not confidently classify. The dogma merges into the argument by infinite stages; and the argument, in which we are expected to infer one part of a whole from the rest, merges by infinite stages into the description of a coherent system, where each of the parts is necessitated by the rest, but the reader is not invited to infer any one of them, but rather to contemplate the connected structure as a whole. If a writer says 'A is B and therefore C is D', that is an argument. But if he says 'A is B and that is why C is D', it is not an argument; for he is assuming that we already believe that C is D, and merely inviting us to realize that it follows from A's being B. When the conclusion is stated before the premisses, then, other things being equal, we more definitely have an argument than when the premisses are stated before the conclusion. The more explicit arguments, as those of geometry, always tell you first what they are proposing to prove.

This state of affairs prevents us from discovering any propositions true of all the arguments of the early dialogues as such. We must therefore concentrate on the more explicit cases (excluding, for example, such passages as *Ap.* 28–35, although we should call them 'well reasoned' and systematic); and these will be for the most part passages in dialogue form where the conclusion to be proved or the proposition to be refuted is clearly indi-

cated at the beginning, even if Socrates does pretend not
to be refuting it.

Let us follow Aristotle and say that every dialectical
argument is either a syllogism or an epagoge (*Topics*
I 12). By 'a dialectical argument' let us mean, as Aristotle
does, any argument put forward in conversation, proceeding on premisses admitted by the other party, and
not requiring any special knowledge. It follows that
every Socratic elenchus is a dialectical argument. By a
'syllogism' let us not mean, in the narrow modern sense,
an argument depending on our insight into the relation
of class-inclusion; but, to translate Aristotle's own words,
any 'argument in which, after certain propositions have
been assumed, there necessarily results a proposition
other than the assumptions because of the assumptions'.
This broad sense of the term is certainly the only one
Aristotle has in mind throughout the *Topics,* from which
the definition comes (*Topics* I 1, 100A25); and probably it is also the only one he has in mind even in the
*Prior Analytics,* although he actually studies only class-
inclusion inferences there; at any rate his definition of
'syllogism' at the beginning of that work is only verbally
different from the definition in the *Topics.*

The meaning of 'epagoge' may be explained later; but
first we must deal with the syllogism in the Socratic
elenchus. In the dialogues themselves there are no cut-
and-dried names for this operation. 'Apodeixis' and its
verb occur occasionally in a broad sense that would include both syllogism and epagoge. The noun 'syllogism'
does not occur until the middle dialogues (*Cra.* 412A
and *Tht.* 186D). The verb 'syllogize' occurs in the
*Charmides* (160D) not as something to be done towards
the end of an elenchus, but as something to be done in
formulating a thesis: you form the thesis by syllogizing
or putting together all the relevant facts. It occurs twice
in the *Gorgias* (479C and 498E). Literally it means 'add
up'; and as we speak of adding up a sum, although
strictly the sum is the result of adding the items, so these
two passages speak of adding up the conclusion; and

therewith we are near to Aristotle's broad sense. The word occurs often in the middle and later dialogues with this sense of 'infer'. The word 'analogize' is also found in the same sense (*Prt.* 332D, *Rp.* I 330E, VII 524D). Another phrase for the same thing is 'What is the consequence of our statements?' (*Euthd.* 281E). The thing itself can often be noticed in the Socratic elenchus, that is, the moment when Socrates, having obtained his premisses separately, explicitly brings them together so that their joint implication becomes evident to the answerer. Here is an example.

> I say, Socrates, ⟨that the rhapsode is competent to judge⟩ all parts ⟨of Homer⟩.—No you do not say all parts, Ion. Or are you so forgetful? Surely a rhapsode ought not to be a forgetful man.—What am I forgetting?—Do you not remember saying that the science of rhapsody was distinct from that of charioteering?—I do.—And did you not admit that if it were distinct it would know distinct objects?— Yes.—Then on your view the rhapsodic science and the rhapsode will *not* know everything. (*Ion* 539E.)

This moment of syllogizing is the moment when all is made clear. The purpose of the separate premisses, the way they fit together, and the fact that they entail the falsehood of his thesis, now become evident to the answerer. In the earlier stages, while the premisses are being obtained, Socrates is not concerned to reveal the tendency of his questions. Sometimes, indeed, he is deliberately trying not to reveal it, in order that the answerer may not refuse to grant him the premisses he needs. This is a trick that the *Topics* recommends; and Socrates is no doubt practising it, for example, when he obtains his premisses in a queer order (as in *Prt.* 332A– 333B). Most of the arguments and fallacies and dodges described in Aristotle's *Topics* and *Sophistical Elenchi* can be exemplified from Plato's early dialogues; and Alexander of Aphrodisias often does so in his commentary on those two works of Aristotle's.

The Socratic elenchus often includes an element prior

to the obtainment of the premisses but subsequent to the obtainment of the thesis or refutand. This is the elucidation and elaboration of the thesis. It serves to make the answerer's conception clearer. It gives Socrates time to think of a refutation. It often allows him to interpret the thesis in a way which the answerer accepts as an interesting extension of his idea, but which enables Socrates to refute it as he could not have done if it had been more moderately or more vaguely formulated. Where this element is absent, the reason is sometimes that the answerer has himself developed his thesis in a long speech, and sometimes that Socrates defines the thesis in another way, by deliberately taking it in a perverse sense, so that the answerer is forced to say more precisely what he means.

### DIRECT AND INDIRECT ELENCHUS

The syllogisms of the Socratic elenchus fall into many types. For some of them we can easily find names from the textbooks of logic. We can recognize here a sorites, there a dilemma, there an argument by elimination or alternative syllogism, there a hypothetical syllogism, there a categorical syllogism in the narrow sense in barbara or one of its other forms. For many more there are no obvious names; and if we tried to make them we might need dozens. But there is one great division which is interesting in itself and important for Plato's theory of hypothesis, the division between direct and indirect argument.

The distinction between direct and indirect applies both to the refutation and to the establishment of propositions. To refute a thesis indirectly is to deduce a falsehood from that thesis; in other words, to show that the thesis entails a consequence which is so repugnant to you that you would rather abandon the thesis than keep it and the consequence along with it. To establish a thesis indirectly is to deduce a falsehood from the contradictory of that thesis; in other words, to show that its contradictory is false because it entails an intolerable consequence.

Reduction to absurdity is a case of indirect argument, for absurdity is one form of falsehood. Direct refutation is best defined as any refutation that is not indirect; but we can also say that it is the refutation that reaches the contradictory of the refutand without at any time or in any way assuming the refutand. Direct establishment is best defined as any establishment that is not indirect; but we can also say that it is the establishment that reaches the demonstrand without at any time or in any way assuming the contradictory of the demonstrand. The argument 'A, therefore B' is a direct establishment of B and a direct refutation of not-B. The argument 'A, therefore B; but not B, therefore not A' is an indirect establishment of not-A and an indirect refutation of A. The indirect argument can be just as valid as the direct; in Aristotle's language, it can really syllogize, and not merely seem to. And it is often more striking than the direct.

Whether an argument is direct or indirect is not always clear. This is a surprising statement when we think of the distinction in general terms, and especially when we have just finished defining it; but it is not surprising when we are reading particular arguments and trying to classify them. Perhaps we can always tell confidently whether a geometrical argument is direct or indirect; but very few arguments are as explicit and as formalized as the geometrical. Moreover, it seems that every direct argument can be converted into an indirect argument; for if we can say 'A, therefore B' it seems that we can say 'Not-B, therefore not-A; but A, therefore B'. And if this is true we can easily believe that an argument could be so vaguely stated as not to have definitely assumed either the direct or the indirect form. The following question of principle adds to the difficulty. When we disprove 'All X is A' by pointing to an X that is not A, is that direct or indirect refutation? To make it indirect we must suppose that our thought is 'If all X were A, this X would be A; but this X is not A; therefore it is false that all X is A.' Yet in practice this would usually appear an absurdly elaborate way of putting the argument; the natural way of putting it is to say 'But this X is not A' and nothing more, that is, to express only the minor premiss of the hypothetical syllogism. The question is important for the analysis of the early dialogues, because they use the negative instance very commonly. Their problem is frequently one of definition; and the most obvious way to refute a definition is to produce a case that falls under the definition but not under the definiend, or contrariwise. The best conclusion is that refutation by the negative instance is essentially indirect; but owing to its extreme simplicity and lucidity it is rarely stated in the full form. If we deny this we shall find ourselves making a wide distinction between narrowly related forms. For example, the following argument is clearly indirect: 'If all X were A, then, since P is an X, P would be A; but P is not A; therefore it is false that all X is A.' Yet it differs from the simple negative instance only in that we need an extra premiss in order to see clearly that P is a negative instance of the thesis that all X is A. I have therefore classified all arguments from the negative instance as indirect.

Taking only the more distinct and more formalized arguments in these nine dialogues, *Protagoras, Euthyphro, Laches, Charmides, Lysis, Republic* I, *Gorgias, Meno,* and *Euthydemus* excluding the sophists' absurdities, I count roughly thirty-nine arguments of which thirty-one seem to be indirect. Thus about three-quarters of the arguments appear to be indirect. The fraction is greatest in *Charmides, Lysis, Euthydemus,* smallest in *Republic* I and *Protagoras.*

Every indirect argument is in outline a destructive hypothetical syllogism: 'If A, then B; but not B, therefore not A'. In this formula let us call not-A the conclusion; not-B the minor premiss; 'if A then B' the major premiss; B the falsehood and also the consequent; A the assumption and also—when the argument is a refutation—the thesis or the refutand. Now in some indirect arguments the consequent follows from the assumption immediately, but in others it does not. From the assumption that

all men are immortal it follows immediately that all
wicked men are immortal; but that Bonzo is immortal
does not follow unless we add the extra premiss that
Bonzo is a man. [Indirect arguments may therefore be
divided into those that require extra premisses in order to
deduce the falsehood from the assumption and those that
do not.] Many of them require many extra premisses and
a great deal of inference; when that is so the major premiss expands into a long deduction and ceases to look like
a hypothetical proposition, and then we lose sight of the
fact that the whole argument is in outline a hypothetical
syllogism. This happens, for example, in almost any reduction to absurdity in geometry. Of the indirect arguments in the early dialogues some employ such independent premisses and others do not. At *Charmides* 170,
for example, from the thesis that temperance is knowledge of knowledge only, Socrates professes to deduce
without the aid of any extra premiss the unacceptable
consequence that temperance, when it knows knowledge, does not know what that knowledge is knowledge
of. The refutation without extra premisses is common in
the *Lysis;* otherwise the arguments in that dialogue
would not be so unusually short.

[In one sense there is an independent premiss in every
indirect refutation, namely, the minor premiss of the hypothetical syllogism. Every indirect argument is a reduction to a falsehood. There must therefore be a premiss
declaring that the falsehood is a falsehood; and that is
the office of the minor premiss of a destructive hypothetical syllogism.] But the above distinction within indirect
arguments was between those that do and those that do
not add other premisses, in addition to the minor, in
order to get the consequent of the major premiss out of
its antecedent.

[When the questioner uses independent premisses in
an indirect refutation, he will naturally obtain them first,
or one of them first. For the thesis is, in this case, barren
of consequences until married to another proposition. Besides, this order conceals the questioner's intention and

thus makes the answerer readier to grant the premiss. When no independent premiss is used, the elenchus sometimes begins with an elaboration of the thesis, and this turns imperceptibly into the deduction from the thesis of an intolerable consequence.

In an indirect elenchus the falsehood to which the refutand is shown to lead may be of any kind or sort whatever, provided that the answerer recognizes it to be a falsehood. The elenchus fails, however absurd the consequence may seem to us, if the answerer himself denies it to be wrong, as we see Socrates denying in the *Gorgias* and the brothers denying in the *Euthydemus*. Obversely, the elenchus succeeds, however dubious the falsehood of the consequence may seem to us, if it seems false to the answerer himself. This is the only thing that can be said about the falsehood universally; but there are certain kinds of falsehood that appear more often than others because of their greater convenience or greater obviousness. In general the two most striking and most useful kinds of falsehood to which to reduce a refutand are absurdity and the contradiction of plain empirical fact. No one cares to maintain a thesis if it has been shown to lead to such a flat denial of our senses as that pigs have wings, or to such an irrationality as that the part is greater than the whole; and Socrates frequently uses both these kinds; and sometimes calls attention to an absurdity by such words as ἄτοπον and ἀδύνατον (*Chrm.* 167C). The most striking form of absurdity is contradiction; and this is frequently in Socrates' mind. At *Laches* 196B Laches implies that the previous argument led to a self-contradiction (he is probably referring to 193D–E). In *Meno* 82A Socrates fears that Meno is trying to entrap him into self-contradiction. At his trial Socrates professed to have shown that Meletus contradicted himself (*Ap.* 27A). In *Gorgias* 460–61 he professes to have exposed a contradiction between one part of Gorgias' thesis and another; and in two later refutations in that dialogue he seems without claiming it to reduce a thesis to a self-contradiction (488–89 and 498). A critic blames him for

enjoying this operation (*Grg.* 461B–C). In the *Phaedo*
(101D) he declares that a standing part of his method
of discovery is to see whether the consequences of a
given hypothesis accord with each other or not. Plato's
dialogues often blame the antilogicians or contradiction-
mongers; and this suggests that the use of the reduction
to contradiction was so common as to lead to abuse.

PLATO'S AWARENESS OF THIS DISTINCTION

We have distinguished between direct and indirect
refutations; and within indirect refutations we have distinguished those that do not use extra premisses from
those that do; and within indirect refutations we have
also distinguished those that reduce the thesis to a self-
contradiction from those that reduce it to another kind
of falsehood. We have applied these distinctions to the
refutations in the early dialogues, and found that some
of the refutations are direct and others indirect, that
some of the indirect refutations use no extra premisses,
and that some of them reduce the thesis to a self-contradiction. The question now arises whether Plato himself also made these distinctions and applied them to
his work.

To say that Plato was as aware of these logical distinctions as we are would be a gross case of 'misinterpretation by abstraction'. Even if we examine his later as well
as his earlier works, we can discover no passage in which
any one of these three distinctions is stated. Far from
realizing the distinctions, he had not even made all of
the abstractions that they presuppose; for he has no word
for 'premiss' and no word for 'indirect argument'. We
have therefore only been pointing out variations that are
actually present in the refutations he depicts. We have
not been saying, and must not say, that he himself was
aware of these variations in the abstract way in which
we have described them. No one can ever be conscious
of all the distinctions that could truly be made about his
own writings; and there is nothing surprising or deroga-

tory to Plato in the view that he had not made these logical distinctions.

On the other hand, to be unaware of a distinction is not necessarily to fail ever to think of either of the distincts; it is more often to think only of one of them, and to apply that one not merely where it is appropriate but also where the other would be appropriate. And this is what Plato seems to have done. Failing to distinguish direct from indirect argument, he thought of elenchus as being always indirect. Not that he explicitly said to himself that elenchus is always indirect, for he did not have the logical term 'indirect'; but that, in stating or discussing any or every elenchus, he habitually *spoke as if* the elenchus consisted in making the refutand lead to a falsehood, which is what we mean by 'indirect argument'. Failing, furthermore, to distinguish the indirect elenchus which uses no independent premiss from that which does, he thought of elenchus as never using an independent premiss. Not that he explicitly said to himself that it never does so, for he did not have the logical term 'premiss'; but that, when discussing or presenting an elenchus, he habitually *wrote as if* the falsehood followed from the refutand without the aid of any extra premiss. Failing, thirdly, to distinguish the indirect elenchus which reduces the thesis to a self-contradiction from that which reduces it to another kind of falsehood, he habitually thought and wrote *as if* all elenchus consisted in reducing the thesis to a self-contradiction. It simply *did not occur to him* that an elenchus might sometimes not be an indirect argument reducing a thesis to self-contradiction without the aid of extra premisses, just as many men have lived to whom it simply never occurred that the earth might go round the sun.

We are liable to object to this interpretation of Plato for three reasons. In the first place, we can point to particular refutations in the dialogues which we should all nowadays agree to be direct. Since these direct refutations are actually there in the dialogues, written by Plato himself and staring him in the face, we feel that he can-

not possibly have supposed all refutations to be indirect.
In the second place, whether or not there are any direct
refutations in the dialogues, the logical possibility of such
a species is so obvious to us that we assume that it was
obvious to Plato. We feel that a great philosopher cannot have 'overlooked' such an elementary logical point.
In the third place, we feel that the proposed interpretation attributes to Plato an actual logical error too gross
for him to commit, namely, the error of supposing that
a proposition ever can entail its own contradictory without the aid of extra premisses. Surely, we say, there are
very few theses that by themselves give rise to pairs of
contradictory statements, or that of themselves contradict themselves. A few queer propositions excogitated
by modern logicians may do so, such as 'The class of all
classes not members of themselves is not a member of
itself', but surely not any proposition examined in Plato's
early dialogues.

Although the first of these objections appeals to Plato's
text, all three of them rest on the belief that certain logical doctrines *must* have been obvious to Plato because
they *are* so obvious to any intelligent person. This belief
is destructive of any true history of human thought, and
ought to be abandoned. Evidently there must have been
a time when the human race, or its immediate ancestor,
possessed no logical propositions at all, true or false. Nor
is there any necessity that logical propositions, when they
did arise, should at once be those which seem obvious
to us. Nor did logical propositions in any scope and ab-
stractness arise with Socrates or with the early Plato,
but, as Stenzel has shown, with the later Plato and his
pupil Aristotle (*Plato's Method of Dialectic*, translated
by D. J. Allan). The history of thought cannot succeed
if we assume from the beginning that some idea or other
is innate and necessary to any human mind.

PLATO'S CONCEPTION OF THE LOGIC OF ELENCHUS

A genuinely empirical approach to Plato's dialogues
gives a result other than that asserted in these objections;

for, while it shows that there are many direct refutations in the text, it also shows that Plato regarded these refutations as indirect reductions to a contradiction.

In the *Gorgias* the proposition, that the professor of rhetoric is not responsible for the use his pupils make of their skill, is refuted in a perfectly direct manner, by first obtaining and then syllogizing the two premisses, (1) that if the pupil does not already know the truth about justice the professor will tell him, because the orator must know this, and (2) that he who knows the truth about justice is just. Yet this direct refutation is referred to beforehand as a demonstration that some of Gorgias' statements 'do not exactly follow from or harmonize with' others (457E), and afterwards as a demonstration that Gorgias has contradicted himself (487B). The latter passage also declares that Polus contradicts himself; but each of the three refutations of Polus is direct. Here then we have a striking example of the loose way in which Plato can make Socrates use the term 'contradiction'.

The same looseness appears in later dialogues. In the second book of the *Republic* (380C) Homer's and Hesiod's tales about the gods are abruptly said to contradict themselves, after a discussion which gave no evidence of self-contradiction. Later in this dialogue (V 457C) the logos or argument is said to agree with itself in a way which seems to imply that it might have contradicted itself. The *Theaetetus* (155B) contains a curious passage of this sort. Plato there brings forward four propositions of such a kind that, as we should put it, the first three together conflict with the fourth. His own description of the situation, however, is that the first three conflict with each other when we add the fourth to them.

This misinterpretation of direct refutations as being indirect reductions to self-contradiction came easier to Plato because of a certain confusion, or rather because of his failure to make a certain distinction. Every elenchus makes the answerer contradict himself in one sense, namely, in the sense in which the man who changes his opinion thereby contradicts his former opinion. For the answerer agrees to the premisses of the elenchus, and he

agrees that they necessitate the conclusion, and the conclusion contradicts his original opinion. But it is one thing
to make the answerer see the force of an argument that
contradicts his former theory, and another thing to make
the theory contradict itself. Plato confuses that contradiction of a thesis which constitutes an elenchus as such
with the special form of elenchus which consists in showing that the thesis contradicts itself. The fact that every
successful elenchus persuades the answerer to deny his
former opinion, that is, to contradict it, made it easier
for Plato to assume that every elenchus achieves this result by showing that the former opinion contradicts itself.

The strongest evidence of all is the passage in the
*Phaedo* (101D) where Socrates makes it an essential
point of method not to discuss an hypothesis itself until
you have 'considered its results to see if they accord or
disaccord with each other'. This passage entails that Plato
was consciously assuming, or making Socrates assume,
first, that the consequences of a single thesis may contradict each other; second, that if they do so the thesis is
thereby disproved; and third, that the consequences of a
single thesis may contradict each other without the aid
of any extra premiss. The nineteenth-century readers of
Plato saw these implications clearly, and shrank from
them. They could not believe that Plato would assert
such things, which seemed to them logical monstrosities.
Jackson and Archer-Hind accordingly proposed to expel
this phrase from the text as spurious. Goodrich (*Classical
Review* XVIII 8 ff.) saved the text from mutilation by
going through the arguments and pointing out that in
reality Plato uses extra premisses. We must understand
the term 'hypothesis' in a large sense, he said, as including
besides some special proposition the general body of
standing propositions on which the questioner may draw
for premisses. But both Goodrich and the expungers assumed that Plato's logical views were like ours in a point
in which they are not. Even in mathematics, even in
logic, the human race changes its opinions from age to
age, although much less than in history and politics. The

evidence of the unmutilated *Phaedo*-text, and of the dialogues themselves, is that Plato assumed that any thesis may without marriage give birth to quarrelling twins.

The assumption that there are no extra premisses is a natural accompaniment of the assumption that every elenchus reduces the thesis to self-contradiction. For if additional premisses are introduced, the thesis does not contradict itself by, so to speak, its own unaided efforts. It contradicts itself only because tempted thereto by the evil demon of an extra premiss. Whatever X may be, X plus Y will always produce not-X if you choose Y judiciously.

The assumption that there are no extra premisses is made easier by the ambiguity of the phrase 'according to your logos', which Socrates frequently uses in refutations, especially in drawing the conclusion. The word 'logos' can cover every premiss and every inference in virtue of its meaning 'argument', and yet imply that there has been no extraneous premiss in virtue of its meaning 'thesis'; for in the early dialogues it often means the same as our 'proposition', and the same as 'hypothesis' means in the middle and in some of the early dialogues.

Plato's way of regarding the process of refuting a thesis comes out clearly in his *Parmenides*. Zeno there explains that his book was 'a defence of Parmenides' theory against those who try to make fun of it by showing that, if everything is one, many consequences follow that are ridiculous and contrary to the theory itself' (128C–D). This sentence implies very distinctly that certain persons thought that the theory of Parmenides gave rise to consequences that contradicted itself. Nothing is said about any extra premisses that might be required to produce the contradiction. The speaker assumes that the theory by itself generates its own contradiction; and it does not occur to him that the contradiction might really be between Parmenides' theory and certain other propositions that both sides were accepting. Plato goes on to make Zeno say that his own book was an attempt to show that

the opposite theory led to even more ridiculous consequences; and here too there is no suggestion that the
absurdity was due to the clash of the theory with other
accepted beliefs.

Later in the *Parmenides,* after the theory of Ideas has
been examined, Parmenides recommends to Socrates the
exercise of drawing the consequences of an hypothesis,
and of its contradictory, each set of consequences to be
drawn out in the fullest detail. Here again the assumption is that these consequences will follow from the hypothesis alone, and not from the hypothesis together
with a standing body of other postulates (136).

The last part of the *Parmenides* consists of a long example of this mode of intellectual exercise. Here the
hypotheses 'if there is a one' and 'if there is no one', are
each separately made to give rise to a great many consequences. In each case these consequences are divided
into those concerning the 'one' itself and those concerning
the 'others', thus giving four sets of consequences. Each
of these four is again divided into two violently conflicting subsets, so related to each other that, roughly speaking, each proposition in one subset is the contradictory
of some proposition in its fellow subset. A vast mass of
contradictions is thus produced in each of the four sets
of consequences. The important point for our present
purpose is that in each set this mass of contradictions is
represented as flowing simply and solely from the single
hypothesis with which it begins. A modern logician, an-
alysing the deduction, would say at once that many additional premisses are introduced; but Plato does not think
so. A modern logician would say also that some of the
supposed 'consequences' are really definitions; but Plato
does not think this either. To put it in modern terms,
Plato makes Parmenides proceed as if the number of
the postulates in the postulate-set for each deduction
were one and only one. Here, then, is overwhelming
evidence that Plato thought of refutation as the deduction of contradictions from the refutand alone, without
the aid of any other premisses.

So much by way of establishing the proposition that Plato, without ever clearly envisaging the alternatives, regarded all elenchus as the deduction of a contradiction from the refutand alone, without any additional premiss.

# 6. SOCRATIC DEFINITION

RICHARD ROBINSON

## THE WHAT-IS-X? QUESTION

The Socrates of Plato's dialogues is continually asking questions. Let us distinguish these into the primary question and the secondary questions. In each discussion he first proposes some important problem, usually ethical; and that is the primary question. As soon as an answer is suggested, he proceeds to examine it by means of a series of questions to the answerer; and those are the secondary questions. This chapter is concerned only with Socrates' primary questions.

These primary questions have, roughly speaking, one of two forms: either 'Is X Y?' or 'What is X?' Examples of 'Is X Y?' are: 'Is justice better than injustice?' in the *Republic;* 'Are those who become friends like each other?' in the *Lysis;* and 'Ought Socrates to escape?' in the *Crito*. Examples of 'What is X?' are: 'What is justice?' in the *Republic;* 'What is temperance?' in the *Charmides;* and 'What is courage?' in the *Laches*. Of these two types it is the What-is-X? form that stands out and catches the attention of every student of Plato's early dialogues. This is not, apparently, because there is actually more space devoted to the discussion of What-is-X? questions than to the other type; for only three or four of the early dialogues are primarily and directly engaged in such discussion throughout their philosophical parts, namely the *Euthyphro,* the *Laches,* the *Charmides,* and the *Hippias Major*. The *Gorgias,* the *Meno,* and *Republic* I (which we may count an early dialogue) all abandon the question 'What is X?' for the question 'Is X Y?'; while the *Ion,* the *Hippias Minor,* the *Apology,* the *Crito,* and the *Protagoras,* never raise the question at all. The explicit question of the *Lysis* is not what friendship is but what

its condition is, although the former question is present
as a faint undercurrent, and there is perhaps some confusion between the two. The What-is-X? question therefore owes its prominence in the early dialogues not to
spatial predominance but to the emphasis which Socrates
puts upon it.

Socrates often expresses dissatisfaction with the answer
he receives to his What-is-X? question, on the ground
not that it is false but that it is not the *kind* of answer
he had in mind when he asked 'What is X?' Thus in the
*Theaetetus* (146), which in this respect is just like an
early dialogue, Socrates, having asked 'What is knowledge?' and been told that it is geometry and shoemaking
and so on, replies that he asked for one and has been
given many. 'You were not asked what things there is
knowledge of, nor how many sorts of knowledge there
are; for our aim in asking was not to count the sorts of
knowledge but to know what knowledge itself is'. He
then gives an illustration of the kind of answer he wants:
if he had asked 'What is clay?', he would have wanted,
not a list of the various sorts of clay, but simply 'earth
mixed with liquid' (147C). In this explanation there are
two key phrases that Socrates uses to indicate his desire.
One is the opposition between the 'one' and the 'many';
he wants the one knowledge and not the many knowl-
edges. The other is 'what X itself is'. These phrases constantly recur when Socrates is talking about his What-is-
X? question.

He explains his question at length in the *Meno* (71–
77). Here also he gives examples of the sort of answer
he requires: if he asked 'What is figure?', a good answer
would be 'the limit of a solid' (76A). Here also he uses
the opposition of the one and the many (77A): he explains that he wants not some virtue but virtue (73E),
that which is the same in all the Xes (75A). The *Meno*
also has two other ways which are of great importance
to Socrates in explaining the nature of his question. One
is the use of the word εἶδος or form; he wants, he says,
'some one identical form possessed by all the virtues,

through which they are virtues, to which the answerer ought to look in explaining to the asker what virtue really is' (72C, cf. *Euthyph.* 6D). The other way of explaining the question is by means of the word οὐσία or being or essence; when he says 'What is X?' he wants the being or essence of X (72B, cf. *Euthyph.* 11A).

Socrates frequently asserts that the question What is X? is prior to certain other questions about X, in the sense that we cannot find sure answers to those other questions until we have found sure answers to this one. You cannot, he says, know what *sort* of thing X is until you know *what* X is. Thus you cannot really know whether virtue is teachable until you know what virtue is (*Men.* 71, 86D–E, 100B; *Prt.* 360E), nor whether justice is a virtue until you know what justice is (*Rp.* I 354C). You must also know what X is before you can know whether it is beneficial (*Rp.* I 354C and *La.* 189E–190A), or how it is to be obtained (cf. *La.* 189E–190A and all the passages on the teachability of virtue). The most surprising of all his assertions in this line is that at the end of the *Lysis*: 'Well, said I, we have become ridiculous, Lysis and Menexenus, both I who am old and you. For as these people go away they will say that we think we are friends of each other—for I count myself among you— but we have not yet been able to discover what a friend is.' This is surprising because it seems to imply that until you know what X is you can never say whether this is a case of X. That our knowledge of X is prior to our knowledge of its cases is implied also in the *Euthyphro* (6E), where Socrates says that when Euthyphro has told him what X is he is going to use it as a paradigm or pattern to determine which things are X and which not. In fact, the impression vaguely given by the early dialogues as a whole is that Socrates thinks that there is no truth whatever about X that can be known before we know what X is. He never explicitly says so; nor, on the other hand, does he ever set any limits to the priority of this question. Prior to ascertaining what X is, he seems to think, we can form more or less probable opinions that X, whatever it may be, possesses the character Y, but can never be certain of such a thing ( cf. *Tht.* 196D–E ).

Nor does Plato represent Socrates as seeking to answer his What-is-X? question by looking to cases or examples of X. On the contrary, as we have seen, he makes Socrates rebuke those answerers who give him some of the many Xes instead of the one X itself. Only when an answer of the desired sort is already given does anything like a case appear in the Socratic discussions; and then it is used not to establish but to refute the proposed answer.

If we look in the early dialogues for justifications of this principle, for reasons why the question What is X? must always be answered prior to any other question about X, we do not find them. On the contrary, the principle is offered as self-evident and too obvious for discussion. There is, however, something like an argument to this point in the mature *Phaedrus* (260). Imagine, says Socrates, that I were to urge you to use a horse in war, while neither of us was acquainted with horses, but I knew that you thought a horse to be that domestic animal which has the longest ears. This would be absurd. But it is like what actually happens in cities, for ignorant orators persuade ignorant cities to do bad things, both parties being under the impression that they are good things. Before you can say anything useful about horses you must know what a horse is; and before you can say anything useful about the good you must know what the good is. A twentieth-century philosopher would reply that it is a matter of experience that we can and do make useful statements about X without being able to say what X is in the way Socrates desires; and therefore the above argument must conceal some false premiss or fallacious inference.

The presentation of the What-is-X? question in Plato's early dialogues is no more abstract than I have represented it above. If we describe it, as I have so far refrained from doing, by means of such words as 'definition' and 'example', if we extract from it explicit rules and principles of definition, we pass to a stage of abstraction higher than the dialogues themselves display. We can, indeed, pick out an occasional word to be appropriately translated by 'example' or 'definition', and we can very easily formulate, from Socrates' instructions to his hearers, rules resembling those in a modern textbook; but that is only to say that each level of abstraction is near to the next! The actual picture in the dialogues is not more but less abstract than the picture here given; for Socrates does not use the letter X; he never gives the function but always one of its arguments.

Throughout the long series of his dialogues Plato continued to believe in the propriety and importance of this search for essences which he had depicted at the beginning of his writings. He can laugh at himself from time to time, and represent the demand for the 'one' instead of the 'many' as a piece of sophistical perversity (*Sph.* 239E–240A); but it remained his own demand. It is what he refers to as 'taking the logos of the essence' (*Rp.* 534B) or simply 'giving a logos'. It came to seem to him much more difficult than he had at first assumed it to be (*Letters* VII, 342–43. is one of his most despondent discussions of it); and he was thus led to spend much thought on devising methods to accomplish it. The great theory of dialectic is the theory of the method of discovering essence. Especially is this so in the *Sophist* and later dialogues, when the instrument of dialectic was division; for the purpose of division was precisely to give the definition of the essence. It is somewhat less so in the middle dialogues; for the method of hypothesis, which is the form dialectic takes there, is not so much a way of discovering essence as a way of evading the search for essence while still paying lip-service to the principle that you cannot know anything else about X until you know what X *is*. At least this seems to be the purpose of the method of hypothesis in its first appearance, which is in the *Meno*. The problem of that dialogue is whether virtue is teachable. Socrates declares that to answer we must first ascertain what virtue *is*. The attempt to ascertain this fails, however; and rather than abandon the discussion they are led to *hypothesize* a certain account of the essence of virtue and consider whether it would be teachable on this assumption (87).

Repeated failures in the effort to discover any particular essence only increased Plato's eagerness and his certainty that the essences were there. He thus came to introduce an element not found in the early dialogues at all, namely reflection on *essence in general, or the essences as a body,* as opposed to concentrating always on one particular essence; and these reflections are what is called Plato's theory of Ideas.

### CRITIQUE OF THE WHAT-IS-X? QUESTION

If we now cease to confine ourselves to something like English translations of Plato's words, and make use of modern terms and higher abstractions in order to criticize the What-is-X? question, the first thing we notice is that Socrates is looking for equivalences. He wants an answer, say 'X is AB', such that every X is AB and nothing else is AB. If given an answer, such as 'X is A', where A is not equivalent to but broader than X, he points out that other things besides X are A, and asks to have marked off the part of A that is equivalent to X (e.g., *Prt.* 312; *Grg.* 449 ff., 453 C ff.).

There are, however, various sorts of equivalence or convertible proposition; and it appears that Socrates is not ready to accept any kind. In the first place, there are verbal definitions, such as 'Hund means dog'. Socrates does not want these. He is not asking for a dictionary-definition of some word previously unknown to him. On the contrary, the X in his questions is always some word which he and his companions use every day of their lives, some word which, in unphilosophical circles, they would be said to know the meaning of perfectly well. Thus, while, in the ordinary sense, he knows what the word X means (and what it means is surely the thing X), he nevertheless does not know what the thing X is. Yet he expects the answer to his question to be itself a set of words. It seems, therefore, that his procedure implies, though he was unaware of it, that there is a word or set of words which gives or enshrines a knowledge of the thing X in some way in which the word X does not enshrine a knowledge of the thing X even for those who understand it and use it correctly. If the desired answer is 'X is AB', then, although he understands the word X just as well as the words AB, and although they both indicate the same entity, yet when he has the whole phrase 'X is AB' he knows satisfactorily what that entity is, and when he only has the word X he does not.

Any equivalent of X may serve as a means by which someone identifies X or distinguishes it from something else; but, among such equivalents, some, as we vaguely say, 'give the essence of X' and others do not. It is possible to identify X without giving its essence, by making use of other elements of reality and their relation to X. The proposition that 'virtue is the only human character which can never be misused' identifies virtue by referring to human character and misuse; and it evidently does not give its essence. It simply gives virtue a unique place in the context of reality, as two numbers give a point a unique place in a system of plane coordinates. Every statement giving X's essence serves to identify X; but not every statement serving to identify X gives its essence.

Now will Socrates be satisfied with any sort of identification, or does he insist on an identification through essence? The answer is that he has not made this distinction, and speaks sometimes one way and sometimes the other.

On the one hand, many passages suggest that all he wants is a mark that shall serve as a pattern by which to judge of any given thing whether it is an X or not. In the *Euthyphro* (6E) he describes his aim in just this way. In the *Meno* (74B–C) he gives the fact that there are figures other than roundness as the reason why roundness is a bad description of figure. In the same dialogue (75B) he offers the following as an example of the kind of answer he wants: 'Figure is that which alone of all things invariably accompanies colour'. This is clearly nothing more than a designation or identification; and, though Meno objects to it, he does so on the ground not that it ought to be more than a designation but that it would not identify the thing for a person for whom the word 'figure' by itself did not already do the business. The same purpose is suggested again by Socrates' habit of illustrating his What-is-X? question by cases where X is an individual (*Men.* 71B, *Tht.* 209, *Grg.* 453C); for surely a convertible proposition about an individual cannot be more than an identification. It is suggested again by a word he often uses to describe the process of answering a What-is-it? question, namely ὁρίζειν. For this term, never losing the feel of its original connexion with boundary-stones, suggests laying down a mark to distinguish a field from the next, without in any way describing the soils or the crops in the fields so delimited. And in Plato's dialogues the translations 'distinguish' and 'determine' are suitable as often or more often than 'define'.

In many other passages, however, Socrates' purpose in asking What is X? is evidently not, or not merely, to distinguish X from everything else. It is to get at what he calls the essence or the form of X, the one in the many, that single identical something whose presence in all the many Xes is guaranteed precisely by the fact that we call them all Xes (*Men.* 74D).

There is thus a duality in Socrates' conception of the question What is X? On the one hand it is merely the search for an equivalent of X, for any description convertible therewith. On the other hand, it is the search for something felt to be narrower than this, for one special equivalent of X which is felt to be X in a more intimate way than any of the others.

There is a curious trace of this duality in the *Theaetetus*. The last ten pages of that dialogue contain a rather careful discussion of the conception of logos, and distinguish three meanings of the word. The first of these meanings is the expression of a thought in words. Now

Aristotle often narrowed this meaning of logos down to the expression in words of a thought that gives a definition. Logos thus came to mean the formula of a definition, the description that gives the essence; and this is prepared by a passage in the *Republic* (534B), where Plato says that the dialectician takes the logos of the essence of each thing. In this sense, then, logos means the expression of an answer to the question What is X? The interesting point is that Plato's other two senses of logos in the *Theaetetus* appear to reflect the two ways in which Socrates regards the What-is-X? question in the early dialogues. According to one of these senses the logos is that in which the thing differs from all other things; here we have clearly the notion of the What-is-X? question as the effort to differentiate and distinguish. The notion of it is as a search for essence is reflected in the other sense, according to which the logos of X is a statement of the elements of X; for that the essence of a thing is to be found in its elements is a notion that always arises when the search for essence is pushed very far.

Socrates almost invariably assumes that his term X is univocal. He has no fear of ambiguity. Since you call all these things by one name, he says, tell me what is the one thing you mean every time (*Men.* 74D). 'We are accustomed to posit some one form for each set of things to which we apply the same name' (*Rp.* 596A). There is, however, one curious passage where his answerer tentatively suggests that X is not the same in all the Xes, and Socrates rebuts the suggestion with a strange and puzzling argument. It comes in the first six pages of the *Meno*, which are the longest piece of methodology in the early dialogues; and it will be worth our while to quote it at length.

> Do you think the health of a man is different from the health of a woman? Or is it the same form everywhere, so long as it is health, whether it be in a man or in anything else?—The health of a man and the health of a woman seem to me to be the same.—And so with size and strength?

If a woman is strong, she will be strong with the same form and the same strength? By 'the same' I mean that it makes no difference to strength as strength whether it occurs in a man or a woman. Or do you think it does?—No, I do not.—And will it make any difference to virtue as virtue whether it occurs in the young or the old, in woman or in man?—I somehow feel, Socrates, that this is not like those others. —What? Did you not say that the virtue of a man was to manage a city well, and of a woman to manage a household well?—I did.—And can one manage a city or a household or anything else well unless one manages it temperately and justly?—No, indeed.—And if they manage justly and temperately, they will be managing with justice and temperance?—Necessarily.—Then the man and the woman, if they are to be good, both need the same qualities, namely justice and temperance.—Apparently.—What about the young and the old? Could they ever become good if they were intemperate and unjust?—No, indeed. —They would have to be temperate and just?—Yes.—Then all men are good in the same way; for they all become good by obtaining the same qualities.—It seems so.—But they would not have been good in the same way, unless their virtue were the same.—No, indeed.—Since therefore the virtue of everyone is the same, try to say, &c. (*Men.* 72–73.)

In this passage Meno's reply, 'I somehow feel, Socrates, that this is not like those others', gives expression to an inkling that virtue is not the same in all virtuous persons. This is the only occasion in the early dialogues where it is suggested that the term proposed for definition might be ambiguous. The suggestion is made to come from an answerer, and not from one of the most intelligent and attractive answerers in these dialogues. Socrates is represented as not entertaining it seriously for a moment; he regards it as a view natural to those who have not reflected but evidently false to those who have.

The argument which Socrates offers to convince Meno that virtue is the same in all cases apparently consists in pointing to an identity in all of them, an identity which he indicates by the words 'justice and temperance'. Now pointing to an identity in all the Xes does not prove that X is a univocal word unless the identity to which you point is the very thing that X means. (For example, the premiss that all tops are material objects does not prove that 'top' has only one meaning, because what 'top' means is certainly not 'material object'.) Hence Socrates' argument proves that the word 'virtue' always means the same only if the thing that he points to, and that Meno admits to be present in all cases of virtue, is the very thing that the word 'virtue' means. But, if Socrates can thus point to the very thing that 'virtue' means, and Meno can thus instantly recognize it, why are they asking what virtue is and, according to their own account, failing to find out? They seem to know already what is the one virtue in the many virtues.

Socrates is also assuming some sort of realism as opposed to nominalism, though this again is nothing that enters his head, but only one of the logical consequences of what does enter his head. He is assuming that this form or essence or one in the many is not a word in the mouth, nor a concept in the head, but something existing in the particular Xes independently of man. Earth-mixed-with-liquid, for example, is one essence really occurring in many different things, such as fuller's earth and brickmaker's clay and so on. 'In every action the holy is the same as itself, and the unholy is opposite to all the holy and like itself, and everything that is to be unholy has some one form according to its unholiness' (*Euthyph.* 5D). The identical character appears and reappears in different parts of experience, irrespective of what man may think or say.

Someone might say that, if you ask what is common to all the virtues, and expect a verbal answer, the perfect answer is 'virtue', and any other word or words will necessarily be wrong. The early dialogues contain no trace of such a suggestion. Socrates' behaviour implies that there will always be some correct answer which does not contain the word 'virtue' or a synonym. Now if your account of the essence of X is not to contain the word X or any synonym, it seems that it will have to consist in an explication of the structure of X, an exhibition of X in a more extended form. It will have to give X seen through a telescope, as it were, though the magnification must not be too great for the whole of X to remain in the field. Thus Socrates' behaviour further implies that X will always have a structure that can be unfolded. It will always be like the planet that becomes bigger in the telescope, and not like the star that remains a point. It will never be a simple entity having no true analysis. This implication, undetected in the early dialogues, had risen into Plato's consciousness to some extent when he wrote the *Theaetetus;* for he there conceives of a man maintaining that the primary elements have no logos, which is to say that no account can be given of their essence (201E); on this hypothesis the question What is X? would have no true answer when X was a primary element.

The foregoing discussion reveals several assumptions that must be made if Socrates' question is to be a legitimate question admitting of a true answer. First, we must assume that the word X is univocal. Second, we must assume that the thing X has an 'essence'. Third, we must make some sort of realist assumption about the ontological status of this 'essence'. And, fourth, we must assume that this 'essence' is not a 'primary element' but has a structure that can be explicated; for otherwise we must already know what X is in asking the question in Socrates' sense.

In view of all these assumptions, and of the possibility that we already know what X is when we raise the question, it is surprising that we are all of us so willing to ask What is X? in Socrates' sense, and so unsuspecting of the difficulties it may lead us into. One cause of our willingness seems to be the vagueness of the What-is-X? form itself. For it is, perhaps, when unsupported by a context, the vaguest of all forms of question except an inarticulate grunt. It indicates less determinately than any other the sort of information the questioner wants. The most pre-

cise form is Is X Y?, since the answerer then knows that
the asker wants precisely the information that X is Y or
that X is not Y, whichever is true. Less precise are Where
is X? and When is X?; they tell us that a time or a place
is wanted, but not by reference to what we are to determine the time (whether, for example, by reference to
the birth of Jesus or to a certain collision of carriages),
nor how narrowly we are to define the time (for example whether to a minute or to a century). Vaguer still
is Why is X?, since there is an indefinite plurality of facts
that are causes or reasons or explanations of any given
fact. Vaguest of all is What is X?, for it amounts only to
saying 'Please make some true statement about X'. Some
examples will make this clearer. Who is Abner? He is a
painter. Who is Abner? He is the man who painted the
portrait of Lorme in this exhibition. What is a rhombus?
A thing you learn about in geometry. What is a rhombus? A plane figure. What is a rhombus? A rhomboid
having two adjacent sides equal. Each of these five is a
reasonable answer to a What-is-it? question; yet each is
a very different kind of proposition.

The vagueness of the form of a question is usually
lessened by its context. The situation in which I ask 'Who
is Abner?' may show clearly that I want you to tell me
some relation in which Abner stands to you and no one
else does, or that I want you to tell me his business. The
situation in which I ask 'What is potassium?' may show
that I wish to know what the word 'potassium' means, or
whether this substance is an element, or to what class of
element it belongs, or what is its atomic weight. Instead
of putting the question vaguely and relying on the context to make it clear, I might do better to use a more
precise form. Thus for the above four cases of 'What is
potassium?' I could say respectively 'What does that
word mean?', 'Is potassium an element?', 'What sort of
element is it?', 'What is the definition of it?'

The explanations which Socrates gives of his question
provide a context determining this vague form to mean
the search for essence as above described. But it is the

half-felt presence of all the other possible meanings of
What is X? that prevents our seeing the pitfalls in this
search for essence. Whenever a difficulty arises, we interpret the question in some other way to avoid it. For example, if the conception of essence becomes momentarily
embarrassing, we take What is X? as merely a request for
identification. Such an evasion is always possible, because there are several other, non-Socratic senses in
which What is X? is always a proper question. One of
these is 'What does the word X mean?', the request for a
verbal definition. Another is 'Give a unique designation
of X', the request for a mark of identification. A third
seems to be, 'Make some true statement about X', for
What is X? is sometimes as vague as that. The vague
form What is X? is an especial temptation 'to answer
questions, without first discovering precisely *what* question it is which you desire to answer' (G. E. Moore,
*Principia Ethica* vii).

Another cause of our willingness to ask What is X?
without restriction is that it really is a useful habit to
turn to definition when in perplexity. Very often, after
we have pressed an inquiry a certain distance, we cannot go farther until we use more precise terms. A What-
is-X? question is then in place; and, though this is always
a verbal definition, the useful habit thus acquired will,
in combination with our usual failure to distinguish
the senses of this question, lead to our putting it in some
senses and some cases where it is not useful.

Again, it often happens that a theory is put forward
in the form 'X is YZ', where this is supposed to be a convertible proposition; and that after some debate this
theory is disproved. 'X is *not* YZ.' Then it is very natural
to think: 'Well then, what *is* X?' So we slide into the
What-is-X? question without full consciousness of doing
so. The *Republic* does not open with the question, What
is justice? but with the question, Is justice honesty and
paying what one owes? (331C). Not until five pages
later (336C), after this and another theory about justice

have been refuted, is the question raised 'What *is*
justice?'

Lastly, we ask the What-is-X? question unrestrictedly
because the following seems such a plausible argument:
'If we know what a thing is, we can surely say what it is'
(*La.* 190C, cf. *Chrm.* 159A). Conversely, we feel that
we do not know what a thing is unless we can give some
description that is convertible with it and does more than
merely identify it.

# 7. ELENCTIC DEFINITIONS

GEORGE NAKHNIKIAN

In the Socratic dialogues[1] there are scattered remarks about the nature of definitions and the criteria for good definitions. There are also examples of what Socrates seems to believe are good definitions—of courage in the *Protagoras* (360D); of quickness in the *Laches* (192A). The definition of courage in the *Protagoras* emerges in the course of the Socratic elenchus. The definition of quickness in the *Laches* does not; it is stated flatly, without defense or argument, as if it was obviously a paradigm of a correct definition (*La.*, 192A–B). Such definitions as the one of courage in the *Protagoras* I shall call "elenctic definitions," meaning a definition (typically of an ethical term) in the purported discovery of which the Socratic elenchus plays an essential role. To correspond to the division of dialogues into the Socratic and the

This is a previously unpublished article, written especially for this volume. The author is grateful to Gregory Vlastos and A. D. Woozley for a number of helpful suggestions.

[1] The majority of Platonic scholars believes that a line can be drawn between the early (or Socratic, or ethical) and the later dialogues of Plato, and that the early dialogues express the views of Socrates while the later ones contain doctrines that are Plato's own invention. Although there is no complete agreement as to exactly which dialogues are Socratic, there is consensus. A representative list of the early dialogues, compiled by Richard Robinson in his contribution on Plato for the *Oxford Classical Dictionary*, consists of the *Hippias Minor, Laches, Charmides, Ion, Protagoras, Euthyphro, Apology, Crito, Gorgias, Meno, Lysis, Menexenus,* and the *Euthydemus*. Robinson omits *Republic*, Bk. I, from the *Dictionary* list, but includes it among the Socratic dialogues in *Plato's Earlier Dialectic*. In this essay I shall proceed on the supposition that Robinson's list, including *Republic*, Bk. I, is acceptable, and that Socratic and Platonic teachings are roughly separable in the manner suggested. If these suppositions are false (and I do not know whether they are or not), nothing substantial would have to be changed in the main philosophical points I wish to make.

later ones, I shall distinguish elenctic definitions in the
Socratic dialogues (Socratic definitions, for short) from
elenctic definitions in the later dialogues (Platonic definitions, for short). My object in this essay is to explain the
nature and availability of elenctic definitions. I shall proceed by comparing and contrasting the theory and practice of Socratic and Platonic definitions. Inasmuch as the
theory and practice of elenctic definitions is a *locus
classicus* of philosophical explications, this is also an essay
on philosophical analysis.

My terminology makes it true by definition that the
elenchus plays an essential role in the attempted discovery of both Socratic and Platonic definitions. Moreover,
Socrates and Plato are essentially in agreement as to the
nature and criteria of good definitions.

In the *Meno* Socrates presents the rudiments of a theory of what we would call definitions today. Although he
does not formulate his views on what definitions are by
means of sentences of the form "A definition is ——,"
still it is clear in context that what he is thinking can be
formulated by means of such sentences. These, then, are
some of the things that Socrates believes as to what a
definition is.

(1) A definition is an answer to such questions as the
following. What is the nature of the bee? What is virtue?
What is health? What is strength? (72A–B)

(2) A definition focuses upon a common nature, the
self-same *eidos*, that unites many individuals under one
head.

> Do bees differ as bees, because there are many and differ-
> ent kinds of them; or are they not rather to be distin-
> guished by some other quality, as for example, beauty,
> size, or shape? . . . And so of the virtues, however many
> and different they may be, they all have a common nature
> which makes them virtues; and on this he who would answer
> the question, "What is virtue?" would do well to have his
> eye fixed (72A–C).

(3) A definition states what is the same in, common to (and peculiar to?) a number of entities, namely, those entities that are *bona fide* instances of the *definiendum*.

> Ever and anon we are landed in particulars, but that is not what I want; tell me, then, since you call them by a common name, and say that they are all figures, even when opposed to one another, what is that which they have in common, which you designate as figure—which comprehends straight as well as round, and which is no more one than the other? (72D)

(4) Taken together, (2) and (3) suggest that in seeking to understand the kind of thing a thing of a certain kind is, we seek to identify uniquely by means of a definite description, or to understand the structure or constitution of a [relevant] Form (*eidos*) that is common (and peculiar?) to things of that kind.

Here and in (3), I put a question mark on the parenthetical clause to note the fact that Socrates does not explicitly *say* that the thing or the *eidos* in question must also be peculiar to the things in question; he only *says* that it must be common to them. Still, I take it that what Socrates means to say is that the thing or the *eidos* must be both common and peculiar. That this is what he means to say is evident from counterexamples he produces on numerous occasions in the course of elenctic refutations of definitions that are too broad.

The definition of figure at 75B is not by a genus and a specific difference. By means of a definite description it provides a way of identifying figure. Figure is the only existing thing that always follows color. Socrates says that this is a true account. But at 76A he gives what he believes to be another true account, one that Meno will find easier to understand: Figure is "limit of solid." This sounds like a definition by a genus and a specific difference. Socrates thus believes that in some cases there are true alternate definitions of one and the same thing.

This poses a problem for us. How should we describe

his view? Is it that there are alternate true definitions of
one and the same *eidos?* Or is it that given a class of particulars similar in some respect, there may be at least two
logically independent Forms each one of which is common and peculiar to these particulars, and that in such
cases it is up to us to legislate on pragmatic grounds and
relative to certain purposes or congeries of purposes
which Form is to be definitive of being that kind of particular? In spite of its anachronistic flavor, it is not wholly
implausible that Socrates at times inclines to the second
alternative. A case in point is provided toward the end
of this paper. According to this alternative, figure defined
as limit of solid is a different property or Form from figure defined as the only existing thing that always accompanies color. This is what makes the two definitions true
but different.

According to the first alternative, and assuming that
the relation between *definiendum* and *definiens* is one of
identity, limit of solid and the only existing thing that
always accompanies color are one and the same property.
But in the context of the *Meno* there are complications.
Meno is supposed to understand the definition of figure
in terms of solid but not to understand the one in terms
of color because he is not clear about color. This is not to
be explained by saying that Meno is unfamiliar with, or
does not understand, the Greek synonym for our *word*
"color." His complaint is that he is not clear about what
*color* is. The definition of figure in terms of solid offered
by Socrates as an alternate true definition of the same
*eidos,* figure, is, therefore, not an alternate unless its
*definiens* is composed of properties that are clear to
Meno. But it would then seem to follow that the two
*definientia* consist of distinct properties. For Meno cannot be clear and unclear about the same property at the
same time and in the same respect. And that those should
be distinct properties is inconsistent with what is implied by the assumption that one and the same *eidos* is
being defined and that the relation between *definiens*
and *definiendum* is one of identity.

Perhaps in some cases the relation should be weakened from identity to logical or some other kind of strong equivalence. Perhaps further reflection would show only that limit of solid is necessarily present if, and only if, the only existing thing that always accompanies color is present. But there is something *ad hoc* here. The definition of figure in terms of solid is by a genus and a specific difference. Presumably, Socrates wants to hold that in all such definitions the relation between *definiens* and *definiendum* is one of identity. The definition in terms of color is not by a genus and a specific difference. It is in terms of an invariant and necessary correlation. Must Socrates resort to the *ad hoc* device of saying that in a correlating definition the *definiens* and *definiendum* are not identical, that they are only strongly equivalent? Perhaps he would be doing better were he to say instead that correlating definitions are not properly classified as definitions. And to say this would take nothing away from their power to characterize uniquely, and to help us identify, and to understand the nature of a certain property.

Actually, there is another way out. What we have lurking here in the *Meno* may be the paradox of analysis. In the preceding paragraph my argument assumed that if Meno is unclear about the property of being the only existing thing that always accompanies color and clear about the property of being limit of solid, then these must be distinct properties. This argument is not conclusive by any means. We can argue exactly analogously as follows: Meno is unclear about figure but clear about limit of solid. Therefore, figure and limit of solid cannot be identical. But "Figure = Df. limit of solid" may nevertheless be true. Meno cannot be clear and unclear about the same property at the same time and in the same respect. But being unclear that P is identical with Q *prior* to reflection and clear that there is no difference *after* reflection is a difference in respect. (This, of course, is also the answer to the misological paradox that "a man cannot inquire either about what he knows or about what he does not know" [*Men.* 80D–E] ).

Socrates then has the following option: Figure is identical with the only existing thing that always accompanies color. Figure is also identical with limit of solid. Prior to reflection one may not be cognizant of either identity and also not cognizant of what they entail, namely, that the only existing thing that always accompanies color is identical with limit of solid. After reflection one may know this. Now at the beginning of the dialogue Socrates says that he does not know what virtue is *at all*, that he is *utterly ignorant* about virtue (*Men.* 71B, my italics). If we take this literally, we must suppose that when at 75C Meno hints that he does not know what color is, he means that he has no idea of color, that he is utterly ignorant about color. But this is sheer nonsense. Unless Meno has the concept of color he cannot even hint that he does not know what color is. The claim must mean that he has no clear and adequate idea of color. Meno may have to get his concept of color straight before he can see that limit of solid and the only existing thing that always accompanies color are not two properties but one. But it is in principle possible for him to do this. In fact, Socrates undertakes to help him understand color in the Empedoclean terms that are familiar to Meno. Socrates does not think much of this particular account of the nature of color, but he seems to be going on the assumption that Meno needs to achieve clarity about what color is as a condition for seeing that limit of solid and the only existing thing that always accompanies color are identical.

In short, one can consistently hold that in all definitions, including correlating ones, the *definiendum* and *definiens* are identical even though there are at least two different true definitions of the same property. Upon reflection Meno might come to see that figure is limit of solid. But presumably he needs to reflect further to see that limit of solid is identical with the only existing thing that always accompanies color. This is the feature that makes the two definitions of figure different without disturbing the identity of *definiens* and *definiendum*.

That Socrates construes the relation between *definiens* and *definiendum* as one of property identity is implied by the kinds of argument he uses against false definitions. A typical case is the elenctic refutation of Charmides' proposal that temperance is modesty (160E). Here is the argument (*Chrm.* 160E–161B). Temperance is honorable. That is evident. It is also good. For all temperate men are good, or, more exactly, the presence of temperance makes men good, and not bad. (We might put this by saying that temperance is always a good-making property). But a property that is always good-making is itself good. Modesty, on the other hand, is sometimes a good making and sometimes a bad-making property. Hence, it is not itself always good. Therefore, temperance cannot be the same as modesty.

Notice that the argument is in two steps. Socrates is not content merely with the observation that there is no perfect coincidence between the class of temperate men and the class of modest men. He goes on to argue to the conclusion that the *property* of temperance is not the same as the *property* of modesty.

I have explained the two different ways of construing the belief that one and the same thing may be truly defined in alternate ways. There is no evidence that Socrates was aware of this distinction. In practice he seems to proceed sometimes according to the first and at other times according to the second (the pragmatic) alternative. There is no plausible interpretation of the ways he treats the definition of figure to make it accord with the second alternative. But Socrates' practice in crucial places in *Republic*, Bk. I accords best with the second alternative. Toward the end of this paper I shall take note of the fact that Socrates selects rational animality, and not some other property logically independent of this that may be common and peculiar to men, as being the essential ingredient in a morally relevant definition of man. The theory of this practice is the second and not the first alternative. Note that there is no contradiction in the position I am attributing to Socrates.

I have so far listed four propositions that are a part of Socrates' theory in the *Meno* as to what a definition is. The following four propositions are also a part of that theory:

(5) Definition [of being, e.g., a virtue] seeks the single thing [a single virtue] that runs through and is common to many particulars [individual virtues] (74A–B).

(6) There is a very strong suggestion at 74A–C that virtue is not alone in being a single thing that runs through and is common to many particulars. Figure and color are, in this respect, said to be like virtue. And, presumably, this by no means exhausts the list. Socrates seems to be implying that whenever there is this relation between one thing and many things then the many things are of a kind, and that it is possible to define with reference to that one thing what it is to be a thing of that kind.

(7) That definition is possible can be seen from another though not wholly unrelated perspective. Many things are called by a *common name*. This is possible only because the things in question have a common nature. "Figure" is the common name that applies to the straight and the round. The common name refers to the common nature that is manifested in all the relevant particular things, but is other than those particular things (74E).

(8) Definition looks for that which is the same element common to all these things, i.e., to the things that bear a common name (75A). Socrates may well be assuming that things that are called by the same name because they are all alike in some respect are alike because there is some one element common to them all. At this stage Socrates gives no explanation of the relation *being common to*.

Again in the *Meno* Socrates lays down certain criteria for good definition.

(1) A definition may be true, although the interlocutor is either unclear about, or does not understand at all,

some of the terms in the *definiens*. A definition that is true is good, but one that is both true and either clear or understood to some degree is better from "the dialectical point of view."

Thus, in 75C Socrates says that he "would have told the truth," that is, he would have given a true definition of figure in 75B, even if the interlocutor had not understood some of the terms in the *definiens*. But Socrates does go on to say that a "more dialectical" definition would use only terms that the interlocutor understands. And the language he uses in saying this makes it clear that he believes "a more dialectical" definition to be superior to one that is true but unclear or recondite.

(2) A definition must not be viciously circular. To define virtue as the power of governing by virtuous means violates this requirement. Likewise, there is a violation if we define virtue as the power of acquiring goods by virtuous means (78E).

(3) Related to this is another error that I think Socrates notes at 78C–79E. Suppose we define:

Virtue = Df. the procuring of goods justly, or courageously, or temperately, or wisely, or in a pious manner. (78D–E)

It follows immediately that procuring goods justly entails being virtuous. But all parties in the conversation agree that justice is only a part of virtue. Hence, procuring goods justly entails that one is acting in a wholly virtuous manner and also that one is acting in a manner consonant with only a part of virtue. As Socrates says to Meno at 79B: "Then it follows from your own admission that doing whatever one does with a part of virtue is virtue itself." And this is a contradiction. One and the same action cannot be both wholly virtuous and only partly virtuous. The general point behind this example is sound. If we assume that justice is one among a number of virtues, then any definition of virtue that entails that justice is the whole of virtue is unacceptable.

Moreover, "Do you suppose," Socrates asks, "that anyone can know a part of virtue when he does not know
virtue itself?" A man who is totally ignorant of what
virtue is cannot understand when told that this, that, and
the other are parts of virtue, and that the whole of virtue
consists of these parts taken together.

Such a definition of virtue as the one at *Meno* 78D–E
is unacceptable to Plato as well, but for reasons that are
not given until we come to the Platonic books of the
*Republic*. Plato clearly distinguishes justice as a certain
condition of soul from just actions, defining the latter in
terms of the former. The definition at 78D–E, together
with the assumption that justice is one among a number
of virtues, would have the consequence that justice is
an action consisting of the procuring of goods justly, or
courageously, or temperately, or wisely, or in a pious
manner. This statement is necessarily false of justice as
a certain condition of soul. A condition of soul is not an
action. It is an act but only in the technical sense of
actuality as against potentiality. The definition at 78D–E
cannot satisfy Plato because it is incapable of conveying
the Platonic doctrine that justice as a characteristic of
individual human beings is fundamentally a certain condition of soul.

The Socratic definition of virtue and the Platonic elaboration of it are wholly in accord with the methodological guidelines in the *Meno*. A human virtue will turn out
to be a character trait the presence of which is a necessary condition of having the sort of character that causes
a man to perform well the functions of a man *qua* rational animal. Consequently, a good or virtuous man is,
by definition, a man who possesses all the human virtues.
Equivalently, a good or virtuous man is, by definition, a
man whose character is such as to cause him to perform
well the functions of a man *qua* rational animal. But,
upon reflection, Socrates and Plato conclude that the human virtues are justice, temperance, courage, and wisdom. (Socrates often adds piety to this list.) Therefore,
a man is good or virtuous if, and only if, he is just, wise,

temperate, and courageous. A virtuous man will have the ability to procure goods justly, wisely, courageously, temperately (and piously, Socrates might want to add). Moreover, he will never desire to procure goods unjustly, unwisely, intemperately, or in a cowardly or impious manner because he will know that no good that he can so procure can outweigh the evil that he incurs in wrongdoing.

(4) At 76C–77A there appears to be another criterion for good definitions, but the point is very obscure. Socrates suggests that a definition of color based on the efflux theory of vision propounded by Empedocles is somehow deficient. A better definition is that of figure as the termination of solid. We already know that Socrates likes this definition because he thinks that it is both true and clear to the partners in the dialogue. But why does he poke fun at the Empedoclean definition of color? Socrates acknowledges that that definition given "in the manner of Gorgias" would be clear to Meno. For Meno was a pupil of Gorgias who, in turn, learned his science from Empedocles. Is the definition then false? Socrates does not say so. He seems to dislike it because it is "in the high poetic style." Does this mean that although the terms of the *definiens* are clear to Meno, they are in themselves imprecise? Or does it mean that the definition is inferior for being based upon a questionable speculation about the nature of vision? If these are the defects that come under being "in the high poetic style," then we have two additional Socratic criteria for a good definition. The terms of the *definiens* must be not only clear to the interlocutor, but they must be also precise in themselves, and they must not be based upon questionable speculations.

These excerpts from the *Meno* are quite representative of Socrates' views on definition in the Socratic dialogues, and they are consistent with the Socratic elenchus in practice. In later dialogues Plato introduces the method of division in the *Phaedrus* and elaborates on it in the *Sophist* and *Statesman.* The aim of this method is to articulate definitions by a genus and a specific difference, the latter being a mark or condition that distinguishes a class under that genus from other classes under it. These are the only definitions that Plato can admit consistently with his theory of collection and division. In fact he admits none others. Definitions such as "Father = Df. male parent" pose no problem. But there are more sophisticated examples of definitions by a genus and a specific difference, and there is reason for thinking that Plato would approve of them. For example, Plato would not, I think, balk at a definition such as "Grandfather = Df. father's father or mother's father." There is by implication such a "disjunctive" definition each disjunct of which is in terms of a genus and a specific difference at *Theaetetus*, 147D–148D. According to Fowler's translation and interpretation in the Loeb edition (but not according to the Cornford or the Jowett translations), Theodorus and his students set out to define what it is to be the square root of a number. They first define "length" and "surd," each by a genus and a specific difference. They do not go on to say in so many words that the square root of a number is either a length or a surd. But this is what their analysis would require them to say, if they were to go on and complete the task that they set out to accomplish.

Socrates (speaking for Plato) warmly commends the definition of "surd," and invites Theaetetus to define knowledge along similar lines. But is there any reason to suppose that Socrates would not have commended the definition of the square root of a number that on Fowler's reading is implied by Theodorus and his students? In the absence of evidence to the contrary, why should we suppose that Socrates would reject the plainly discernible logical consequences of propositions that he accepts? The availability of the Fowler rendition of the admittedly imprecise passage at *Theaetetus* 147D–148D leaves room for the hypothesis that Plato would not be unhappy with disjunctive definitions, provided that each disjunct is in terms of a genus and a specific difference.

The hypothesis is confirmed at *Republic* 352E, 353A. Socrates defines "the work of a thing [to be the work] which it only or it better than anything else can perform." As this definition occurs in Bk. I, it is Socratic. But it is also Platonic by implication. For the Platonic definitions of human virtue and of the virtues in the individual, and some Platonic arguments for the proposition that justice as a state of soul is a man's most valuable possession, are formulated in terms of the Socratic concept of the work of a thing. Thus, the generic Platonic analysis of the justice of a thing is that each part of the thing is performing its own work without interfering with the work of any of the other parts. Clearly this notion of the work of a thing is the Socratic one.[2]

Although the vast majority of formulations that Socrates regards formally as definitions are by a genus and

[2] Because of these examples, if not for other reasons, a Platonic definition by a genus and a specific difference must not automatically be identified with an Aristotelean definition *per genus et differentiam*. It is by no means certain that Aristotle's theory of definition can countenance the above definition of the square root of a number. Theodorus and his disciples begin by dividing numbers into the square and the oblong. They then go on to define "length" and "surd" in terms of square and oblong numbers. This is perfectly in line with the Platonic method of division. *Diaeresis* involves "the division of things by classes [or kinds], not taking the same Form for a different one or a different one for the same" (*Sph.* 253D). Division must come "at the natural joints" (*Phdr.* 265E). The closer division comes to the real structure of the Forms the better it is (*Statesman* 265E). A generic Form must be divided only where it divides into two specific Forms. Plato stops short of saying that for a correct definition there is exactly one correct choice of where a generic Form divides into two specific Forms. If Theodorus can throw light on what it is to be the square root of a number by starting with a division of numbers into the square and the oblong, well and good. Nothing that Plato says rules out the possibility that some other division, some choice of another "natural joint," may have been equally serviceable. Aristotle, I suspect, is much more rigid than this. For him there seems to be exactly one correct way of specifying the *differentia* of a given genus, one that culminates in a formula of the form: Being a P is, by definition, being a Q that is R, where neither Q nor R is a "disjunctive" property.

a specific difference, the earlier Socratic method for achieving clarifications of meaning admits definitions that may not be of this type as, for example, the definition of figure (*Men.* 75B), or the definition that "Temperance is modesty" (*Chrm.* 160E). Thus, the method of division is not merely a new recipe for discovering definitions. It is also a somewhat new theory of what a definition is. For Plato definition is analysis by a genus and a specific difference. For Socrates it is that, but not exclusively.

Cornford says some misleading things about the differences between the earlier elenchus and the later method of diaeresis.[3] He says that the method of division "has nothing in common with the deductive movement of the Socratic elenchus, which terminates in the rejection of a suggested definition." This is too sharp a contrast. In the Socratic dialogues the analytical techniques of the elenchus are not purely destructive. In the vast majority of cases the Socratic elenchus does "terminate in the rejection of a suggested definition"; but not always. In the *Laches* (195A), Nicias defines courage as knowledge of what one ought to fear and ought not to fear. Socrates rejects this definition because of a certain argument that he seems to think tells against it. (The argument is actually a piece of bad reasoning). In the *Protagoras* (360D), the elenchus leads to the definition rejected in the *Laches*. Whatever uncertainties we have (and we have some) about Socrates' accepting this definition we do not have them because Socrates thinks that the elenchus disposes of it. We are uncertain only because at the end of the dialogue Socrates hints that perhaps he and Protagoras are no clearer at the end than they were at the beginning of their conversation about any of the problems that they discussed. The definition of courage in the *Protagoras* is the only elenctic definition of an ethical term in the Socratic dialogues. It is the only one that is arrived at by an elenctic process and not

[3] See F. M. Cornford, *Plato's Theory of Knowledge* (London: Kegan Paul, 1935), pp. 184–85.

rejected by an elenctic process. This single exception is enough to refute Cornford's allegation.

There is another way in which the Socratic elenchus is not purely destructive. I shall argue later that in *Republic*, Bk. I, the Socratic elenchus against Cephalus, Polemarchus, and Thrasymachus yields positive guidelines that Plato uses in Bk. IV in formulating what he believes to be correct definitions of justice, courage, temperance, and wisdom. It is interesting to note that the definition of courage in Bk. IV is exactly the same as the one in the *Laches* (195A) and the *Protagoras* (360D). What is a Socratic definition in the *Protagoras* is a Platonic definition in the *Republic*. The definition is a Platonic definition because it appears in a Platonic dialogue, and the purported discovery of it makes essential use of results obtained by means of the Socratic elenchus.

It is, moreover, important to note that the guidelines for a correct definition of such terms as justice, courage, temperance, and wisdom that emerge from the Socratic elenchus in *Republic*, Bk. I, are just the sort that Plato would have needed in order to accomplish a fruitful diaeresis, had he been employing in the *Republic* the method of collection and division. Cornford is wrong again about there being "nothing in common" between the Socratic elenchus and the Platonic method of diaeresis. As an analytical tool for arriving at definitions by a genus and a specific difference, the method of division is not feasible in the absence of the sorts of guidelines that the Socratic elenchus yields. I shall have more to say on this later on.

Cornford is also misleading when he makes the following contrast:

> The Socratic method contemplates a single Form . . . and the many individual things which partake of that Form. Only one Form is in view, and the definition is to be gained by a survey of the individual instances. . . . But [in the method of collection and division] Plato's attention is now transferred from the group of individuals with

its common Form to the relations of Forms among themselves, and in particular to the relation between the Forms
which occur in the definition of a specific Form.[4]

This is a faulty contrast. Even if some commentators
should be right that "Plato's theory of Ideas," namely,
"reflection on *essence in general, or the essences as a
body,*" is "not found in the early dialogues at all,"[5] once
Plato proffers the theory of collection and division he
cannot consistently think of definitions except in terms
of the relations between the Forms which constitute a
specific Form, or, in more aseptic language, in terms of
the relation of identity between the property that is being analyzed and the properties that constitute it by a
genus and a specific difference. The earlier Socratic
method seems to allow for definitions that are not of just
this sort. But there are plenty of examples in the Socratic
dialogues of definitions that are of just this sort. Hence
the method of elenchus and the method of diaeresis do
not differ in the way suggested by Cornford. Independently of the ontological status assigned the Forms, the
method of diaeresis commits Plato to an exclusively analytic theory of definition. But nothing in the earlier Socratic method implies the rejection of such definitions.

A close study of any random sample of the Socratic
elenchus convinces me that as a method of discovering
real definitions, the elenchus is superior to, and more
fundamental than, the method of division. Neither
method is mechanical; but the earlier method shows a
more realistic appreciation of the subtleties and complexities involved in deciding whether or not a proposed
*definiens* is relevant or appropriate relative to the purposes that it is to serve. Cornford believes that the
generic Form to be divided is "divined by an act of intuition."[6] This is a harmless statement provided it is under-

[4] *Op. cit.,* p. 185.
[5] See Richard Robinson, *Plato's Earlier Dialectic* (Ithaca: Cornell University Press, 1941), p. 55.
[6] *Op. cit.,* p. 186.

stood that the intuition must be based upon a knowledge of such relevant features of our *analyzanda* as the elenchus reveals. The choice of a right genus prior to division, or the choice of a right specific difference at each step of the division depends upon precisely such knowledge. What, for instance, is the correct genus for defining the kind of creature that you and I are? Is our genus anthropoid? Is it animal? What is our criterion of correctness here? Exactly similar questions arise in connection with the problem of selecting a correct specific difference. The method of diaeresis provides no clues to an answer. The elenchus does. I shall explain how the elenchus does this by examining briefly a lengthy sample of the Socratic elenchus: the argument with Cephalus, Polemarchus, and Thrasymachus.

But first we should understand what it means to say that Socratic and Platonic definitions are intended to be true or correct real explicit definitions of properties the nature of which, prior to analysis, we may but dimly apprehend.

Neither the early nor the later dialogues contain an explicit definition of what a real definition is. The emphasis on diaeresis in the Platonic dialogues suggests that Plato's view of a real definition may be put thus. In a real definition a property, P, is said to be identical with a finite conjunction or disjunction of properties, none of which is identical with any of the others or with P. A correct or true real definition is one in which the alleged identity obtains. The Socratic conception of a real definition has to be characterized somewhat more broadly. In the Socratic dialogues Socrates does not object to the *forms* of such definitions as "Temperance is modesty" (*Chrm.* 160E), or to such definitions as the one of figure at *Meno* 75B. Charmides says that temperance is the same as modesty. This is not an analysis in terms of a genus and a specific difference. It is an identification. Temperance and modesty are said to be not two properties but one. If modesty is not analyzable, and if it is true that temperance is modesty, then there can be no definition of temperance by a genus and a specific difference. Socrates questions only the *truth* of this definition. He never questions its *form*. Again, the definition of figure at *Meno* 75B provides a unique specification of figure by means of a definite description, not by an analysis by a genus and a specific difference. Although the vast majority of definitions actually considered in the Socratic dialogues are of the genus–specific difference form, the fact that there are examples of other sorts indicates that the Socratic conception of a real definition must differ somewhat from the Platonic one. The Socratic conception may be put thus: In a real definition, a property may either be uniquely identified by means of an ineliminable[7] definite description; or it may be said to be identical with a finite conjunction or disjunction of properties none of which is identical with any of the others or with it, and any one of which may itself be definable; or finally, it may be said to be identical with some property that itself is not a conjunction or disjunction of distinct properties. ("Temperance is modesty" would illustrate the last clause, if in fact modesty was itself not a conjunction or disjunction of distinct properties). A correct or true real definition is one in which the alleged identity obtains.

These conceptions have one serious drawback. Inasmuch as there exists no satisfactory criterion of identity of properties, there exists no criterion for deciding when a Socratic or Platonic real definition is true. However, we do have the ability in many instances to see, beyond the shadow of a doubt, that being P is or is not different from being Q. The Socratic elenchus relies on this ability, and it is a very effective tool for piecemeal philosophical analysis.

The Socratic and Platonic conceptions of what a real definition is do not indicate any awareness of the pos-

---

[7] In "Figure is the only existing thing that always accompanies color," the definite description is ineliminable. In "x is a father = Df. x possesses the property of being a male parent," the definite description is eliminable.

sibility or need for other forms of definition, viz., contextual and recursive definitions. They are really conceptions of what a real *explicit* definition is. These conceptions have linguistic counterparts, for we can also speak of a real explicit definition of a given linguistic expression.

The Platonic conception of a real explicit definition of a linguistic expression, E, satisfies the following conditions:

(1) It is of the form: E = Df. E'.
(2) E and its *definiens*, E', are different expressions.
(3) E has a certain standard use.
(4) The *definiens* undertakes to give the meaning of E for that standard use by listing a number of conditions that, either conjunctively or disjunctively, constitute logically necessary and sufficient conditions by a genus and a specific difference for being the sort of thing to which E, in that standard use, applies.

The Socratic counterpart would be the same except for (4), which would read as follows: The *definiens* undertakes to give the meaning of E for that standard use either by listing a number of distinct conditions that, either conjunctively or disjunctively, constitute logically necessary and sufficient conditions by a genus and a specific difference for being the sort of thing to which E, in that standard use, applies; or by listing a simple condition, that itself is not a complex of distinct conditions, that constitutes a logically necessary and sufficient condition for being the sort of thing to which E, in that standard use, applies; or, by providing, by means of an ineliminable definite description, a logically necessary and sufficient condition for being the sort of thing to which E, in that standard use applies.

No such definitions of "real explicit definition of a linguistic expression" exist in either the Socratic or Platonic dialogues. But they are definitions in line with facts that Socrates and Plato recognize, and more importantly, they are wholly in line with the elenchus.

In the passages cited from the *Meno*, we saw that
Socrates takes note of the fact that there are "common
names," such as "red," "man," "cow," "figure," "bee,"
"number." Now in order to be a "common name," an expression must have a meaning. Many a "common name"
is defined by a genus and a specific difference. But must
they all be so defined? Socrates does not think so. The
definition of "figure" at *Meno* 75B does not appear to
be by a genus and a specific difference. Yet Socrates says
that it is a true definition. There is another question,
however, that Socrates and Plato seem to have left unanswered. Can all "common names" be defined by a
genus and a specific difference? We do not know what
Socrates and Plato thought about this. We do not know
if they ever resolved to their own satisfaction the problem of whether or not there are indefinable elements.
The things Plato says about this in the *Theaetetus* and
*Cratylus* seem to provide meager evidence as to what
his well-considered opinion was. And I do not recall
that there is anything definitive about this in the Socratic
dialogues, either. Thus, we do not know if Socrates or
Plato would have said that in our linguistic framework
the "common name," for example, "red" is not definable,
while "man" is.

Still we do know that Socrates and Plato believed that
many "common names" associated with analyzable properties can be defined explicitly. And the above definitions of "real explicit definition of a linguistic expression" reflect the underlying assumptions of the elenchus
when it is employed as a propaedeutic to the discovery
of real explicit definitions. One of these assumptions is
that the word we are trying to define is in the standard
vocabulary of educated speakers of the language; another is that a necessary condition for correctness in an
explication of meaning is that the explication shall not
contradict any pre-analytically accepted facts about the
entities to which the *definiendum* applies. A good illustration of all this is to be found in Socrates' criticisms of

Cephalus', Polemarchus', and Thrasymachus' definitions of "justice." We shall come to this shortly.

If we concentrate on the Socratic and Platonic notions of real definition in terms of identity of properties, a relevant contrast would seem to be that between real, on the one hand, and verbal and dictionary definitions on the other. This is precisely where a modern Platonist, the G. E. Moore of *Principia Ethica,* places the emphasis in a well-known passage in Chapter I of that book. The implication is that while the philosopher's job includes the dissection of complex properties into their constituent elements, it is no part of his task to worry about words or to report their meanings either as recorded in authoritative dictionaries or as revealed to an investigator who is exquisitely attuned to the contours and nuances of educated discourse.

But in the presence of either the Socratic or the Platonic definition of "real explicit definition of a linguistic expression," the significant contrast is not between real versus verbal and dictionary definitions. It is between real and arbitrary definitions. A dictionary definition may be a perfectly good example of a real explicit definition, e.g., the definition of "father" as it is used in such sentences as "My father died of a heart attack." So used, it is clear that the word "father" means *male parent,* and the dictionary lists this as one of the meanings of "father." Webster's Third New International Dictionary gives a precise definition of "vector" as it is used in such a sentence as "The concept of a vector is a key concept of classical mechanics." Someone introduced the concept of vector into astronomy and physics. Someone used the word "vector" for the first time to mean *vector.* Before this happened there was no such standard use for "vector." There was no such word in English. But when the stipulation that "vector" is to mean such and such was adopted by physicists, the word acquired a standard use, and its definition in the New Webster is now a precise real definition.

The same dictionary defines arithmetical addition as

"the process denoted by the sign + of combining two or more numbers so as to obtain their sum." In the judgment of the lexicographer this definition presumably articulates the educated layman's notion of arithmetical addition. It is, therefore, presumably a real definition of what the layman understands by "+." However, it is imprecise and unsatisfactory as compared with Peano's recursive definition or with a set-theoretic explicit definition. There is no reason why the latest dictionaries should not also include the more precise definitions. If they did, they would be giving real definitions that articulate correctly and precisely the meaning of "+" as it is standardly used in arithmetical contexts such as "$1 + 1 = 2$." The layman's meaning reported in the dictionary represents a relatively superficial understanding of the relevant meaning of "+."

The technical definitions are the result of a more profound understanding. The technical definitions presuppose knowledge of such facts about natural numbers as these: That they may be serially ordered to constitute a discretely infinite sequence with a first but no last member, each member in the sequence having exactly one successor; that $1 + 1 = 2$, $1 + 2 = 3$, etc.; that addition is commutative. The technical definitions are not stipulations. They are each a correct way of explicating the nature of addition for natural numbers. There is a standard of correctness here. The definitions accord perfectly with the facts of arithmetic and with the salient facts about natural numbers. These facts are universally recognized by arithmeticians. Peano is the first to provide a clear and precise explication or analysis of addition. We could equivalently say that Peano is the first to provide a clear and precise explication or analysis of the meaning of "+" as this symbol is used in such arithmetical sentences as "$1 + 1 = 2$." There is no significant contrast between discovering what the exact nature of an arithmetical operation is and discovering what the exact definition of an arithmetical symbol is for one of its standard uses. The interesting contrast is this: that Peano made a discovery. He accomplished an explication. He did not make a linguistic stipulation. His definition gives us a clearer idea of what addition is than does the layman's definition. Whichever way we describe his accomplishment, as the explanation of the exact nature of addition or as the discovery of an exact definition of "+," what matters is that we judge the accuracy of his analysis by the same standard: conformity to the pre-analytically known facts about natural numbers and sums.

Plato in the *Republic* and Socrates in the early dialogues are trying to discover a clear and precise real explicit definition of what it is to be a good man. They are trying to do something essentially like what Peano did. Even in our day, consulting the standard lay dictionaries or the best dictionaries and encyclopedias of philosophy does not provide the sort of formulation Plato is looking for. The lay dictionaries define a good man as a man of praiseworthy character. This is not wrong. In fact, it is absolutely the right beginning. What we next want to know is what are the essential features of a praiseworthy character. Socrates' exchanges with Cephalus, Polemarchus, and Thrasymachus make it abundantly clear that Socrates is working on the assumption that a correct real definition of a good man is one that will conform to the true judgments we make as to what a man ought to do and what sort of person he ought to be. These true judgments correspond to the truths of arithmetic and the salient properties of natural numbers. As conformity to the latter is a necessary condition for a real definition of addition to be a correct explication, so conformity to the former is a necessary condition for a real definition of what it is to be a good man to be a correct explication. Conformity here amounts to this, that none of the logical consequences of the proposed explication contradict the pre-analytically recognized facts.

Socrates and Plato, I think, are insufficiently sensitive to the complexities involved in the above standard of correctness. How do we tell which of our ought-judgments about human actions and character are true?

And who are the "we" whose true ought-judgments are
to provide the crucial test? Nevertheless, their procedure
is sound. We do need a standard of correctness, and it
does seem unreasonable to look for it elsewhere than in
just the sorts of judgments Socrates and Plato select.
There is a clear indication at *Republic* 442E that Plato
himself is committed to the principle that analytic definitions are defective unless they can stand the test of
conforming to pre-analytic data. He wants to "confirm
completely" his own definition of the justice of the individual "by applying commonplace and vulgar tests
to it."

I have already called attention to the fact that we do
not have a criterion of identity for properties. Add to
this the enormously complex and controversial issues
that are involved in the standard of correctness, and we
see that the Socratic elenchus is not a routine, mechanical, wholesale method of analysis. Still, it is a method
that works very well piecemeal.

Consider the criticism of Cephalus' remarks about telling the truth and paying one's debts, if these are construed as a definition of justice in the individual.[8] The
main thrust is the Socratic open-question:[9] "Are not these
acts [telling the truth and restoring anything we have
been trusted with] sometimes right and sometimes
wrong?" The answer is "Yes." Hence, being a just man
cannot be definitionally or otherwise necessarily connected with telling the truth and keeping one's end of a
bargain, no matter what. For being a good man entails
being a just man. And being a good man cannot be definitionally or otherwise necessarily connected with doing
such actions. The opening move of the elenchus against
Cephalus is at the very least a legitimate *ad hominem*

[8] Cephalus' remarks are quite casual. There can be little doubt
that Cephalus has no idea of what a definition is. Socrates is the
one who interprets Cephalus' remarks as though they were meant
to formulate a definition.

[9] The Socratic open-question is very much like G. E. Moore's, as
will be explained on p. 151, n. 10, below.

argument. Cephalus, the individual, is supposed to have offered a definition. That definition has logical consequences that are inconsistent with certain ought-judgments that Cephalus, the individual, believes to be true. Therefore, at the very least, Cephalus has to give up either the definition attributed to him or the ought-judgments.

In this instance, however, the opening move in the elenchus proves to be more than just a legitimate *ad hominem* argument. If paying one's debts is constitutive of being just, then it would follow that a man is just only if he keeps every promise he makes, for keeping a promise is one way of paying one's debts. The judgment that it is false that no matter what, the truth must be told and promises kept, is one that we have no reason to doubt. Indeed, granted that ought-judgments can be true or false, then we can see that if there are incompatible promises, then it is false that one ought to keep every promise, no matter what. But there are incompatible promises. Therefore, it is false that one ought to keep a promise, no matter what. Hence, assuming that ought-judgments are true or false, Cephalus' judgment that after all not every promise ought to be kept is not just a private opinion. It is demonstrable. Hence, it is Cephalus' definition of just man that is at fault.

We can ask Cephalus another open-question that Socrates did not ask but legitimately could have: "Are these acts—telling the truth and keeping promises—the only acts that we can do rightly or wrongly?" The answer is plainly "No." We make ought-judgments about other kinds of actions, and this fact shows that Cephalus' definition cannot be a correct explication.

The elenchus against Polemarchus is an equally good illustration of how it can be a devastating piecemeal method of refuting false definitional claims. In one place Polemarchus defines a just man as a man who helps his friends and harms his enemies. One defect of this definition, one that Socrates neglects to point out, is that like Cephalus' definition, it is too narrow. The Socratic open-question can be asked here, too. For it is a fact that we can act rightly or wrongly in relation to strangers and mere acquaintances.

The definition has other consequences that are inconsistent with facts about how we deliberate. We judge that mere friendship and mere enmity are not reason enough to steal, kill, cheat, and lie. Polemarchus' definition implies that doing such things in order to harm an enemy and benefit a friend is not only right but is required of a man who would be just. Furthermore, we can be friends with disreputable and evil individuals, and we can be enemies with good men. There is something wrong with a definition that implies that in order to be good a man must at times harm a good man, and further the interests of, aid and abet an evil and disreputable man who is engaged in doing disgraceful things, just because the good man happens to be an enemy and the bad man happens to be a friend.

These difficulties can be avoided by revising the definition to say that a just man is a man who benefits those he truly believes are upright and harms those who he truly believes are wrongdoers. Apart from the fact that this is a viciously circular definition, it implies that it is a man's duty to injure a wrongdoer whenever he can. But we have every reason to believe that this conclusion is false.

The review of these familiar matters serves to remind us of the power of the elenchus to dispel faulty notions. But the elenchus is not purely negative. It prepares the way for constructive work. It has positive results.

The positive results of the elenchus against Cephalus and Polemarchus include the following: (1) That no list of kinds of actions, no matter how finitely long, can provide a real definition of goodness in a man, if of any action of the kind on the list we can ask, "Are not actions of this kind sometimes done rightly and sometimes wrongly?," knowing that the question is rhetorical. This is a special application of the sort of question that has come to be called the open question. G. E. Moore used it in *Principia Ethica,* pp. 15 ff., and made it fashionable in contemporary discussions in ethical theory. Socrates is the first Western philosopher on record to have used the open-question tactic to demolish incorrect definitions of ethical terms, and Plato is the first to have seen the power of such questions to elicit certain specific criteria of adequacy for analyzing ethical concepts.[10] (2) That human goodness is a matter of character involving dispositions, attitudes, sympathies, antipathies, loves, and aversions. The demarcation of good character is to be sought in the features that distinguish a good character from a bad one. Thus, any attempt to define human goodness in terms of particular relations, such as friendship and enmity, family, tribe, or country, is bound to fail.

The elenchus against Thrasymachus is less decisive as a critical tool. The first point that Socrates scores against Thrasymachus is a legitimate *ad hominem,* and nothing more. Socrates shows that Thrasymachus is incoherent in his initial exposition. Thrasymachus asserts two propositions: (1) Whatever the ruler (or the stronger) decrees the subject (the weaker) ought to obey, and (2) The subject is acting rightly or as he ought only if he acts in the interest of the ruler. The first of these is an ought-

---

[10] The Socratic use of the open-question tactic is in some ways superior to Moore's. According to Moore, no list of "natural" (scientific, metaphysical, religious, and otherwise non-evaluative) properties can be identical with goodness, for of anything described purely in terms of such "natural" properties we can always "sensibly" ask: But after all, are things of that kind good? One very difficult task this formulation imposes is to provide a criterion for distinguishing "natural" from "non-natural" properties, the latter being the same as "evaluative" properties. In the second place, the rhetorical question can be asked even of things that are described in evaluative terms. Consider one of Polemarchus' definitions, the one in which a just man is said to be a man who does good to friends whom he truly believes to be good men, and harm to enemies whom he truly believes to be bad men. The *definiens* contains evaluative terms, such as "good man." Still the Socratic open-question can be asked of it: Is it, after all, not the case that the actions described can sometimes be done rightly and sometimes wrongly?

judgment that Thrasymachus believes. The second is a logical consequence of his definition of what justice is. Socrates observes that a ruler may decree a law falsely believing it to be such that if obeyed it will serve his own interest. By (1) a subject ought to obey such a law. By (2) he ought not to obey it. What this shows is that Thrasymachus cannot admit that a ruler can make mistakes about what is to his own interest, and at the same time consistently assert both (1) and (2). Socrates does not argue directly against either (1) or (2). Instead he attacks Thrasymachus' defense against the *ad hominem*. The defense is that a ruler in the strict sense (one who makes no mistakes about what is to his own interest) always legislates in his own interest.

Socrates' argument that this proposition is false is inconclusive. His major premise is that every *techne* serves the interest of its subject. This is false, if "subject" means a thing that is not brought into existence by exercising the *techne*, but is something upon which the *techne* is practiced. A front-line soldier is not serving the interest of the enemy he kills. If, however, "subject" means that product or state of affairs that the *techne* is meant to realize, then in the case of some *technai* there can be no question as to what they are meant to realize. Their aim or function is logically implied by the very concept of the *techne* in question. A shepherd, for example, is *defined* by his function, which is to look after the welfare of the sheep in his charge. A good shepherd is one who performs his function well, and in doing so he inevitably serves the interest of the individual sheep that are under his care. But it is by no means obvious that from the very definition of a ruler in terms of his function it follows that in performing his function well, a ruler inevitably serves the interest of his subjects. A good ruler is one who performs well his function of acting as the supreme executive official of a given body politic. But a good ruler, like a good thief, may not be a good man or a wise man. Or, he may be both good and wise, but he might find it necessary to sacrifice the individual interests of the present generation of his subjects for the sake of the long-range safety of the state. So it seems by no means to follow that a good ruler is a ruler who serves the interests of the individuals who are his subjects.

Socrates' own argument is thus inconclusive, but the Socratic elenchus can be used effectively against Thrasymachus. We can ask the same questions about his definition as we did about Cephalus' and Polemarchus'. Is it, after all, true that just and right action consists in nothing more or less than serving the interest of the stronger? Moreover, are not these actions themselves sometimes right and sometimes wrong to do? In view of the facts about ought-judgments we actually make, believe to be true, and have no reason to doubt, the correct answer to the second question is "yes," and to the first question "no."

And again, the elenchus does not provide solely destructive criticism. The participants in the dialogue think that the elenchus in Bk. I against Thrasymachus devastates Thrasymachus's theory as he states it in Bk. I. In Bk. II Glaucon and Adeimantus play devil's advocates by undertaking to "revive the argument of Thrasymachus." In their brief for Thrasymachus they seem to suggest that Thrasymachus' theory of justice is premised upon two assumptions: (1) that the standard of man's goodness is to be found in his nature, and (2) that the justice that accords with nature profits him who is just and natural injustice harms him who is unjust. Plato himself accepts these assumptions. His basic disagreement with Thrasymachus is over what the nature of man is and what profits a man. From this disagreement arise their different conceptions of what justice and goodness are.

With the positive results of the elenchus in the background and serving implicitly as criteria of adequacy for the constructive analysis, Plato proceeds to work out his own theory of what a good man is. This contention is perfectly consistent with the supposition that *Republic* Bk. I is Socratic, the rest Platonic. Organically the *Republic* gives the impression of being a coherent unit. Bk. I does not stand apart from the rest. There is a continuous development of ideas from beginning to end. This is one reason for supposing that in Bks. II–X, Plato goes beyond Socrates not by developing an altogether independent doctrine but, among other things, by building upon the results reached by Socrates in Bk. I. Another reason for thinking this is that some recurrent themes in the Socratic dialogues that may have been written before Bk. I of the *Republic* are given in the *Republic* a much more positive and definitive formulation, viz., (1) that man's goodness is a composite of "parts," these being justice, courage, temperance, and wisdom. (From time to time in the early dialogues other virtues are added—piety or holiness, for example; but the aforementioned four appear in every catalogue of the presumed parts of virtue); (2) that virtue is in some essential way connected with knowledge; (3) the definition of courage apparently rejected by Socrates in the *Laches* and apparently accepted by him in the *Protagoras,* finally reappears in Bk. IV of the *Republic* bearing Plato's approval.[11] The definition in Bk. IV is built upon the Platonic doctrine of the tripartite soul (= the essential man). In the Socratic dialogues there is no positive analysis to compare with Plato's sure-footed systematic explication of virtue in terms of the nature of man. But the Platonic theory of man and the Platonic explication of virtue based upon

[11] The approval is not unqualified. At *Republic* 435D Socrates says that "this matter," namely, the soul's tripartite constitution and the attendant definitions of justice, courage, temperance, and wisdom (cf. 504B) will never be apprehended "accurately from such methods as we are now employing in discussion. For there is another longer and harder way that conducts to this." The reference to the longer way is that only those who have knowledge of the good can fully and accurately understand the nature of man and of human virtue. But what this means is not precise. Is Plato implying that the theory of the tripartite soul and the consequent definition of justice are accurate and exact, but that only those who come to know the Good will know that they are accurate and exact? Or is he implying that only those who come to know the Good will have a perfectly precise conception of human nature and human virtue? 504D–E seems to favor the latter.

that theory contain nothing that Socrates must needs repudiate. On the assumption that the nature of justice and goodness in man depend upon the nature of man, the first thing to do is to find out what man's nature is.

There is more than one logically independent set of properties that are unique and peculiar to man. Which among these should the moral philosopher choose to define man? Physical anthropologists have found it useful to define man as an anthropoid that exhibits all four of the following properties: (1) erect posture, freeing the forearm for carrying and manipulation; (2) the hand structure with thumb-finger opposition, permitting manipulation and grasping, thus freeing the lips and mouth for use in speech; (3) the vocal cord structure, which together with chest cavity is sufficiently under central nervous control to permit the finely differentiated response which we call speech, and (4) the highly organized brain which permits complex learning and complex co-ordinated responses. Such a definition of man may be wholly adequate for the purposes of physical anthropologists, but it is obvious that it is inadequate for the moral philosopher. The presence of these physical characteristics permits the development, but does not entail the presence, of such centrally relevant factors as the needs, wants, interests, attitudes, dispositions, beliefs, ideals, sympathies, and antagonisms that are characteristic of man as a rational creature. As Socrates says in the *Phaedo,* it is because of such factors as these that he is sitting in prison waiting for the hemlock, not because his body has muscles, bones, ligaments, and joints.

Accordingly, any conception of human nature, even if framed in terms of properties that are unique and peculiar to man, is bound to be inadequate, if not irrelevant, for the purposes of inquiry into the nature of justice and goodness in man, if it ignores the essential factor of rationality in man's nature. This factor is duly emphasized in the Socratic dialogues. Witness Socrates' preoccupation with the theme that virtue is knowledge. Socrates never doubts that a morally relevant conception of man

cannot overlook his rationality. But is Socrates overly intellectualistic? Does he overlook the passions and the
*thumos* that Plato emphasizes? It is difficult to be sure
about the *thumos*, but it is fairly clear that Socrates does
not ignore the animal in man. The theory of punishment
in the *Gorgias* assumes that instruction by direct appeal
to the intellect may not suffice for curing a man who is
dominated by his animal drives. Socrates regards all
wrongdoing as at bottom being due to ignorance. Still, he
gives evidence of maintaining a distinction between
those who may need to be prepared, through punishment, for instruction, from those who can be cured of
their wrongdoing by instruction alone, without the in-
tervention of punishment. This distinction makes sense
only on the supposition that a man's animal drives may
sometime get so out of hand that before he can listen to
reason his passions must be subdued by punishment.

Socrates, then, gives ample evidence of believing that
both rationality and animality are essential ingredients
in a morally relevant conception of human nature. This
is in line with the positive results of the elenchus against
Cephalus, Polemarchus, and Thrasymachus. One of the
positive results of the elenchus is the conclusion that human goodness is a function of human character. The
standard dictionaries are wholly in accord with this. But
they do not go on to provide an illuminating distinction
between good and bad character. The explication of
that distinction, the discovery of a specific difference for
good character, calls for an original explication. The key
to a successful analysis is the recognition that for the purposes of moral philosophy man is essentially a rational
animal. Socrates' explication of what it is to be a man of
good character is based on the assumption that the goodness of a thing of a certain kind consists in its performing
well the functions of a thing of that kind (*R.* 352E–
353E). A good shepherd is a shepherd who performs
well the functions of a shepherd. The good performance,
to be sure, must not be a matter of accident or luck. The
agent or the instrument (e.g., a bread knife) must be in

such a condition that his or its being in that condition is a causal determinant of his or its praiseworthy performance.

Accordingly, the first step in the Socratic analysis of a good man is that he is a man whose character is such as to cause him to perform well his essentially human functions, viz., the functions of a rational animal. In the language of the *Meno,* we have just described the "common nature" of any human virtue. A human virtue is an essential ingredient in the sort of character that causes a man to perform well the functions of a rational animal. The fully fledged Platonic moral philosophy builds upon these Socratic results. Plato's analyses of ethical concepts are elenctic definitions.

There is in the Socratic dialogues no elenctic definition of the particular virtues of justice, courage, temperance, and wisdom with which Socrates appears to be decidedly happy. There is no satisfactory explanation of why the Socratic paradoxes are not paradoxes. There is nothing like the intricate argumentation in the later books of the *Republic* to prove that justice pays. There is no elaborate theory of what man is. Plato has his own answers to these problems. They are based upon distinctively Platonic views about the nature of human knowledge and the nature of the human soul. These views go beyond anything we find in the Socratic dialogues. But there can be no doubt that the Socratic dialogues contain the essential groundwork for the Platonic solutions.

# 8. SOCRATES ON THE DEFINITION OF PIETY: *EUTHYPHRO* 10A–11B

Plato's *Euthyphro* is a clear example of a Socratic definitional dialogue. The concept to be defined is that of holiness or piety (τὸ ὅσιον), and the need for a definition is presented in a manner characteristic of the early dialogues. Euthyphro is about to prosecute his father on a charge of murder, Socrates expresses surprise at Euthyphro's action, and Euthyphro defends himself by saying that to prosecute his father is pious, whereas not to prosecute him would be impious. Socrates then wonders whether Euthyphro's knowledge of piety and impiety is sufficient to guarantee that he is not acting impiously in prosecuting his father. The trap has been set; Euthyphro's vanity is stung, and the search for a definition begins. The outcome of the search is also familiar; all of Euthyphro's efforts miscarry. The dialogue ends with no satisfactory definition of piety either produced or in the offing.

The central argument in the dialogue is the one Socrates advances (10A–11B) against Euthyphro's definition of piety as "what all the gods love." The argument is interesting on several counts. First, the argument is sufficiently unclear as to warrant discussion of what its structure is. Second, it is at least open to question whether there is any interpretation or reconstruction of the argument according to which it is valid and non-fallacious. Third, there are a number of points of contemporary philosophical interest that inevitably arise in any adequate discussion of the argument. Fourth, the argument has been traditionally thought to have an important moral for contemporary ethical theory, and not just for ancient theology. Before beginning a detailed examination of the argument itself, I will comment briefly on the moral the argument has been traditionally thought to have.[1]

For Euthyphro, the question whether or not he ought to prosecute his father is to be settled by determining whether or not it would be pious for him to do so. Whether or not his doing so would be pious is determined by finding out whether all the gods love it, or, as we might now say, approve of it. For Euthyphro, then, moral questions (such as "Ought I prosecute my father?") are settled by appeal to moral authorities—the gods. Euthyphro is offering an authoritarian normative ethical theory. But he apparently wishes to offer an authoritarian meta-ethical theory as well, since "pious" is for him *defined* in terms of the approval of an authority. Moreover, Euthyphro must have thought of his authorities as pre-eminently wise and rational; after all, they are the gods. Their wisdom and rationality is part of what makes them moral authorities. It is their wisdom and rationality that enables them to perceive, where mere mortals may fail to perceive, whether a given act is pious. Socrates' argument may then be thought of as having the following force. If "pious" is to be defined in terms of the gods' approval, then the piety of a given act cannot be that upon which the gods base their approval of it. If the gods' approval of a pious act has any rational basis, then, it must lie in their perception of some *other* features of the act. And then it is *these* features in terms of which "pious" should be defined. In general, if one's normative ethics are authoritarian, and one's authorities are rational and use their rationality in forming moral judgments, then one's meta-ethics cannot also be authoritarian.

[1] Cf. A. E. Taylor, *Plato the Man and his Work* (London: Methuen, 1949), p. 151, and Robert G. Hoerber, "Plato's *Euthyphro*," *Phronesis*, III (1958), pp. 95–107, esp. n. 1, p. 102, and p. 104.

I want to argue in support of this somewhat traditional interpretation of the *Euthyphro*. I shall try to show that Socrates' arguments should be taken as supporting this conclusion (indeed, that they cannot be taken to support anything else).

I

Socrates begins his argument against Euthyphro's proposed definition by asking him this question: "Is the pious loved by the gods because it is pious, or is it pious because it is loved?"[2] (10A2–3). Socrates hopes to get Euthyphro to affirm the first and deny the second of these two alternatives, but Euthyphro fails to understand the question. Socrates agrees to "speak more plainly" (10A5) and then produces the most baffling part of the argument.

Before examining the explanation that Socrates offers, we might note that it seems somewhat surprising that Euthyphro does not realize that he cannot, consistently with his own definition, deny the second of these alternatives. For if "pious" is to be defined as "loved by all the gods," then surely, in some sense of "because," it will be because it is loved that the pious is pious. But I think it is easy to see why Euthyphro cannot be expected to have realized this. First of all, it has not been stated explicitly that Euthyphro was to be offering a *definition*. When the question was first raised, Socrates simply asked Euthyphro to "say what the pious is" (5D7); later, Socrates asks for "the characteristic[3] in virtue of which everything pious is pious" (6D10–11). And it is not hard to imagine that Euthyphro, not appreciating the force of the phrase "the characteristic in virtue of which" (τὸ εἶδος ᾧ),

[2] Translations, unless otherwise noted, are my own.

[3] I translate εἶδος throughout as "characteristic" rather than (the more usual) "form" since it seems clear that in this dialogue, and at this stage in Plato's philosophical thought, to give the εἶδος of F is to say what all Fs have in common and not to introduce a supra-sensible Platonic Form to which Fs are (somehow) related.

would find it sufficient to produce a formula which he feels will serve to pick out all and only pious things. After all, the philosophical topic of definition was just being invented, and Euthyphro could hardly have been at home in it. And part of Plato's point will surely be that the definition of a term "F" cannot be *just* a formula which applies to all and only F things. If this is a mistake that Plato wants to show up, then Euthyphro must surely be given the opportunity to make it. At this point in the dialogue Euthyphro is content to say that pious things are the ones the gods love; and if this is what he wishes to say, then he need not be expected to answer Socrates' question "Is the pious pious because it is loved?" in the affirmative, even if he understood the question. But he has not even claimed to understand it.

II

The next part of Socrates' argument, in which he tries to explain to Euthyphro what his question meant, has produced more confusion on the part of commentators and translators than has anything else in the dialogue. Everything starts out well enough: Socrates notes that we speak of a thing being carried and a thing carrying, a thing being led and a thing leading, etc., and that the first member of each pair is different from the second (10A5–8). The first member of each pair is a passive participle (*pheromenon*, "carried"; *agomenon*, "led"; *horōmenon*, "seen") and the second an active participle (*pheron*, "carrying"; *agon*, "leading"; *horōn*, "seeing").[4] The distinction is surely intended to be a grammatical one; as has been frequently noted, the grammatical terminology in which the distinction between active and passive voices would be expressed had not been invented at the time Plato was writing. The distinction is then

[4] In what follows I shall transliterate the Greek terms a Greek-less reader will find it useful to identify in following the argument.

applied to the verb relevant to Euthyphro's definition;
"being loved" (*philoumenon*) is distinguished from "loving" (*philoun*). So far, so good. The distinction Socrates
wishes to draw is clear, even if what he is up to is not.

But having distinguished between active and passive
participles, Socrates immediately drops the active member from the discussion and contrasts, instead, the passive participle with the inflected third person singular
passive. The distinction Socrates is after has to do with
how these forms fit into sentences of the form "p because q." He wants to say that substituting the participle
for "p" and the inflected passive for "q" will yield a truth,
whereas substituting the inflected passive for "p" and the
participle for "q" will yield a falsehood. Thus a thing carried (*pheromenon*) is (1) *pheromenon* because *pheretai,*
but not (2) *pheretai* because it is a *pheromenon.* The
trouble is that whereas Socrates' first distinction was between active and passive voices, this second distinction
is between two different passive forms. Thus, it is hard
to see how the first distinction is meant to bear on the
second. An even greater difficulty is that when we try to
translate Socrates' words when he draws this distinction,
we are faced with the fact that *both* of these forms are
normally translated the same way into English, i.e., "is
carried," "is led," etc. If we try to translate what Socrates
says, then, we get: "a thing carried is (1) carried because
it is carried, but not (2) carried because it is carried."
But this makes Socrates' point nonsense.

This difficulty has reduced translators to babble and
driven commentators to despair. Let me give one example of each. In one translation of the *Euthyphro* we
read:[5]

a thing is not carried because it is in a state of being carried: it is in a state of being carried because it is carried.

[5] F. J. Church, revised by Robert D. Cumming (New York:
Liberal Arts Press, 1956), p. 12.

But even if one can find this intelligible, it is still hard to see why it is supposed to be true. Geach[6] tries translating what Socrates wishes to deny as "A thing is carried because *carried* is what it is" and what he wishes to affirm as "Because a thing is carried, *carried* is what it is" and then gives up, saying that

> this is just whistling in the dark; we just do not know how Plato conceived the difference between the forms I provisionally translate 'so-and-so is carried' and '*carried* is what so-and-so is', nor why it is supposed to be obvious that [the second] is true and [the first] is false.

I think that we can improve on both the translation and the interpretation. Indeed, unless we can understand what Plato is up to here we will be in no position to assess his argument.[7]

Two important points need to be noted if we are to grasp Plato's point. The first is that the passive participle can function as either part of a noun phrase or, by itself, nominally. *Pheromenon ti* means "something carried"; a *pheromenon* is something which is carried. The second point is that the inflected passive entered the discussion in place of the active participle. *Pheretai*—"it is carried" —can, in general, have the sense of "one carries it" or "something carries it"; and it clearly must have that sense in Socrates' argument.[8] It now becomes tempting to try to put Socrates' point this way: The passive participle of a verb introduces the notion of an alteration in something—a thing's being in an altered state or condition. The inflected passive of the verb introduces the notion of a process which results in that alteration—a thing's hav-

---

[6] P. T. Geach, "Plato's *Euthyphro:* An Analysis and Commentary," *The Monist,* July 1966, p. 378.

[7] This opinion is not shared by Geach. Cf. *ibid.,* bottom.

[8] This has been noted by some translators of the *Euthyphro*. *Pheretai* is translated by Fowler (Loeb Classical Library) as "one carries it" and by Cooper (*The Collected Dialogues of Plato,* Hamilton and Cairns, eds.) as "something carries it."

ing been acted on in such a way that it is altered as a result. Then Socrates would be saying that a thing's having been acted on in a certain way explains why it is in an altered condition, whereas a thing's being in an altered condition does not explain why it underwent the process which results in that alteration. Socrates would be seen as putting forward a rudimentary causal doctrine having to do with the relative explanatory powers of causes and effects.[9]

But to try to interpret Socrates' point in this way invites the obvious objection that, owing to a clear disanalogy between the verb "love" and the others that Socrates first considers, the point Socrates wishes to make using these other verbs cannot be applied to the verb "love." For whereas a thing that is carried or led is altered by being carried or led, a thing that is loved need not be altered by being loved.[10]

Let me try to present what I take to be Socrates' point in a way that will leave it immune to such an objection. Let us represent the passive participle of a verb "φ" as "φ-ed thing" or "is a φ-ed thing"; and the inflected passive of the verb either as "is φ-ed by x" where the subject, x, is specified, or as "is φ-ed (by something)" where no

---

[9] Indeed, Socrates' generalization of his examples has often been interpreted as giving voice to just such a doctrine. Socrates' generalization is this: εἴ τι γίγνεται ἤ τι πάσχει, οὐχ ὅτι γιγνόμενόν ἐστι γίγνεται, ἀλλ' ὅτι γίγνεται γιγνόμενόν ἐστιν (10C1–3). Cooper translates these lines as follows: "Whenever an effect occurs, or something is effected, it is not the thing effected that gives rise to the effect; no, there is a cause, and then comes this effect." This mistranslation gives rise to an erroneous interpretation of Socrates' point. It seems to me that Socrates is trying, without an adequate logical vocabulary, to generalize on his earlier examples; lacking the notion of a variable, Socrates uses the all-purpose verb γίγνεσθαι, in effect as a verb-variable. The result of reading Socrates' sentence in this way—with "φ" as a verb-variable in place of γίγνεσθαι—is my pair of principles (α) and (β) below.

[10] Cf. Geach, loc. cit., pp. 378–79. A further reason for not taking Socrates' point in this way is that the verb "see," which occurs in the epagoge, is, like the verb "love," disanalogous to the others in this respect.

subject is specified.[11] Then Socrates' point is that, where "φ" is a verb, a φ-ed thing is

(α)    a φ-ed thing because it is φ-ed (by something)

not: (β)    φ-ed (by something) because it is a φ-ed thing.

Our job now is to try to see whether this claim can be understood in a fairly natural way such as to make (α) true and (β) false. Clearly, this will depend upon the force we assign to the crucial word "because."

It is not hard to see that, on a natural reading of (α) and (β), "because" must be understood to have different senses in the two sentence-forms.[12] Let us begin with (β). We may be at a loss in trying to understand (β), I think, unless we remember that the inflected passive, "is φ-ed (by something)," entered the argument in place of an active form.[18] If we are to understand the earlier distinction between active and passive participles to have any bearing on the later distinction between two passive forms, we must, I think, give the inflected passive in (β) an active sense. Transforming (β) in this way we get:

(β\*)    Someone or something φ-s a φ-ed thing because it is a φ-ed thing.

[11] Bearing in mind that "is φ-ed by x" is taken to be equivalent to "x φ-s it" and "is φ-ed (by something)" to "something φ-s it."

[12] J. L. Ackrill is reported (in a footnote in John H. Brown, "The Logic of the *Euthyphro* 10A–11B," *Philosophical Quarterly*, January 1964, p. 13) to have suggested an interpretation much like the one I develop at length below. The interpretation I offer, however, was arrived at independently of Ackrill's.

John C. Hall ("Plato: *Euthyphro* 10A1–11A10," *Philosophical Quarterly*, January 1968, pp. 1–11) also considers the possibility of understanding the argument to employ "because" equivocally, and even tries out the "person's reason" sense of "because," in much the way that I do below. But he winds up rejecting such an interpretation, on what seem to me to be mistaken grounds. Cf. Additional Note below and Brown, *loc. cit.*

[13] Cf. above, p. 7.

If we understand the context governing the first occurrence of "φ-ed thing" in (β*) to be transparent,[14] we can read (β*) as:

(β*1)　　Someone or something φ-s a thing (which is, in fact, a φ-ed thing) because it is a φ-ed thing.

Leaving out the parenthetical clause we get:

(β*2)　　Someone or something φ-s a thing because it is a φ-ed thing.

Concentrating on just the first part of (β*2), "Someone or something φ-s a thing because . . ." it is easy to see that the "because" should be thought of as introducing a reason for some action or attitude. What sort of reason is being introduced will, of course, depend on the verb that replaces "φ". Where the verb is one which will properly take "someone," but not "something," as the subject (such as the key verb in the argument, "love"), the reason introduced will have to be a person's reason for having a certain attitude or performing a certain action.[15] The first part of (β*2) can therefore be understood as introducing a reason which would serve to answer a question of the form "Why does someone φ . . . ?" The form of answer, "Someone's reason for φ-ing is that . . ." is

---

[14] If a context is transparent, then a quantifier outside the context can govern a variable inside; hence, quantifiers within a transparent context can be moved to the outside. If the first occurrence of "a φ-ed thing" in (β*) is thought of as having the force of "some φ-ed thing," then we can move the quantifier to the outside and obtain:

Some (φ-ed) thing is such that someone or something φ-s it because it is a φ-ed thing

which is equivalent to (β*1). If we omit the parenthetical "φ-ed" the result is equivalent to (β*2).

[15] Where the verb can take "something" as well as, or rather than, "someone" as subject, the "because" might introduce all or part of a purely causal explanation, and not a person's reason. I shall ignore this complication in what follows, as it is not relevant to the point at issue.

clearly what is intended by the first part of ($\beta^*2$), in which "because," rather than "reason for," occurs. ($\beta$), then, can be understood as the claim that someone's reason for $\phi$-ing x is that x is a $\phi$-ed thing. I think that this is a natural reading for ($\beta$); that ($\beta$), so read, is an unacceptable principle I hope to show later.

The "because" in ($\alpha$), on the other hand, cannot be thought of as introducing a person's reason for some attitude or action. The first part of ($\alpha$), "A $\phi$-ed thing is a $\phi$-ed thing because . . ." does not suggest that what is needed to fill the blank is the specification of a person's reason. Rather, it suggests that what is needed is, at least, a logically sufficient condition for applying the participial term "$\phi$-ed thing" to something. Perhaps even more is needed. For we ought to understand ($\alpha$) to be an answer to the question "Why is a $\phi$-ed thing a $\phi$-ed thing?" And this question seems to require an informative answer which provides logically necessary and sufficient conditions for applying the term "$\phi$-ed thing" to something. Transforming ($\alpha$) by replacing the inflected passive with the corresponding inflected active, as we did with ($\beta$), will not alter this reading of ($\alpha$). Transforming ($\alpha$) in this way we get:

($\alpha^*$)  A $\phi$-ed thing is a $\phi$-ed thing because someone or something $\phi$-s it.

Once again understanding the context governing the first occurrence of "$\phi$-ed thing" to be transparent, we can read ($\alpha^*$) as:

($\alpha^*1$)  Something (which is, in fact, a $\phi$-ed thing) is a $\phi$-ed thing because someone or something $\phi$-s it.

Again leaving out the parenthetical clause we get:

($\alpha^*2$)  Something is a $\phi$-ed thing because someone or something $\phi$-s it.

($\alpha$*2), like ($\alpha$), must be thought of as purporting to provide an informative answer to the question "Why is
something a φ-ed thing?" An answer which provides logically sufficient (and perhaps also necessary[16]) conditions for applying the term "φ-ed thing" to something.
In what I take to be the natural readings of ($\alpha$) and ($\beta$),
then, "because" is used equivocally. We must now determine whether, on these readings, ($\alpha$) is an acceptable
principle and ($\beta$) unacceptable.

We can see why ($\alpha$) should be affirmed and ($\beta$) denied by examining some of Socrates' examples. "A carried thing is a carried thing because it is carried (by
something)" has this force: the fact that something or
someone carries x is an informative and logically sufficient condition for calling x a carried thing. This seems
unobjectionable. The condition is logically sufficient because it follows from the fact that x carries y that y is a
carried thing. It is informative because it might instruct
someone in the use of the expression "carried thing."
"Carried thing" is to be applied to something, y, when
there is something, x, which carries y. By contrast, "A
carried thing is carried (by something) because it is a
carried thing" has this force: A reason why x is carried
by someone or something (i.e., a reason why someone or
something carries x) is that x is a carried thing. But this
is clearly objectionable; that x is a carried thing cannot
be anyone's reason for carrying x.

The same point seems to carry over to the verb Socrates is interested in. The fact that someone loves x is an
informative and logically sufficient condition for x's being
called a loved thing; but the fact that x is a loved thing
does not explain why someone loves x. It cannot be any-

---

[16] That Plato thought of ($\alpha$) as providing a necessary condition
as well seems likely. At 10B1–2 Socrates asks Euthyphro whether a
*pheromenon* is a *pheromenon* because it *pheretai* "or because of
something else" (ἢ δι' ἄλλο τι). Euthyphro's answer, οὐκ ἀλλὰ
διὰ τοῦτο, must be understood to mean that *pheretai* and only *pheretai* specifies an informative sufficient condition for being a *pheromenon*, thus making it necessary as well as sufficient.

one's reason for loving x that x is a loved thing.[17] Thus, for Socrates' claim to be made intelligible and acceptable, the *hoti* ("because") in *philoumenon hoti phileitai* and *phileitai hoti philoumenon* must be understood to be used equivocally. But whether this equivocation proves fatal to Socrates' argument remains to be seen.

III

At this point (10D1) Socrates once again poses his original question, and this time Euthyphro is willing to answer. What he says is that the pious is

      (a) loved by the gods because it is pious

not: (b) pious because it is loved (by the gods[18]).

("Loved" translates the inflected passive *phileitai;* the participle *philoumenon* does not appear here.) Now a new term is introduced: *theophiles,* or "god-loved." From the manner of its introduction it is clearly serving as a specific filler for *philoumenon.* To be *theophiles,* I take it, is to be a *philoumenon* which *phileitai hupo theōn.* Next a pair of *hoti* statements, like (a) and (b) above, is put forward (by Socrates, with Euthyphro's assent) about *theophiles.*[19] The god-loved is

[17] One might offer the following objection to this claim. My reason for loving x cannot be that *I* love it, but it can be that *others* love it. And if a loved thing is one that people generally love, then perhaps I *can* give as my reason for loving x that it is a loved thing, i.e., that it is generally loved. Socrates' argument, as we shall see, neatly avoids this difficulty by replacing *philoumenon* ("a loved thing") with *theophiles* ("god-loved") before beginning the discussion of why the *gods* love what they do.

[18] Plato does not actually say *hupo theōn*—"by the gods"—here, but that qualification is clearly intended.

[19] Whether the ὅτι statements about τὸ θεοφιλές enter the argument at 10D9–10 or only later at 10E5–7 is open to question. I have followed Bast and Schanz in amending 10D10 by adding the words τὸ θεοφιλές as the subject of the sentence, which then amounts to an assertion of (a'). If the manuscript tradition is accepted, the subject of the sentence is an implicit τὸ ὅσιον, which would carry over from 10D1. Socrates' point would then be that

      (a′)  god-loved because it is loved by the gods

not:  (b′)  loved (by the gods[20]) because it is god-loved.

Euthyphro has now agreed that (a) and (a′) are true while (b) and (b′) are false. Socrates claims that this shows the pious and the god-loved to be "different from one another" (10D13), for "if they were the same" (10E9), (b′) would follow from (a) and (b) would follow from (a′). The warrant for this inference, not stated by Socrates, can only be that the substitution of "god-loved" for "pious" in (a) yields (b′) and the substitution of "pious" for "god-loved" in (a′) yields (b). At this point it will be wise to stop and assess the argument.

First of all, what does Socrates mean when he says that the pious and the god-loved are different from one another? Does he think he has shown that the class of pious things and the class of god-loved things are not coextensive? If he does think this, he is clearly mistaken. His argument depends on substituting the terms "pious" and "god-loved" for one another in sentences agreed to be true, where the substitutions produce sentences which are agreed to be false. But this result will not show that the terms "pious" and "god-loved" apply to different in-

---

*what is pious* is god-loved because it is loved by the gods. The reason for preferring the emendation is not that this last point would be unacceptable to Socrates (it would not), but that without the emendation the speech at 10D9–10 would have no place in the argument. The construction at 10E2–7 (ὁμολογοῦμεν τὸ μὲν ὅσιον . . . τὸ δέ γε θεοφιλὲς . . .), where (a′) and the negation of (b′) are explicitly asserted, indicates that at least one if not both of (a′) and (b′) have been explicitly formulated already. Burnet, for some reason, feels that the emendation "spoils the argument by making τὸ θεοφιλές the subject instead of τὸ ὅσιον" (John Burnet, *Plato's Euthyphro* [Oxford: Oxford University Press], 1924, p. 49). How this would spoil the argument is unclear to me. But even without the emendation the argument is not spoiled; we need only take the agreement at 10E5 to refer back to 10C9–11, where φιλούμενον ὅτι φιλεῖται is affirmed and φιλεῖται ὅτι φιλούμενον is denied. But this would make the place of 10D9–10 in the argument somewhat mysterious.

[20] Cf. n. 18.

stances unless the sentences in which the substitutions are made are clearly extensional.[21] And sentences of the form "p because q" are not extensional, whether "because q" is thought of as introducing a person's reason for acting or as a logically sufficient condition for the application of a term to something.

But there is no reason to think that Socrates took himself to be showing that these two classes are not coextensive. He has already told Euthyphro that he is not interested in an enumeration of things that are pious, but rather wants to know "the characteristic in virtue of which" each pious thing is pious (6D9–11). Clearly, the point must be that "god-loved" does not introduce the characteristic in virtue of which a thing is pious. And this point is quite consistent with "god-loved" applying to the same things to which "pious" applies. Also, Socrates gives some indication, at the end of his argument, that he realizes he can grant Euthyphro that "pious" and "god-loved" apply to the same things without putting his main point in jeopardy.[22]

So Socrates is trying to show that "god-loved" does not introduce the characteristic in virtue of which a thing is pious. And I think it is safe to say that the phrase which *does* introduce the characteristic in virtue of which a thing is pious would be the definition of "pious." So the principle which Socrates' argument depends on is not, as Geach thinks, "the Leibnizian principle that two expressions for the same thing must be mutually replaceable *salva veritate.*"[23] Rather, it is a principle which might be formulated roughly as follows: two expressions, one

---

[21] In this case it is extensionality with respect to predicate-places that is at issue. For a sentence to be extensional in this sense is for any of its predicates to be replaceable *salva veritate* by any co-extensive predicate, i.e., one true of just the same objects.

[22] 11B2–4. Socrates says that the question of what piety is (τί ποτε ὄν τὸ ὅσιον) arises even if the pious *is* loved by the gods (εἴτε φιλεῖται ὑπὸ θεῶν); and he adds that he and Euthyphro will not disagree about this last point (οὐ γὰρ περὶ τούτου διοισόμεθα), i.e., will agree that what is pious is loved by the gods.

[23] Geach, *loc. cit.*, p. 376.

of which is a definition of the other, must be mutually
replaceable *salva veritate.* We might call this the principle of substitutivity of definitional equivalents, understanding definitional equivalents to be a pair of expressions one of which is a definition of the other. And while
perhaps both principles can be shown to break down in
some intensional contexts, the principle of substitutivity
of definitional equivalents does not seem to be one which
will break down in the intensional contexts in question,
even if the Leibnizian principle will. So if there is a flaw
in Socrates' argument, it does not lie in the intensionality
of "because." But it may lie in an equivocation on
"because."

We saw earlier that in order to render Socrates'
claims about the use of participles and inflected passives in "because" contexts intelligible, we had to interpret *hoti*
equivocally. It is clear that we will have to do the same
here if we are to see why (a) and (a′) are to be accepted as true, and (b) and (b′) rejected as false. Let
us, then, resolve the ambiguity of the troublesome word
*hoti* in the following way: *phileisthai hoti,* literally "to
be loved because" (clearly equivalent in the context to
*phileitai hupo theōn hoti,* literally "is loved by the gods
because"), will be rendered as "the reason the gods love
it is that . . ."; *hosion hoti,* literally "pious because" and
*theophiles hoti,* literally "god-loved because," will be rendered as "a logically sufficient condition for applying the
term 'pious' to it is that . . ." and "a logically sufficient
condition for applying the term 'god-loved' to it is
that . . ." respectively. The referent of "it" will be supplied by the subject of each sentence in which these
phrases occur. The four sentences can now be reformulated as:

(Ra)  The reason the gods love what is pious is that it is
      pious.

(Rb)  A logically sufficient condition for applying the term
      "pious" to what is pious is that the gods love it.

(Ra′) A logically sufficient condition for applying the term "god-loved" to what is god-loved is that the gods love it.

(Rb') The reason the gods love what is god-loved is that it is god-loved.

We may now turn to the question whether (Ra) and (Ra') should be accepted by Euthyphro as true, but (Rb) and (Rb') rejected by him as false.

Since (Ra) is what is going to get Euthyphro into trouble, by turning out to be inconsistent with his definition, one might feel that he should not accept it. But Euthyphro's acceptance of it must be taken to indicate that he thinks the gods do have a reason for loving pious things, that they do not love pious things irrationally, and that *their being pious things* is precisely this reason. (Ra') seems clearly acceptable; that the term "god-loved" correctly applies to something ought to follow from the fact that the gods love it. (Rb), however, should not have been rejected by Euthyphro; for his rejection of it is clearly inconsistent with his definition and it is not apparent that he must reject it in order to maintain that the gods have a reason for loving the pious. But as we will see, Socrates' conclusion does not depend upon Euthyphro's rejection of (Rb); whether Socrates saw that a rejection of (Rb) was superfluous, however, is another matter. But (Rb') must certainly be rejected. For although a person's reason for loving something, x, may be that x has a property P, it is absurd to suppose that this could hold when P is the property of being loved by him. For x's having this property amounts to nothing more nor less than the fact that he loves x. And one's *reason* for loving something cannot be that he loves it. Imagine the following dialogue:

A: "She mistreats you terribly. Why do you love her?"
B: "Just because I do."

B's answer, which amounts to saying "I just love her," is clearly a rejection of A's question. B is saying, in effect, that he has *no* reason for loving her; he just does. Thus, since being god-loved amounts to nothing more nor less than being loved by the gods (a point Euthyphro can be assumed to have at least a dim awareness of, in view of his acceptance of [a']), (Rb') is certainly false. The gods' *reason* for loving something cannot be that they love it.

Socrates, we have seen, equivocates on *hoti* ("because") in the course of his argument. But this is not to say he commits the fallacy of equivocation in the argument. Let us call the "because" which serves to introduce a person's reason a "reason-'because,'" and the one which serves to introduce logically sufficient conditions for the application of a term a "logical-'because.'" Then for Socrates to be committing the fallacy of equivocation would be for him to infer, by substitution, from a sentence which must be understood to contain a reason-"because" one which must be understood to contain a logical-"because," or vice versa. But Socrates does not do this. Although he equivocates on "because" in the argument, the word is used univocally within each of the *inferences* that Socrates draws. Socrates' argument, as we have interpreted it, was that if "pious" and "god-loved" are definitionally equivalent, then (a) entails (b') and (a') entails (b). But the "because" in both (a') and (b) is the logical-"because"; the one in both (a) and (b') is the reason-"because." Socrates' argument, then, does not commit the fallacy of equivocation.[24]

Nor does the argument depend upon Euthyphro's dubious rejection of (b). For the conclusion, that "pious" and "god-loved" are not definitionally equivalent, follows from the acceptance of (a) and rejection of (b') alone.[25] If "pious" meant "god-loved," then something's being pious could not be a reason for the gods to love it, since something's being god-loved cannot be a reason

[24] But see the Additional Note below.
[25] Cf. Lynn E. Rose, "A Note on the *Euthyphro,* 10–11," *Phronesis,* X (1965), pp. 149–50, for a brief discussion of the multiplicity of inconsistencies into which Euthyphro falls.

for the gods to love it. The "because" that is crucial for Socrates' argument is the reason-"because." But the logical-"because" still plays an important, if subsidiary, role in the argument. For the acceptance of (a'), in which the logical-"because" occurs, paves the way for the rejection of the absurd (b').

IV

What, then, does Socrates' argument prove? It does not prove that "pious" cannot be defined as "god-loved." It only proves that "pious" cannot be defined as "god-loved" *if* the gods' reason for loving what is pious is that it is pious. Does this amount to proving that "pious" cannot be defined as "god-loved" if the gods have a reason for loving what is pious? No; the gods might have other reasons for loving what is pious. But this implication is clear at any rate; if the gods do have reasons for loving what is pious, it is to these reasons that we should look in trying to define "pious." If the gods have a reason for loving pious acts, it will be that these acts have, or are thought by the gods to have, certain features. It is these features, then, that should serve to define piety. The fact that the gods have a rational love for what is pious may be relevant to the problem of defining piety. But then it would be in the rationality, and not in the love, that the answer to this problem lies.

The more general point I take to be this. If a moral concept M is such that there is an authority whose judgment whether or not something falls under M is decisive and is rationally grounded, then "M" cannot be defined in terms of that authority's judgment. This may be taken to be a generalization of the conclusion of the central argument in Plato's *Euthyphro*.[26]

[26] I have benefited from discussions of earlier versions of this paper with members of the philosophy departments of the University of California at Irvine, and of Dartmouth College. I owe a special debt of gratitude to Gareth B. Matthews for his help in bringing the paper to its present form.

ADDITIONAL NOTE. There may be a lingering suspicion in the minds
of some that the equivocation on *hoti* ("because") ruins Socrates'
argument in a way that is obscured in my formulation of it. Thus
Brown, *loc. cit.*, claims that Socrates' argument is equivocally fallacious because, he feels, the negation of (b) is *inferred* by Socrates from (a); he similarly feels that Socrates infers the falsity of
*pheretai hoti pheromenon* from the truth of *pheromenon hoti
pheretai*, etc. As I have presented the argument, the denials of (b)
and (b′) are put forward independently of the assertions of (a)
and (a′), not inferred from them. If this is right, there is no reason
to suspect that some inference in the argument is equivocally fallacious.

There is, however, some reason for thinking that the negations
of (b) and (b′) are inferred from (a) and (a′), respectively. For
although no inferential particles precede the introduction of the
negations of (b) and (b′) into the argument, the situation seems to
be different in the *epagoge*. There an instance of (α) is put forward, after which the negation of the corresponding instance of
(β) is introduced, preceded by the (weak) inferential particle ἄρα
(10B4–8). And since the truth of both (a) and (a′) and the falsity
of both (b) and (b′) seem to be inferred from the *epagoge*, the inferential connection between (α) and not-(β) might be thought to
carry over to the later pairs.

Since the inferential particle is the weak ἄρα, rather than the
strong οὖν, one might argue that Socrates is speaking somewhat
carelessly and is not supposing that there is a logical connection
between (α) and not-(β). But the success of my interpretation
does not depend on such an argument, for I think it can be shown
that even if not-(β) *is* being inferred from (α), the inference is not
fallacious *despite* the equivocation on *hoti*.

The sense of (α), as I have interpreted it, might be put in this
way:

Being a φ-ed thing is not a property that a thing can have (or
be thought to have) independently of being (or being thought
to be) φ-ed by someone or something.

The sense of (β) would be:

Someone's reason for φ-ing something is (or can be) that that
thing has the property of being a φ-ed thing.

But despite the obvious equivocation on "because" in (α) and (β),
it still seems quite correct to *infer* not-(β) from (α). For if *both*
(α) and (β) were true, then it would be possible for someone, x,
to φ something, y, and have as a reason for φ-ing y that y has a
property which, it turns out, y cannot even be *thought* to have independently of x's φ-ing it. The absurdity of this seems to be that
it conflicts with the following, which I take to be a conceptual
truth: If x's reason for φ-ing y is that y has property P, then it
must be possible for y to have property P independently of being
φ-ed by x. Otherwise, x's "reason" turns out to be no reason at all.

# 9. SOCRATES AT WORK ON VIRTUE AND KNOWLEDGE IN PLATO'S *LACHES*

GERASIMOS SANTAS

Some of Plato's early works, such as the *Laches* and the *Charmides*, have not traditionally received the attention accorded such Socratic dialogues as the *Protagoras*, the *Meno*, and the *Gorgias*. Yet, these subsequent dialogues discuss themes and problems first broached in these earlier works: the theme that virtue is knowledge of good and evil, and that this knowledge is akin to science; the problem of the unity of virtue; the Socratic insistence that practical, ethical problems be solved by appeal to knowledge, not to votes; the problem of how it is possible to know that oneself or others have such knowledge. All these philosophical concerns are treated in perceptive and illuminating discussions in the *Laches* and the *Charmides*. Both as introductions to the Socratic method and to subsequent Platonic works, and as original contributions to philosophic problems still of concern today, these dialogues deserve greater study and attention than they have traditionally or recently received. In this essay I wish to begin such a study with an analysis of the *Laches*.

The main conversation in the *Laches* is about courage. But the main conversation does not begin till the middle of the dialogue. In the first half Plato sets the stage for the serious discussion that follows. Two elder men of Athens, Lysimachus and Melesias, are worried about the education of their sons. They themselves are the sons of two eminent Athenians, Thucydides (the Elder) and Aristides (the Just), and they feel that while their famous fathers conducted the affairs of the city with great

Reprinted from the *Review of Metaphysics*, 22 (1969), pp. 433–60, by permission of the editors and the author.

energy they did not show a similar concern for the education of their sons. They feel inferior to their fathers and do not want their own sons to feel the same way. They wish their sons to be like their own fathers, not like themselves—active citizens, not idle aristocrats. In this frame of mind, they are most anxious for expert and sound advice about their sons' education. Someone recommended to them for this purpose a new military exercise, fighting in armor. They invited two eminent generals of the day, Nicias and Laches, to see with them an exhibition of fighting in armor, and now they eagerly seek the generals' opinion about the worth of it.

## I. THE GENERALS

Nicias and Laches[1] are surely the right men to ask about fighting in armor, and later about courage. The conversation in the *Laches* is supposed to take place sometime during the long Peloponnesian War, probably after the Archidamian War, and possibly during the short and uneasy peace that goes by Nicias' name; certainly, at any rate, after the battle of Delium in 424 (a battle referred to in the dialogue) and before Laches fell at Mantinea in 418.[2] Both Laches and Nicias had already been elected generals several times, and each had led military expeditions on land and at sea. It is quite possible that at the time of the conversation Nicias was the Athenian leader of the day. Of course we know now that neither general was to go down in history as a great or brilliant military leader; neither had the fortune to win a great or decisive victory. Laches at least had the satisfaction, if that's what it is, to die a soldier's death. Nicias' fate was much worse. He was to come to a sad and even ironic end. Forced by circumstances to lead the disas-

[1] For the lives and careers of Nicias and Laches see Thucydides, especially Bks. VI & VII, Plutarch's life of Nicias; and *The Cambridge Ancient History*, Vol. V.

[2] The date of composition is of course much later, after Socrates' death, probably in the 390's or 380's. See, e.g., W. D. Ross, *Plato's Theory of Ideas*, pp. 2, 10.

trous Sicilian expedition, in pursuit of an aggressive and expansionist policy in which he did not believe and had vainly argued against, he was to see the complete destruction of two Athenian fleets and two armies under him; he himself was forced to surrender, and was put to the sword. Even so, as the central figure of a misfortune that would have collapsed most men, he emerges from the pages of Thucydides as a leader who showed care for his men, who was an example of great fortitude to them, and who even in surrender somehow died without dishonor.

If Nicias and Laches were not great or even fortunate generals, they were still the natural choice for Lysimachus and Melesias to ask about fighting in armor and for Socrates to ask about courage. At the time of the conversation the two generals were already tested and experienced military leaders. They had seen military skills at work, and they had led men to battle, the greatest conceived test of courage in an agonistic society; they had to exhort their men to bravery before battle and lead them by example afterwards; they had seen plenty of courageous men, and cowards too; in short, they had plenty of experience in the subjects to be discussed. Surely, if any men should know about courage—at least the courage of the battlefield—these men should.

## II. SOCRATES

At first sight, Socrates may seem an odd figure in the company of the advising generals. He knows nothing about fighting in armor and he is not a military expert of any kind; we are not even told how he happens to be in the present company. But if we pay some attention to what is said about him and what he does in the first half of the dialogue, his figure and credentials for the discussion begin to emerge.

Socrates is introduced when the generals agree to give advice, but Laches remarks that it would be strange not to ask Socrates' advice also since he is of the same dis-

trict as Lysimachus and spends his time discussing the
pursuits of young people. Nicias concurs, and Lysimachus now recognizes Socrates as the son of Sophroniscus,
with whom he used to be friends, and indeed as the Socrates that his boy has been talking about. Laches continues with testimony of a different kind:

> Indeed, Lysimachus, you ought not to give him up; for I
> can assure you that I have seen him maintaining, not only
> his father's, but also his country's name. He was my
> companion in the retreat from Delium, and I can tell you
> that if others had only been like him, the honor of our
> country would have been upheld, and the great defeat
> would never have occurred.

As Lysimachus remarks, this is fine praise from a man
who should know. In a few lines Plato has introduced
Socrates as a man who has given plenty of time and
thought and talk to the education of the young—the
present subject of the discussion—and as a man of courage also, the very quality to which the discussion will
soon turn.

Socrates, speaking for the first time, is willing to lend
a hand in the discussion, but he defers to the generals as
older and more experienced. Characteristically, he wants
to hear the "experts" first.

The generals, eager and confident, proceed with neat
speeches detailing the pros and cons of fighting in armor.
But, alas, the generals disagree, and Socrates is invited
to cast the deciding ballot. He now makes the first of
two serious moves by which he transforms the whole
conversation. The issue of the worth of fighting in armor
and similar pursuits, he says, should not be decided by
majority vote but on the basis of knowledge, and by an
expert, a man who has knowledge of the matter at hand;
they ought therefore to look for such an expert, in the
present company or elsewhere (the generals, it seems,
are already out of contention—they disagreed about
fighting in armor and need help). Having secured agreement to this by the use of analogies, Socrates proceeds

to his second move. Even before they look for an expert, they should be clear about what they seek an expert *in.* It is not (only) fighting in armor and similar pursuits that they are concerned with, but (also)[3] that for the sake of which these pursuits are undertaken: the treatment of young men's souls or the development of character, and, as it turns out, that particular excellence of character we call courage. If fighting in armor and similar pursuits are intended to develop courage, their worth cannot be estimated before it is known what courage is. Thus we come to the main question of the dialogue. In these two moves Socrates has shifted the mode of the conversation from speeches and votes to Socratic investigation, and the subject of the discussion from alleged means of courage to courage itself.

But before we come to *that* we still have a long discussion (186–90) about how to tell an expert when we find one (a fundamental problem for Socrates, given his insistence on knowledge and experts, and one taken up again in the *Chrm.* when the question is taken up how one can know that oneself or others know something or not); a discussion in which Socrates puts the burden of answering on the generals once more; a discussion in which the generals themselves provide us with further testimony of Socrates' character and talents.

It is perhaps ironic that commentators have thought that Socrates' point about the expert is dropped and the pursuit for an expert abandoned.[4] On the contrary, in this section Socrates is established as the expert! Not an expert in fighting in armor of course. Nor a sophistic expert or orator, one who gives the answers in a great speech, *à la* Protagoras. Not even an expert about courage. Socrates is an expert in a *search* for the nature of courage. Far from abandoning the pursuit for an expert, Plato proceeds, through Nicias and Laches, to establish

[3] "Only" and "also" are my additions. Socrates seems to overstate his point (185C–D) for no apparent good reason. A similar overstatement, equally puzzling, occurs in *Grg.* 367C–E.

[4] See, e.g., G. Grote, *Plato,* Vol. II, p. 472.

Socrates' credentials. When Socrates secures agreement from Lysimachus to a question and answer discussion with the burden of the answers on the generals, the generals make the following speeches:

NICIAS. Lysimachus, it looks to me, in very truth, as though you only knew Socrates at second hand . . . and have evidently not yet had to do with him since he has reached maturer years . . . You strike me as not being aware that whoever comes into close contact with Socrates and has any talk with him face to face, is bound to be drawn round and round by him in the course of the argument—though it may have started at first on a quite different theme—and cannot stop until he is led into giving an account of himself, of the manner in which he now spends his days, and of the kind of life he has lived hitherto; and when once he has been led into that, Socrates will never let him go until he has thoroughly and properly put all his ways to the test. Now I am accustomed to him, and so I know that one is bound to be thus treated by him, and further, that I myself shall get the same treatment also. . . . So to me there is nothing unusual, or unpleasant either, in being tried and tested by Socrates; in fact, I knew pretty well all the time that our argument would not be about the boys if Socrates were present, but about ourselves. . . .

LACHES. . . . Nicias . . . you might think me a lover, and yet also a hater, of discussions: for when I hear a man discussing virtue or any kind of wisdom, one who is truly a man and worthy of his argument, I am exceedingly delighted; I take the speaker and his speech together, and observe how they sort of harmonize with each other. Such a man is exactly what I understand by "musical." . . . But a man who shows the opposite character gives me pain, and the better he seems to speak, the more I am pained. . . . Now of Socrates' words I have no experience, but formerly, I fancy, I have made trial of his deeds; and there I found him living up to any fine words however freely spoken. . . . I therefore invite you, Socrates, both to teach and to refute me as much as you please, and to learn too what I on my part know; such is the position you hold in my eyes since that day on which you came through the same danger with me, and gave proof of your own valor.

Laches tells us that Socrates has *shown* courage, the excellence they will soon be trying to define. Socrates is not ignorant of courage in *that* sense. Nor can he be charged with hypocrisy or insincerity for praising and emphasizing a virtue he has not practiced. Three times Laches testifies that Socrates is a courageous man. Characteristically or not, this general at least does not mind being questioned about courage by a man of courage. Nicias tells us of Socrates' other gifts, particularly what Socrates does *with people* in a Socratic discussion: the talk is "face to face," he draws the person "round and round" in argument, "makes him give an account of himself" and will not let go until he puts "all his ways to the test." Plato does not have the generals tell us what Socrates does *with the subject* while doing all this to people. But that comes from Socrates himself in the discussion that follows. And from that discussion we can indeed tell what sort of expert Socrates is with the subject: he has a conception of the *sort* of thing he is after—a Socratic definition—and he can give examples of it in easier cases; he knows how to formulate correctly the sort of question that leads to such a definition; he is adept at extracting from others the sort of answer he wants; and finally, he has some conception of how to test the answers given— by application to examples, by countercases, and by the internal consistency of the speaker's beliefs. Not unexpectedly, Socrates is indeed the perfect Socratic expert in what is to follow—a Socratic investigation.

How can we participate in this investigation? If we are to enter the discussion as participants and not merely as readers or auditors, we shall have, first of all, our own reactions to contend with. Our reactions may include alternative answers to those that Laches and Nicias give, answers *we* want to give to Socrates' questions. Our reactions may also include faults that we find in Socrates' examinations of the answers given. All these reactions,

if we are to be Socratic participants, we must neither let
go unnoticed nor take at face value; we must try to examine them. But there is another matter, besides our reactions, to be considered, what I may call the *residue* of
Socrates' refutations. True, the dialogue is aporetic: as
in most early Socratic dialogues, all the answers given
are found unsatisfactory, and the participants end up in
the realization that, contrary to what they thought at
first, they don't really know what courage is. This may
indeed be the beginning of wisdom, but it is surely not
the end of it, not even of Socratic wisdom. Not everything in the answers is refuted. Many remarks are left
standing, and are later gathered up by Plato himself in
the *Protagoras* and the *Republic:* the sorts of circumstances in which courage is shown; the objects of courage (the things that one faces dangers for); the feelings
that courage involves; the knowledge that courage requires. Indeed the *Laches* is a rich hunting ground for
what we might call the *variables*[5] of courage (and probably was such a hunting ground for Aristotle).

Of course we cannot fully develop here all these points
—indeed there is no end to them. We can only try to
show by examples how one might participate in the discussion. The object of such participation is not to solve

[5] By the "variables" of courage I do not here mean necessarily
the causes of courage; I mean rather the conditions that constitute
evidence that someone is courageous, conditions such that if one of
them changed, our judgment that a man is courageous would also
change or be modified. The discussion on pp. 188–95 below illustrates the sorts of things that are variables of courage. Evidence-
conditions and causal-conditions may sometimes coincide but often
they do not; a man's eating, for example, is evidence that he is
hungry but it is not of course a cause of his hunger. The causes
of courage may have just as much right to be called the variables
of courage; what is important is not to confuse evidence-conditions
and causal-conditions. In considering questions of how to develop
courage in a person, causal-conditions are more important. In considering what courage is, or how to define courage, evidence-
conditions are crucial. Since Socrates' first concern is to discover
what courage is, evidence-conditions are of greater prominence in
his discussion.

all the difficulties, but to try to understand them and come to appreciate what they tell us about courage.

When finally Socrates invites Laches to say what courage is, the general is ready with a general's answer:

> On my word, Socrates, that is nothing difficult: anyone who is willing to stay at his post and face the enemy, and does not run away, you may be sure, is courageous.

Socrates does not dispute the truth of this answer, but he finds it too narrow, even for a general. Can't one also show courage in retreat or in fleeing and then turning back on the enemy, as the Scythians are said to fight, and even the Spartans at Plataea? At first Laches resists this suggestion, a nice touch on Plato's part since Laches has already testified three times that Socrates showed courage in the *retreat* from Delium! Eventually, Laches admits that one could be courageous in the situations Socrates has brought up; so, staying and facing the enemy is not common to all cases of courage, not even the courage of the battlefield.

But Socrates must widen Laches' horizons even more:

> And so this is what I meant just now by saying that I was to blame for your wrong answer, by putting my question wrongly. For I wanted to have your view not only of brave men-at-arms, but also of courage in cavalry and in the entire warrior class; and of the courageous not only in war but in the perils of the sea, and all who in disease and poverty, and again in public affairs, are courageous; and further, all who are not merely courageous against pain or fear, but doughty fighters against desires and pleasures, whether standing their ground or turning back upon the foe—for I take it, Laches, there are courageous people in all these kinds.

Socrates has listed for Laches different sorts of cases of

courage. This list is part of the residue of the dialogue,
and shows how much wider than the general's is Socrates' conception of courage. The first half of Socrates'
list mentions *circumstances* or *situations* in which courage can be shown (and cowardice too): not only war,
though this heads the list, but also perils of the sea, disease and poverty, and public affairs. All these are social
and natural situations that contain or hint at dangers,
ills, and evils. The second half of the list mentions not
circumstances or situations but *feelings* with respect to
which one can be courageous: pain, fear, desires, and
pleasures. "With respect to which" is vague, as are the
prepositions that Socrates uses, but we can easily cut
down on the vagueness by supplying the key verbs: one
could be courageous in enduring pain, by overcoming
fear, in controlling desires, and in resisting pleasures (in
including desires and pleasures, typically in Plato those
of food, drink, and sex, Socrates foreshadows his difficulty in distinguishing courage from temperance). In-
terestingly enough, these verbs raise the scepter of war
once more, but this time the enemy is not necessarily
external to oneself. The second half of Socrates' list suggests that he thinks that courage can be shown not only
in the battlefield and not only in one's dealings with
society and nature, but also in one's dealing with oneself, with one's own feelings. Some of the feelings he
mentions, like pain and fear, may indeed also be involved in the courage of the battlefield, but others, such
as desires and pleasures, suggest cases of temptation and
inner, moral conflict. As Professor Vlastos has pointed
out,[6] Socrates is extending "enormously" the range of
application of the concept of courage. As Laches' first
answer suggests, courage had been almost exclusively
the virtue of the soldier. Socrates suggests that anyone
can show courage in a great variety of situations other
than war, and with respect to feelings that have nothing
to do with soldiers and battles. This widening of the con-

[6] *Plato's Protagoras*, edited with an introduction by Gregory
Vlastos, (Indianapolis, 1956), pp. xlvii-li.

cept, in addition to the conceptual and moral implications that Professor Vlastos notes, has other important consequences. One consequence is the tendency to move away from behavior and circumstances in trying to define or describe courage—Socrates has introduced enough variety of behavior and circumstances to make such an effort look unpromising; and a corresponding tendency to look for a quality *common in all the agents* that show courage. This last tendency is also a tendency towards greater generality or abstraction, since a quality must now be discovered which can show itself in a great variety of behavior and circumstances. All these points show up in Laches' second try ("Courage is a certain endurance of the soul"): not only does he move away from circumstances and behavior, but he also overgeneralizes, as Socrates points out. In addition, when Socrates includes desires and pleasures in his list of feelings, he seems to overwiden the concept of courage. If a man endures pain or overcomes fear in certain situations we might praise him for his courage; but if he resists certain pleasures or controls certain desires, presumably because he thinks they are wrong or harmful, we are more likely to praise him for his moderation, self-control, or temperance rather than for his courage. In including desires and pleasures, Socrates seems to be blurring the distinction between courage and these other concepts. The net result is that when the participants find themselves in the final difficulty of the dialogue, the difficulty of being unable to distinguish between courage and the other virtues, they have no recourse to behavior, circumstances, and feelings. It is indeed a most remarkable point about the *Laches* that the behavior, circumstances, and feelings that Socrates lists in dealing with Laches' first definition drop entirely out of sight in the rest of the dialogue!

Having widened Laches' horizons, perhaps too much, Socrates next explains what *sort* of answer he wants from the general. He does not want an example of courage, not even lots of examples; he wants what is common, or what is the same, in all the different sorts of cases in which courage is shown. He illustrates the sort of thing he wants with a quick definition of quickness ("the faculty [or 'power'] that gets a great deal done in a little time"), and then returns to his question about courage, amplifying it this time to bring out the point:

> So now try and tell me on your part, Laches, about courage in the same way: what faculty (δύναμις) is it, the same whether in pleasure or in pain or in any of the things in which we said just now it was to be found, that has been singled out by the name of courage?

It is not easy, to say the least, to see what is the same in all the sorts of cases Socrates has mentioned. Though he leads Laches a bit by characterizing the sort of thing he wants as a "power" or "faculty," it is still to be wondered at that Laches, having already been removed from the area in which he could claim some expertize, comes up with anything at all:

> Well then, I take it to be a certain endurance of the soul, if I am to speak of the natural quality that appears in them all.

Having found Laches' first answer too narrow, Socrates now finds this one too wide. Endurance of the soul may be *common* to all cases of courage but it is not *distinctive* of courage; something must be added to endurance if we are to get closer to courage. In particular, one may endure things wisely or foolishly, Socrates points out. Now foolish endurance could not possibly be courage, since it is harmful and mischievous and hence not noble; whereas courage, Laches and Socrates firmly and absolutely agree, is noble (καλόν, a word that can also be translated as "fine," "praiseworthy," and even "beautiful").

This last proposition, that courage is noble, becomes now the anchor of the rest of the discussion with Laches. Wise endurance, Socrates points out, is good and noble;

possibly then, he suggests, wisdom is the additional element they seek, and courage is wise endurance.

It looks like it, says Laches, and Socrates now turns to test this new definition, first by applying it to examples, and then by bringing up countercases:

> soc. Now let us see *in what* it is wise. In all things, whether great or small? For instance, if a man endures in spending money wisely, because he knows that by spending he will gain more, would you call him courageous?

> LACHES. On my word, not I.

We may well agree that this is not a case of courage, but it may also be helpful to ask why. We are not told why this is not a case of courage, but perhaps a plausible answer is the following. Courage, we have been told, is noble. But where is the nobility in this case? This man endures spending money, if endurance it is (presumably he does not like doing so), and the wisdom of this endurance consists in the knowledge that by so spending he will gain more. This knowledge also appears to supply the motive, gain, for the sake of which he endures spending. But the gain motive is more to be expected than admired; there is nothing noble about it and Socrates indeed insinuates that it is a "small" thing. If this is right, the case tells us something specific about the nobility of courage: that it derives, at least in part, from the end for the sake of which the courageous man endures. If the end is not noble, neither is the endurance, and there is nothing to be admired.

But what of the next case that Socrates imagines?

> Or what do you call it in the case of a doctor who, when his son or anyone else is suffering from inflammation of the lungs and begs for something to drink or eat, inflexibly and enduringly refuses?

> LACHES. That is no case of it, in any sense, either.

Surely the end for the sake of which the doctor refuses,
in this case, is good enough: to restore the patient's
health, possibly to save his life. This is no small thing.
And, allowing for ancient medical knowledge, the doctor's refusal is wise. Why then is this not a case of courage? Once more we are not told; but possibly Socrates
is now hinting at another element or "variable" of courage. The case invites the question: What is the doctor
"enduring" in refusing to give food or drink? There is
nothing in sight, except possibly the pleadings of the
patient, which *is* a small thing to endure to save a man's
life. There is no suggestion in the passage that the doctor
refuses at any unusual risk to himself; that, e.g., he or
his career is in danger, that there is fear to be overcome,
pleasures to resist, and the like. Clearly if the imagined
case were changed in any of these particulars, our judgment might also change; if, say, the doctor were ordered
by a madman at the point of a knife to give food or drink
and he refused, we might well say that this is a case of
courage. But as it is, it does not "take courage" to refuse.
To have a case of courage, then, it is not enough that the
end sought is noble; unless there is also some risk or difficulty, whether external or internal, in attaining it, anyone can achieve the end at no cost to himself, and once
more there is little to be admired. Courage is admired
not only because the end is noble, but also because the
achievement of it makes some unusual and personal demands on the agent.

So far Socrates has dealt with cases which do not refute the definition. If our remarks have been correct,
these cases show at most that Laches' definition is incomplete in that it does not include the two elements
we found missing in these cases. But now, characteristically, Socrates moves to cases where these two elements
are present, and extracts from Laches' judgments about
the new cases, which directly contradict the definition:

soc. Well now, when a man endures in war, and is willing
to fight, on a wise calculation whereby he knows that others

will come to his aid, and that the forces against him will be
fewer and feebler than those who are with him, and when
he has besides the advantage of position—would you say
of this man, if he endures with such wisdom and prepara-
tion, that he, or a man in the opposing army who is willing to stand up against him and endure, is the more
courageous?

LACHES. The man opposed to him, I should say, Socrates.

SOC. But yet his endurance is more foolish than that of the
first man.

LACHES. That is true.

Incidentally, Socrates does not explicitly say whether
the man in the opposing army has the same estimate of
the situation as his enemy or whether he thinks mis-
takenly that *he* has the advantage of numbers, assistance,
and position. Presumably the former, otherwise Laches
would not be so confident in his judgment that this man
is the more courageous. And this brings out a point that
we might well expect from the discussion so far: whether
a man is (judged to be) courageous depends not only
on the objective situation—the actual circumstances he
faces and what he does in them—but also on his estimate
of the situation, what we might call the psychological or
intentional aspects of courage.

Socrates continues with three other cases where the
man judged (by Laches) less courageous has the advantage not of numbers or assistance or position but of
knowledge or skill in what he is doing: knowledge of
horsemanship, skill in slinging and shooting, adeptness
in diving in wells. In all these cases two men are compared, two men who endure dangers equally, presumably for the same or similar noble ends, but one of whom
has the advantage over the other of numbers or assistance or position or knowledge or skill. And in all these
cases Laches makes two judgments: that the man with
the lesser or no advantage is more courageous, and also

that *his* endurance is less wise (or, as Socrates over-
states it, "more foolish"). Socrates has no difficulty in
bringing Laches to see that these two judgments contradict his own definition of courage. If courage were
wise endurance, where the endurance is the same or
equal, as in the present cases, "more courageous" should
correlate with "wiser endurance"; but now the opposite
has been judged by Laches to be true; and he seems also
to be implying that in some cases foolish endurance can
be courage.

No wonder Laches becomes perplexed! He has been
led by Socrates to contradict not only his own last definition, that courage is wise endurance, but also their previous agreement that courage is noble whereas foolish endurance is not.

These contradictions, however, though they are effective in reducing Laches to a state of Socratic ἀπορία or
perplexity, do not by themselves show that Laches' definition is mistaken, as Socrates seems to imply. The fault
could be in the earlier agreements that Laches made, that
courage is noble whereas foolish endurance is not, or in
the comparative judgments Laches made about the series
of cases that Socrates imagined. The agreements we cannot touch, but the judgments that Laches made were, I
believe, hasty and faulty. Perhaps the man with the
lesser or no advantage is not *more* courageous; or possibly his endurance is *not necessarily* more foolish or even
less wise than that of the man who has the advantage.
On this last point, Socrates is guilty of not supplying
enough information about the case, and Laches is even
more guilty in not asking for clarification. Plato, I believe,
provides us with some clues for the clarification that is
necessary. He has Socrates say that the present discussion is *about what* the man who wisely endures is wise.
And later he has Nicias instruct Laches on an important
distinction (Nicias presumably learned it from Socrates): a distinction between being wise or knowing
*what* the alternatives before one are and which alternative is likely to materialize, *and* being wise or knowing

the comparative *values* or worth of the alternatives before one (the distinction between knowledge of fact and knowledge of value).[7] The cases that Socrates described for Laches contain information only on the first sort of knowledge, the agent's estimate of what the situation is and what are his chances of success; we are told nothing about how the agents conceived the values of that for the sake of which they were enduring and the values of the alternatives to enduring. But clearly information on these points will make a difference to our judgment whether the agent's endurance is wise or foolish. If, say, the man with the lesser or no advantage conceives what he is fighting for (say, the defense of his city) as high enough in value and/or the alternatives to enduring (say, the enslavement of his city and family) as low enough, his endurance in fighting on may be anything but foolish, even though he knows that he has the lesser or no

[7] The distinction between knowledge of good and evil and knowledge of "facts" that Nicias draws, and which is also drawn in the *Chrm.* by Socrates himself, is not necessarily the same as Hume's distinction between "ought" and "is." The Humean distinction is usually associated with two doctrines: (a) that no ought-propositions can be derived validly from is-propositions alone, and (b) that knowledge of ought-propositions is unlike, with respect to origin, evidence, and certitude, the scientific or logico-mathematical knowledge of is-propositions. It is very doubtful that these doctrines can be attributed to Plato (or Socrates). For one thing, Plato, as we know from the *R.*, places knowledge of good and evil within the province of reason, whereas Hume argues that our knowledge of ought-propositions has its sources in sentiment —reason is neutral on ought-propositions. Moreover, Plato tends to distinguish knowledge of good and evil from, say, knowledge of medicine, in a parallel way that he would distinguish between, say, knowledge of medicine and knowledge of farming: All three are distinct in that they have different sorts of things as their objects (what is known). There is, however, one point of significant similarity: It is by living in accordance with knowledge of good and evil that we can become happy (living in accordance with knowledge of other things would not by itself have that result), says Socrates in the *Chrm.*; and it is knowledge of ought-propositions (and their source, sentiment) that is the proper guide of prudential and moral choices in Hume, not (Hume's) reason (except instrumentally).

advantage. Indeed, the men in the opposing army, in Socrates' first example, the men with the lesser or no advantage in numbers or assistance (and even position, after they had been betrayed), could well be the Spartans at Thermopylae! It is this sort of case, one supposes, that Laches had in mind when he judged the man in the opposing army to be more courageous—but hardly this sort of case when he assents to Socrates' suggestions that this same man is more foolish in enduring; instead of replying "That is true," he should have said "That all depends."

Similar points can be made about the subsequent cases that Socrates brings up. To dive into a well, with no skill in such diving, in order to show that one is not afraid of anything, is foolishness indeed—boldness or daring at best since the end is foolish. To dive into a well, with no skill in diving, in order to save a child's life, when there is a skilled diver at hand willing to try, may also be foolish. But to dive into a well, with no skill at diving, in order to save a child's life, when there is no one else to do it, is anything but foolishness. What these and similar variations show is that whether or not we have a case of courage depends not only on the objective situation, and not only on what one knows or believes the risks are and what the chances of success, but also on how the agent conceives the value of what he risks, the value of what he tries to achieve, and the value of the alternative to be avoided. The wisdom or the foolishness of what one is doing, and the nobility too, depends as much on the values as on the facts.

But Laches is not aware of the distinction on which all this turns, as Nicias' later instruction shows; or at least he is not aware of the bearing of the distinction on the judgments he made. His perplexity is a direct consequence of this. Even though Laches has been perplexed, however, his last definition has not been shown to be false. If our diagnosis of his troubles is near the mark,[8]

[8] Socrates supports this diagnosis when he recommends at 193E–194 that he and Laches retain the element of endurance, thus im-

Socrates has shown, not that Laches' definition is false, but that it is grossly incomplete. Laches' definition is in fact not a bad beginning at all, but it is no more than that.[9]

## IV. THE ROUND WITH NICIAS: COURAGE AS KNOWLEDGE

Socrates professes to be as perplexed as Laches and asks Nicias to help. What does *he* think courage is?

Nicias is willing to make a fresh start, but he does not heed Socrates' advice that they retain the element of endurance. Nor does he give us, like Laches, his own beliefs about courage. Instead, he relates how he once heard Socrates say that every man is good in the things he is wise about and bad in those he is ignorant of. Hence, he says, if the courageous man is good he must be wise. From this it certainly does not follow that courage is a kind of wisdom, but this is perhaps Nicias' meaning, Socrates suggests. When Laches asks, "What kind of wisdom?" Nicias produces the new definition:

> Courage is the knowledge of what is to be dreaded or dared, either in war or in anything else.

It should be clear at once that Nicias' definition, unlike Laches', does not merely imply that courage *requires* knowledge or wisdom; it states that courage *is* knowledge of certain things, it is a species of knowledge.[10]

---

plying that Laches has gone wrong in the matter of what the enduring man is wise about.

[9] The Greek term, καρτερία, which has been translated "endurance," can also have the sense of "standing steadfast," and even the more active sense of "perseverance." Socrates never questions or rejects this element in Laches' definition, though it is not retained in Nicias' new definition. Perhaps καρτερία is too passive a quality to suit all cases of courage, and may be more suitable to the later notion of fortitude.

[10] Though this definition is put in the mouth of Nicias, clearly we have now left the generals' views, if not the generals, behind, and we are in Socratic territory—the definition is really Socrates' own. For this we have not only the evidence of the *Prt.*, in which

Laches' reaction to this would probably be the reaction of most people. Surely, he says, one can have knowledge without having courage; Nicias is just babbling and talking nonsense, he adds. Though his reaction merits attention, Laches seems resentful at having been shown ignorant of courage and wants to reduce Nicias to the same state. *He* therefore undertakes a quick refutation of Nicias, *à la* Socrates. But he fails. He fails because of the distinction already mentioned, the distinction between knowledge of fact and knowledge of value. Nicias' definition does not have the false implication that every expert, craftsman or scientist, farmer or doctor, is courageous because each knows what is to be dreaded or dared in his own field. The doctor, for example, knows, as a medical expert, what is diseased and what healthy, and what causes these states—one hopes; but whether, say, disease is always more dreadful than health, or whether it is better for one to die than to live diseased, these things the doctor's science does not tell him. Nor is it the seer that has the knowledge in question, as Laches sarcastically suggests. The seer may know what is yet to come, whether a man will meet with death, disease, or poverty; but whether it is better for one to suffer or avoid these things, it is not for the seer to decide.

Laches replies that he is still unable to understand

---

Socrates offers as his own the definition offered by Nicias (the only change being that he uses σοφία rather than ἐπιστήμη). Plato gives us plenty of clues in the *Laches* itself: Nicias has said that he is well acquainted with Socrates and has been in many of his talks, and he introduces the definition by indicating that it was suggested to him by something Socrates had said, that every man is good in the things he is wise about and bad in those he is ignorant of. Socrates readily assents to this—it is probably a generalization that Socrates drew from his observations of craftsmen, artists, and medical men—and it is probably as good a source as any for the Socratic paradox that virtue is knowledge. In any case, we have considerable evidence for supposing that in the round with Nicias, Socrates is examining his own favorite doctrines (a situation that is repeated in Socrates' examination of Critias in the *Chrm.*), and that, at another level, Plato is examining and turning over in his mind central Socratic doctrines.

Nicias, and accuses the other general of dodging. Though Nicias is not dodging, Laches is raising important questions. Who has the kind of knowledge that is Nicias' courage? If not the ordinary experts in the arts, crafts, and sciences, then who? Can anyone have this sort of knowledge or are there experts in it?

Socrates now undertakes to question Nicias, interrupted by rounds of acrimony between the generals.

Anyone who holds Nicias' view of courage must deny that animals are courageous, since they can hardly be supposed to have this rare knowledge Nicias has been hinting at; and yet, as Laches is quick to interpose, everyone admits certain animals, lions for example, to be courageous.

But Nicias escapes once more, by making more distinctions. He who through ignorance has no fear of the dreadful is fearless and foolish, not courageous. In his opinion, he says, very few people are endowed with courage and forethought, while rashness, boldness, and fearlessness are to be found in a great number of men, women, children, and animals.

Socrates remarks that Nicias seems to have gotten his wisdom from Damon who constantly associates with Prodicus, the cleverest of the sophists in distinguishing terms like these. Nicias' wisdom may be wisdom by association, but his distinction between courage and fearlessness seems clear enough. His "boldness" and "rashness" are not so clear, but Socrates does not press him. Instead, he turns to examine what Nicias considers courage proper, and involves Nicias in a final difficulty from which the general this time is not able to escape.

Let us pick out the steps in Socrates' final argument:

(1) Courage is a "part" (not the whole) of virtue; other "parts" are temperance, justice, and similar things.

(2) Things to be dreaded are those things that cause fear, things to be dared are those things that do not cause fear.

(2.1) Those things that cause fear are not past or present

evils but expected evils; for fear is the expectation of future evil.

(2.2)   Things to be dreaded are future evils, things to be dared future goods or future non-evils.

(2.3)   [Accordingly] Courage [*à la* Nicias] is the knowledge of future evils and future goods or non-evils.

(3)     Concerning the various things about which there is knowledge, "there is not one knowledge of how a thing has happened in the past, another of how things are happening in the present, and another of how a thing that has not yet happened might or will happen most favorably in the future, but it is the same knowledge throughout. For example, in the case of health, it is medicine always and alone that surveys present, past, and future processes alike; and farming is in the same position as regards the productions of the earth. . . . And in matters of war . . . generalship (not the seer's art) makes the best forecasts . . . because it knows better what is happening or about to happen."

(4)     "Then courage is knowledge not merely of what is to be dreaded and what dared, for it comprehends goods and evils not merely in the future but also in the present and past and in any stage, like the other kinds of knowledge."

(4.1)   ". . . courage is knowledge not merely of what is to be dreaded and what dared, but practically a knowledge concerning all goods and evils at every stage."

(5)     A man who "knew all good things, and all about their production in the present, the future, and the past, and all about evils likewise" would lack nothing in virtue; such a man would be not only courageous but also just, and temperate, and pious too.

(6)     "Hence what you now describe, Nicias, will be not a part but the whole of virtue." [And this contradicts premiss (1).]

(7)     "Thus we have failed to discover, Nicias, what courage really is."

This is Socrates' final argument against Nicias' definition of courage. It is a remarkable argument. Remarkable not only because Socrates propounds it in the face of the many faults that it contains—faults in its logic and on the question of the truth of the premisses—but also because the premisses of this argument seem to have two consequences that can only be described as difficulties for Socratic and Platonic ethics. These two matters, of faults and consequences, take work but are not really difficult to disentangle. What *is* difficult to discover—and yet necessary to discover for an adequate philosophic understanding and assessment of Socratic and Platonic ethics—is why Plato and/or Socrates found the premisses of this argument persuasive: to discover the conceptual sources that led them to this argument. In the rest of this paper I shall take up these three issues.

First, the consequences. The first consequence is the doctrine of "the unity of virtue": that if a man has any one virtue he has them all.[11] To obtain this consequence from the present argument we only need to add to premiss (5) a proposition that Socrates often assumes, plausibly enough: that to have any one of the virtues a man must have knowledge of good and evil.[12] If having knowledge of good and evil is a necessary condition for having (and practicing) any one virtue, and if having knowledge of good and evil is a sufficient condition for having all the virtues, it follows directly that if a man has

[11] It should be noted that this consequence, and the second one, are not valid consequences of Nicias' original definition (knowledge of what is to be dreaded or dared), but rather of the definition that Socrates derives from it (knowledge of all goods and evils). I argue below that this derivation is mistaken.

[12] That knowledge of good and evil is a *necessary* condition for having and practicing any one virtue is the uncontroversial part of the Socratic paradox that virtue "is" knowledge (the other, the controversial part, is that such knowledge is sufficient for all the virtues). Socrates suggests the uncontroversial part when he points out to Laches that they must add wisdom to endurance if they are to get a definition of courage (wisdom being knowledge of good and evil, though Laches does not catch on). The point is suggested again when Socrates points out to Critias (as an objection to the latter's definition of temperance as "the doing of good things") that a man may on occasion do a good thing without knowing that it is a good thing; in such a case, Critias readily agrees, the man would not be temperate.

any one virtue he has them all. This consequence is certainly paradoxical in the sense that it contradicts ordinary
factual beliefs about people and their behavior; and
Plato was certainly aware of this, as Laches' and Protagoras' protestations show.[13] How paradoxical the doctrine
of the unity of virtue is we can see by stating it another
way: each man either has all the virtues or none of them!
Why should Socrates and/or Plato maintain such a paradoxical doctrine in the face of stiff opposition, opposition
with which they do not deal on its own grounds (that is,
by appeal to observations of human nature and behavior)? I think the answer is that they maintained it because and so long as they thought it was a direct logical
consequence from the two Socratic premisses from which
we ourselves just derived it. To give it up, they would
either have to give up the Socratic premisses themselves
—an unlikely story at least up to the *Republic*—or they
would have to find fault with the derivation.

The second consequence presents an even greater difficulty, for it is a conceptual, not a factual, difficulty. If
we grant the two Socratic premisses that imply the unity
of virtue, it would seem that any attempt to *define* any
one virtue as knowledge of good and evil will end up in
failure in that we end up defining the whole of virtue,
whereas we were trying to define some one virtue which
is part and not the whole of virtue. This is indeed the
punch line in Socrates' argument against Nicias: in defining courage as knowledge of good and evil, Nicias has
not succeeded; for his definition is a definition of the
whole of virtue and hence not a definition of courage,
since courage is part of virtue, not the whole of virtue.
This argument can be repeated—indeed, appropriately
enough, it can be repeated against Socrates himself. For

[13] We have already noted Laches' first reaction to Nicias' definition. In the *Prt.* 329D–E, when Socrates asks Protagoras to choose
between the two analogies he has brought up, and Protagoras picks
"the face analogy," and Socrates asks him whether if a man has
one "part" of virtue he must have them all, Protagoras replies: "By
no means, since many are brave but unjust, and many again are
just but not wise."

example, towards the end of the *Charmides*[14] Socrates
suggests that knowledge of good and evil would be a
better candidate for a definition of temperance than the
candidates Critias has brought up. Now all we have to
do is cite to Socrates his own premiss (5) and his own
conclusion (6) and point out to him that these count as
much against his definition of temperance as they count
against Nicias' definition of courage. To maintain his definition of temperance, and Nicias *his* definition of courage, they would have to give up the propositions that
courage is part and not the whole of virtue, that temperance is part and not the whole of virtue, and that courage
and temperance are not identical.

It should be noticed that giving up these three propositions is a different and a much stronger (logically) consequence than the *first* consequence I discussed above.
The first consequence is that the virtues cannot be found
apart, each from the others, in a man. The second consequence is that the virtues cannot be distinguished even
*in definition*, each from the others. The second consequence is stronger than the first in the sense that it implies the first; whereas the first consequence does not imply the second (for example, equilateral triangles are not
found apart from equiangular triangles, nor the latter
apart from the former, but the definition of equilateral
triangle is different from the definition of equiangular
triangle). Moreover, the first consequence is factually
paradoxical in the sense that it contradicts a factual belief (e.g., that some men are temperate without being
courageous); whereas the second consequence seems
conceptually paradoxical (for if someone, for instance,
thought that "courage" and "temperance" meant the
same we would be inclined to say that he was confused
and we might refer him to a dictionary—and Socrates in
in his non-philosophic moments might send him to
Prodicus!).

Now in the *Protagoras* Socrates accepts these consequences (though it is not clear that he distinguishes be-

[14] Cf. 174 ff.

tween them). Indeed not only does he accept these consequences; he fights for them in long and elaborate
arguments that have recently received considerable attention.[15] In the *Laches* Socrates accepts the view that
courage is part and not the whole of virtue; in the *Charmides* he accepts or presupposes the view that temperance is one of the virtues and not the whole of virtue;
and in the *Euthyphro* he distinguishes between justice
and piety.[16] But in the *Protagoras* he gives up these views
and bravely argues, in the face of stiff opposition from
Protagoras, that the virtues are not distinct each from the
others and that the Greek equivalents of "justice," "temperance," etc. are really different names for one and the
same thing.[17] The only passage that I know of that can
account for this change is Socrates' argument against Nicias in the *Laches*. Nicias' definition of courage is really
Socrates' own, as we learn in the *Protagoras*.[18] And Socrates thought that this argument against Nicias, or rather
against himself, was a good one. He thought therefore
that he had to give up his favorite definition of courage
or the very center of his ethical teaching (that knowledge
of good and evil is a necessary and sufficient condition
for the virtues) or the proposition that courage is part
and not the whole of virtue. Somewhat understandably
perhaps, he chooses the last course—or at least he decides

[15] Vlastos, *op. cit.* Vlastos' examination of the arguments for the
unity of virtue in the *Prt.* stimulated a great deal of discussion.
The most recent article is by D. P. Gauthier, "The Unity of Wis-
dom and Temperance," *Journal of the History of Philosophy*, Vol.
VI, No. 2 (April, 1968) which is a criticism of an earlier piece by
D. Savan.

[16] See, e.g., *La.* 190C–D, *Chrm.* 159C, *Euthphr.* 12–13.

[17] *Prt.* 329D.

[18] *Prt.* 360D. There are a few differences between Nicias' and
Socrates' definitions, but they do not seem significant. For example,
Socrates uses σοφία rather than ἐπιστήμη, but earlier (357–58)
Socrates used both terms to refer to knowledge of good and evil;
and the conclusions that Lyons reaches regarding the relations be-
tween the two terms further confirms that no great significance can
be attached to this difference (John Lyons, *Structural Semantics*,
Oxford, 1963, pp. 227–28).

to give it a good try. In the *Republic* of course the story has a different ending. In all probability Plato could not bring himself to accept the outrageous paradox of the unity of virtue in its strong version. Though he retains the view that knowledge (or at least true belief) of good and evil is necessary for virtue, he gives up the view that it is sufficient; and he brings in new elements for the definitions of the various virtues, the three elements of the soul, their functions and relations; and through the analogy of social virtues and virtues in the individual he even makes circumstances and behavior relevant again to the definition of the virtues. Possibly, a case can be made that in the *Republic* Plato still holds the view that the virtues are not found apart each from the others; but no case can be made that he still supposes that the virtues cannot be distinguished in definition each from the others.

In view of the centrality and importance of Socrates' argument against Nicias in the development of Socratic and Platonic ethics, it becomes a matter of some interest to determine the soundness of Socrates' argument. Does the Socratic definition of courage (given by Nicias) and the Socratic view of the relation of virtue to knowledge, plus the auxiliary premises of the argument, really commit Socrates, as he seems to have thought, to giving up the view that courage is part and not the whole of virtue? I think not. Despite a certain plausibility, Socrates' argument has several disabling faults.

Socrates' argument rests on three crucial inferences. First, that if a man has knowledge of what is to be dreaded or dared in war or anything else, he must have knowledge of future evils and future goods (or non-evils); this is supported by statements (2), (2.1), and (2.2) which are of a definitional character. Second, if a man has knowledge of future goods and evils, he must have knowledge of goods and evils at every (temporal) stage, whether these occur in the past, present, or future; this is supported by the analogy between courage as knowledge and knowledge in other areas. Finally, if a man has knowledge of *all* goods and evils, and of their production and destruction, at every (temporal) stage, he will have all the virtues, not just courage; this inference is readily granted by Nicias and is not supported here by any evidence. The first inference has to be restricted, the second is dubiously supported, and there is a missing link between the second and the third that cannot be validly supplied.

To begin with, we may grant that things to be dared are future goods or non-evils, and things to be dreaded or feared are future evils. But it should be noted that not all future goods (or non-evils) are things to be dared. Taking my vitamins tomorrow is a future good, but what is daring about that? Taking vitamins in certain quantities at certain intervals is known to have beneficial consequences and no harmful side-effects; there is therefore no risk to be taken, danger to be faced, or evil to be endured in doing so. To know what is to be dreaded and dared I need not know *this* future good. When it comes to future evils and things to be dreaded (or feared), we might perhaps grant that in a sense all future evils are to be feared. But then we must notice that not all our dealings with future evils are cases of courage or cowardice —some are irrelevant to courage and knowledge of them is not necessarily to be included in the knowledge that is required for courage. I look at the coming rainstorm and foresee that it will ruin my beans and my new suit if I stay outside, but there is no good reason for me to stay. Going inside is only good sense, and staying outside only foolishness; neither is courage or cowardice. Generally speaking, goods that come unaccompanied by evils and evils that come unaccompanied by goods are irrelevant to courage and cowardice, and knowledge of them not necessary for the knowledge required for courage.

The upshot is that knowledge of what is to be dreaded or dared in war or anything else need not be or include knowledge of *all* future goods and *all* future evils. Now this point carries over to the second crucial inference of

Socrates' argument. If we grant what Socrates says about knowledge in other areas in step (3) and we also grant that knowledge of what is to dreaded or dared is similar in those respects, what follows is what Socrates says in step (4), *not* what he says in (4.1). That is, what follows is that if a man has knowledge of the future goods and evils that are relevant to courage he will also have knowledge of *such* or *similar* goods and evils generally; it does not follow that he will have knowledge of *all* goods and *all* evils. This "all" is the missing link, a link that Socrates has no right to supply (since he has not shown that things to be dared are all future goods, and we have seen how false this is), as he in fact does in step (4.1). The reason why he does in fact supply it is clear: he needs it in order to bring his favorite doctrine (5) to bear on the argument. Step (5) starts with "knew *all* good things . . . ," and without the "all" even Socrates would hold (5) to be false.

Thus Socrates' argument fails even if we grant two crucial premises in it, which represent Socrates' two most favorite and central ethical doctrines: the analogy of virtue (as knowledge) to knowledge in the arts, crafts, and sciences, and the sufficiency of knowledge of good and evil for virtue. These two doctrines by themselves do not, fortunately, have as a consequence the outrageous paradox of the unity of virtue. Where then has Socrates gone wrong? Clearly he has stretched beyond endurance the concept of things to be dared; and consequently he has overwidened the concept of courage. And what is the source of this mistake? This is a more difficult question to answer, but the answer I believe is to be found back in Socrates' conversation with Laches. Laches had a very narrow conception of courage, narrow both in terms of the behavior that can be described as courageous and the circumstances (war and fighting) in which one can show courage or cowardice. Socrates sets out quite correctly to widen in both these respects Laches' conception of courage. He cites other types of behavior, even within war and fighting, that can be called courageous, and he probably supposes that there is too much variety of behavior that can be called courageous for any description of behavior to be successful as a definition of courage. Eventually he allows behavior to drop entirely out of sight. This may be a mistake, but it is not a mistake that concerns us here. In listing *circumstances* other than war (perils of the sea, disease and poverty, public affairs) in which one can be courageous or cowardly, Socrates is also widening—so far as Laches is concerned, anyway—the range of application of the concepts of courage and cowardice, and rightly so. But in doing this he fails to set any limits at all to the range of application of these concepts—the question of limits is not even raised at all. He probably supposes that his list of circumstances is open-ended and that it contains too much variety for any description of circumstances to enter successfully a general definition of courage. But he does not see that this does not preclude him from using his list of circumstances for setting at least some rough limits to the range of application of the concepts. His list, open-ended or not, could have served this function. But he allows it to drop completely out of sight. This tendency either to forget or not to consider at all limits of application shows itself again later when Nicias defines courage as the knowledge of what is to be dreaded or dared in war or *anything else* (or, more literally, "in all the other things"). Well, what "other things"? The other circumstances that Socrates listed besides war? That would have been useful to determine, but the point is not raised. The final straw is Socrates' extrapolation of "future goods" from "things to be dared"; here Socrates has gone from a concept that retains some connection with courage as distinct from other virtues to a concept that has no such connection. In the *Protagoras* the mistakes about range of application are repeated, indeed compounded.[19] But

---

[19] For example, see *Prt.* 331A–B: "Is not holiness something of such a nature as to be just, and justice such as to be holy, or can it be unholy? Can holiness be not just, and therefore unjust, justice unholy?" The language that Socrates uses contains the distinctions between "not just" and "unjust" (μή δίκαιον and ἄδικον) and

in the *Republic* Plato saves the day—or at least the hour —by bringing back into relevance circumstances and even behavior. And in Aristotle the lesson is finally brought home.

The other premises of Socrates' argument can also be questioned of course. For example, even if we concede Socrates' analysis of knowledge in medicine, agriculture, and the like, we might still wonder whether knowledge of good and evil can be like that. Can we really have this general, law-like kind of knowledge of good and evil that Socrates seems to be hinting at? This is a matter of no small importance. If such general, scientific-like knowledge of good and evil can be had, with its comforting assurance, courage may indeed be dared with confidence—and the other virtues as well. For no matter what the risks, we would at least know that we were doing the better thing. But if not, we are left with the agony of existential decision.

In the *Laches*, however, these issues are not examined. Socrates hurries along. Having assumed without question that such knowledge of good and evil can be had, he proceeds to extol its power beyond belief: a man who has such knowledge, he says, will have all the virtues; he will be not only courageous, but just and temperate and pious as well.

In this final pronouncement, the crowning piece of the whole dialogue and a bold statement of the Socratic paradox that virtue is knowledge, Socrates has again forgotten something he said earlier or at least he has failed to consider its relevance. Just as he failed to consider the relevance of the circumstances he listed in connection

---

between "not holy" and "unholy" (μή ὅσιον and ἀνόσιον), but Socrates runs over them like a tank. Justice has to be holy or unholy (and who can be shameless enough to say "unholy"?) and holiness has to be just or unjust (and who dares say "unjust"?). He does not catch Protagoras in this round, but he has a little more success in the next one: "Tell me, does a man who acts unjustly seem to you to be temperate in so doing?—I should be ashamed, Socrates, he replied, to admit that, in spite of what many people say." But where is the shame in admitting that a man who acts unjustly may be neither temperate or intemperate in so doing?

with a definition of courage, so he fails now to consider the relevance of the *feelings* he mentioned earlier to his final pronouncement. And yet the feelings are very much relevant to this favorite doctrine of his. Isn't it possible, we want to ask, that a man has all the knowledge that Socrates is talking about, and yet fails in virtue because he cannot endure the pain? Or, he is near-paralyzed with fear? Or, because he is unable to control his desires or resist pleasures? Socrates has listed the feelings that play an important part in courage and cowardice, but he has not dealt with them. He begins to do so in later dialogues, the *Protagoras*, the *Republic*, the *Philebus*, the *Timaeus*. In the *Laches* Plato has made only a beginning, but a very fruitful one. For a comparison between Socrates' list of feelings and his final pronouncement, in which the feelings are so prominently absent, cannot but invite an important question: What are the relations, causal and conceptual, between the feelings Socrates has listed and the knowledge of good and evil he has talked about? Indeed, not only these relations, but a whole triangle of them comes into view. For clearly, there are not only these relations to be considered, but also the relations, causal and conceptual, between knowledge of good and evil and virtuous *behavior;* and the relations, causal and conceptual, between these feelings and behavior. Can we really understand courage and the other virtues without some understanding of these complex relations?

The merit of the present dialogue is that it brings these questions into view, not that it answers them. In the *Laches* Socrates has not really given us any answers about courage. But by doing things and leaving things undone, by questioning and rejecting, by comparing and contrasting, by twisting and turning—in short, by a paradigmatic show of his method, he has succeeded in bringing into view nearly all the important questions about courage. Appropriately, the dialogue ends with a resolve to continue the discussion on another occasion.[20]

[20] I wish to thank the American Council of Learned Societies for a Fellowship that made it possible for me to do this study.

# 10. VIRTUES IN ACTION

M. F. BURNYEAT

## INTRODUCTION—APOLOGY 30A–B

It is a familiar feature of the tradition of moral philosophy which began with Socrates that its primary concern
is with virtues and vices, with what it is to be a good man
and why one should aspire to perfection of the soul. By
contrast, the focus of much modern ethics is on actions
rather than on character, the primary concern being with
principles of right conduct.

This difference of approach has been thought to reflect an impoverishment in contemporary philosophy,[1]
but perhaps the more common reaction is doubt that the
opposition between being and doing will bear much examination; after all, if a man's character is revealed in his
actions, the ancient approach through goodness of character and the modern through goodness of behaviour
should in the end go over the same ground from different directions. The doubt is likely to be influenced
or reinforced by trends in moral psychology which encourage an all-purpose use of the concept of a disposition; for the content of a disposition derives from its
exercise in action. Thus a recent introduction to ethical
problems does not think it seriously controversial to propose

> that we regard the morality of principles and the morality
> of traits of character, or doing and being, not as rival kinds
> of morality between which we must choose, but as two
> complementary aspects of the same morality. Then, for

This is a previously unpublished essay, written especially for this
volume.
[1] Cf. e.g., G. E. M. Anscombe, "Modern Moral Philosophy"
(*Philosophy*, 1958), or Bernard Mayo, *Ethics and the Moral Life*
(London, 1958), chap. XI.

every principle there will be a morally good trait, often going by the same name, consisting of a disposition or tendency to act according to it; and for every morally good trait there will be a principle defining the kind of action in which it is to express itself.[2]

If, however, we go back to Socrates in search of this complementarity or symmetry of treatment, we find, instead, that virtue is spoken of as something capable of dominating and organizing the whole pattern of a man's life. Consider this famous declaration from Plato's *Apology*, giving Socrates' version of the activities which his accusers represented as corrupting the young:

> All I do as I go about is try to persuade you, both young and old, to make your first and chief concern not your bodies or your valuables but the soul and its improvement —what I say is, 'Virtue does not come from valuables, but from virtue valuables and all other good things come to men in their private and public affairs' (30A–B).

No doubt some listeners, like some modern translators, would understand Socrates to be making the implausible claim that virtue pays in a straightforwardly financial sense, although to confine the thrice-repeated "valuables" (χρήματα) to money is to miss the Socratic challenge to common notions of what is a valuable possession. On the other hand, Socrates is evidently thinking of virtue as something more than the virtuousness of a good man's way of life, in the sense of a tendency to perform virtuous acts. For he goes on to make, in the closing paragraph of his speech, the correlative claim, "To a good man no evil comes either while he lives or when he is dead" (41D), and his meaning here is surely not a simple definition of goodness as the absence of evil. Rather, the thought is that a good man's existence is so dominated by virtue that he recognizes no evil but the loss of virtue's benefits.

In modern discussions of the theme, to ask whether

[2] William K. Frankena, *Ethics* (Englewood Cliffs, 1963), p. 53.

virtue is a good to a virtuous man is to ask about the benefits he obtains from his virtuous way of life, and there are two main ways of dealing with the question: either to consider whether or not a life so led results, in at least the normal course of actual events, in the attainment of such personal ends as wisdom, power, or happiness; or to reject all concern with "the profits of moral action" as reducing morality to expediency, principle to policy, and quite missing the special point or value that resides, intrinsically, in virtue.[3] Socrates and Plato might accept that regarding virtue as a good is an attitude that comes, perhaps only comes, with the acquisition of virtue itself; but in accordance with the Socratic precept "The unexamined life is not worth living" (*Ap.* 38A), they treat the attitude as very much in need of justification.[4] However, they centre the problem, not on the intrinsic or consequential values of the actions which make up a particular way of life, but on virtue conceived as something which the soul both has and benefits from in much the same way as the body both has and benefits from health (cf. e.g., *Cri.* 47D–E). The analogy, with its implication that "virtue" is more than an abstraction for the virtuous life, suggests that being is in some way prior to doing. This is the subject I want to investigate.

CHARACTER OF THE PROBLEM—LACHES 190D–191E

Trivially, courage is exemplified in courageous deeds, but what else can be said of these which would be informative about their relation to the virtue of courage? This is the problem posed in Plato's *Laches*, and it is

[3] Cf. Philippa Foot, "Moral Beliefs" (*PAS* 1958–59) *versus* D. Z. Phillips, "Does It Pay to Be Good?" (*PAS* 1964–65).

[4] Contrast Peter Winch's interesting paper "Can a good man be harmed?" (*PAS* 1965–66), which articulates an attitude that seeks expression, but *not* objective justification, in the idea of its being worse to do than to suffer wrong. His detail is drawn less from Socrates than from Kierkegaard and Wittgenstein, and I doubt that ancient and modern will bear too close assimilation, even with account taken of the "divine sign."

equally a problem for a dispositionalist in search of some type or types of action which courage is a disposition to perform.

Laches, asked to say what courage is, replies, "If someone is willing to stand fast in the ranks and fight back at the enemy without running away, such a man you may be sure is courageous." Socrates does not disagree,[5] but reminds Laches of the varied tactics which have earned a high reputation in warfare, explaining that he did not mean to ask only about those who are brave in a particular type of fighting, nor indeed to confine the question to military matters as such; he wanted also to include courage in dangerous situations at sea and in political affairs, courage in the face of disease and poverty, pain and fear, and even courage in contending with desires or with temptations to various kinds of pleasure.

This sort of list is typical of the range of a virtue concept like courage. A number of the items on it would have been controversial at the time,[6] and one might reasonably baulk still at the notion that Socrates could show courage in resisting the sexual allure of Alcibiades as well as in disregarding the menaces of the Thirty Tyrants. But it is equally typical of a virtue concept that its range should be liable to controversial extension or modification. For to state and defend criteria for collecting manifestations of a virtue is to articulate a way of grouping certain phenomena which exposes something of one's outlook on life in general; such exposure, Nicias warns early on in the *Laches* (187E ff.), was one of the risks of conversation with Socrates.

[5] His initial "Well said!" (190E–7) compliments Laches, but on the way he replied to a question other than the intended one. In the course of clearing up the misunderstanding he restates the definition, but with a qualification or hesitancy marked by the particle που in 191A–1. Only when Laches reacts sharply to this (191A–4) does he admit at 191A–5 that the man described *is* courageous. The admission may reasonably be read as a polite device for keeping up dialectical momentum.

[6] Cf. Gregory Vlastos, Introduction to the Library of Liberal Arts Volume, *Plato's Protagoras* (Indianapolis, 1956), pp. xlvii ff.

Given, then, that the *Laches* survey of courage illustrates how a virtue concept is likely to have very various
and often contestable applications, the question to ask is
what *kind* of criteria would be appropriate for deciding
that many different actions were all manifestations of the
same virtue. Several distinguishable approaches to the
problem are tried out in Plato's early dialogues. Each
implies a certain conception of what a virtue is, and each
suffers an *elenchus* or critique which illustrates some difficulty about characterizing a virtue in terms of the actions in which it is revealed. The arguments involved are
of interest both in their own right, for their contribution
to the problem of the relation between virtue and action,
and as examples of the way Socrates sought to recom-
mend his own view that each and every virtue should be
characterized as knowledge. A brief comment on this
second aspect will sketch in the dramatic function and
overall philosophical purpose of the passages to be
examined.

In Plato's early dialogues Socrates is shown exposing
difficulties in his interlocutor's notions about virtue, not
in order to construct an argument from their inadequacy
to the conclusion that virtue is knowledge, but to free the
other person's mind from the mistaken beliefs which stop
him trying the Socratic approach to the problem at hand.
The idea of virtue as knowledge is indeed less a conclusion at which discussion can rest than a starting-point
for a new approach—a better one to be sure, but not
without difficulties of its own to be cleared up before its
philosophical benefits can be finally confirmed.[7] All the
more reason, then, why the interlocutor must be jolted
out of his misplaced confidence in inadequate views and
made to share with Socrates that strong feeling of dissatisfaction with one's own ignorance which the elenchus
aims to arouse and sustain; successful practice of the
method will secure a companion in the search for truth,

---

[7] This point is perhaps most clearly seen in the last section of
the *La.* (194C ff.); cp. also *Euthphr.* 14B ff., *Chrm.* 164D ff.,
*Prt.* 361A–D.

not merely refute some error. Hence too what Robinson calls "the personal character of the elenchus":[8] the target is an opinion held by the respondent of the moment and the only worthwhile form of attack is through premises which have and keep his assent. Such, in outline, is the philosophic mission portrayed in these dialogues as the larger setting within which particular passages find their dramatic function. The programme is one there is every reason to accept as no less a genuine mark of the historical Socrates than the recurrent irony which enlivens its execution.

The arguments themselves, however, are no doubt the creation of Plato. One may be confident that Socrates' mission would bring him again and again to problems about explaining a virtue in terms of action, yet sceptical of his having attacked precisely the targets in exactly the ways represented in the dialogues. This does not mean doubt as to how accurately various passages embody some residue of views and reasonings from one or more actual conversations. Arguments conceived in and for the context of a particular discussion with, say, Protagoras, are what Socrates produced and what Plato dramatized, not a refutation of Protagorean doctrines in the abstract such as is credited to Democritus. The testimony of a Socratic dialogue is dramatic rather than historical. It offers something of deeper significance than some arguments Socrates might have used against a certain type of opponent: a dramatic action which displays characteristic traits of the Socratic approach to moral philosophy. Some of these traits will become apparent as we consider in turn three different conceptions of what a virtue is and the objections that Plato's Socrates finds appropriate to them.

[8] Richard Robinson, *Plato's Earlier Dialectic*[2] (Oxford, 1953), pp. 15–17, with further details in chaps. 1–6.

### VIRTUES IN STYLE—CHARMIDES 159B–160D

The *Charmides* starts off its inquiry into the virtue which the Greeks called *sophrosyne,* with Charmides defining it as a restrained composure or quietness in a person's bearing—whatever he does, he does it quietly. More generally, R. S. Peters has suggested that terms for character-traits have a "primarily adverbial" significance and "usually indicate a *manner* or *style* of behaving."[9] And perhaps the problem of the *Laches* would look more manageable if it was reformulated as a problem, not about what the brave man does, but about the way he does it.

The distinction between what is done and how it is done is, of course, relative to the description under which the action is contrasted with the manner of its performance, as represented by some adverbial phrase or clause. A victory bravely won can also be described as a brave deed, and so described admits of its own adverbial qualifications, as performed, say, unflinchingly or with panache. But then with the new description bravery becomes an essential ingredient of the action instead of a feature of it suitable for adverbial expression. To give a genuine contrast between what is done and how it is done, the description and its adverbial qualification should be logically independent, allowing for the same action to be done in a contrary manner. In particular, if a virtue like *sophrosyne* is to be interpreted as some kind of "good style" or way of going about things, able to confer a special merit on widely different actions, it should be possible to perform those same actions in a different, and even vicious, way. The *Charmides* discusses whether, as an "adverbial" interpretation requires, all the actions that manifest *sophrosyne* are done in the same way, and this too is only a genuine issue while the actions them-

[9] "Moral Education and the Psychology of Character," *Philosophy* 37 (1962), p. 38.

selves are considered under descriptions which do not entail the presence of the virtue.

*Sophrosyne* is untranslatable, because the phenomena it grouped together for Greek culture do not form a whole to our outlook. But it may be represented here as modesty (Charmides is embarrassed about explaining how to verify his own presumed possession of the virtue), and the definition of *sophrosyne* as quietness can be taken as a claim that modest behaviour has distinctive stylistic features which an observer can identify without prior assessment of the agent's character. No doubt Charmides chose quietness in an attempt to picture the unobtrusiveness he feels to be distinctive of a modest manner. Socrates' rebuttal takes this observer's view of modesty further still: treating "quietly" as equivalent to "slowly" and "arduously" enables him to object that there are many, or even more, actions where the manner which "looks well" (makes a performance unobtrusive) is not slowness, but speed and agility.

"Fast" and "slow" here mean fast and slow for the type of action, not fast and slow for the agent or for anyone or any action. So the introduction of "arduously" does not have to imply that a slow performer *feels* his task to be a difficult and cumbrous one. It could be enough that he shows little ease in getting through it, like a beginning reader working slowly and (we might justly say) arduously through his first story-book, unconscious of any need to improve his pace. The focus, then, is on what an observer could find to praise as a good way of doing an action of the given type, and so long as it is a type performable with or without modesty, Charmides can hardly object to the way his definition is treated.

Reading may seem an odd candidate for modesty. As in the *Laches*, Socrates' examples of actions that can and should be graced by the virtue under discussion include a number—playing a piece of music and solving a problem are others—which might reasonably be contested. But the main thrust of his accumulation of examples is against any attempt to equate modesty with whatever manner gives merit to the performance of a particular type of action, on the grounds that this may vary from action to action: to the extent, indeed, of involving contrary modes of execution, like fast and slow. And although the argument oversimplifies by assuming there is only one such feature to be isolated in an action, as if a modest manner was the only meritorious one, the fact even that "unobtrusively," let alone "modestly," can be applied to totally dissimilar and sometimes logically incompatible styles of behaviour is a fair objection to the view that such adverbs express a typical "look," style, or manner that distinguishes the actions of an unobtrusive or modest person.

This is not to deny that some traits do seem to be associated with a characteristic manner. Roughly, they are those that lend themselves to mime or pretence: vices more often than virtues, because vices frequently involve the natural expression of an emotion or impulse which the corresponding virtue would check. For example, cowardice would be easier to mime than courage, greed than temperance, while a show of patience requires signs of impatience. Hence the virtues easiest to fake are ones like generosity and veracity where action is the natural expression of an inclination or attitude. But even in these cases there is more to the trait than an imitable style of behaviour, and it is traits to which character adverbs primarily refer; where the adverb can ascribe to an action the typical "look" of a certain trait, as is perhaps the case with "patiently," the use is a secondary and derivative one.[10]

For consider in this light the view of judicious behaviour which Gilbert Ryle presupposes when he lists "behaving judicially" (judiciously) with "talking like a pedagogue" and "has an elliptical look" as descriptions involving comparison with the behaviour or appearance typical of a certain class of subject, *viz.* (at least some)

---

[10] Cp. J. L. Austin, "A Plea for Excuses" in his *Philosophical Papers* (Oxford, 1961), pp. 147–48.

judicious persons, pedagogues, or elliptical platters.[11]
The suggestion is that to behave judiciously is to do
something in the way a judicious person would typically
do it. One difficulty is that while there are general laws by
which to compare the looks of tilted round objects with
those of untilted elliptical ones, and no doubt there are
thought to be some generalizations about how pedagogues talk, it is arguable that the ways of judicious men
neither follow a set pattern nor vary as a simple function
of their circumstances. More important, discovering how
judicious people typically behave would at most show
whether an action was done in the way a judicious man
might be expected to do it. The task of deciding how, in
response to a given occasion, a judicious man would actually do it, though a theoretical one, may call for the
good judgement requisite in judicious practice itself.
(Similarly, there may be occasions when how to do a
thing modestly can only be determined by consulting or
watching someone whose modesty is independently attested.) It is a further question again whether, in acting
as a judicious man would, an agent is behaving judiciously; for that his action must be informed by good
judgement, not merely endorsed by it.[12]

This confirms the point which the argument in the
*Charmides* is evidently designed to emphasize, that there
is a significant difference between an adverb of manner
like "slowly" and virtue adverbs like "modestly" or "judiciously." To read as a slow reader would is to read
slowly, and it is how he reads that distinguishes the actions of a slow reader. But to talk as a modest or judicious person would—whether this refers to the way he
typically does or to the way he actually would here and
now—is not *eo ipso* to talk modestly or judiciously. Accordingly, what distinguishes the speech of a modest or
judicious man is not how he talks—the conclusion the
*Charmides* reached from the premise that a modest man
does different things in different ways.

[11] *The Concept of Mind* (London, 1949), pp. 217–18.
[12] Cp. Aristotle, *Eth. Nic.* 2.4.

The conclusion is not, of course, directed against the truism that a modest man behaves in a modest way, but against interpreting this as a style or manner in a less formal sense. The moral in brief is that modesty is not an elevated kind of mannerism. The modest manner named after the virtue Charmides sought in it exists, at best, as a social grace, to be put on and off without serious prejudice to what one does.

### VIRTUES IN RULES—EUTHYPHRO 10A–11A

Peters would reply that the manner is to be identified by reference to what he calls "rules of social appropriateness."

> A man who is ruthless, selfish, honest, punctual, considerate, does not necessarily have any particular goals; rather he behaves in a certain manner, according to or not according to certain rules.[13]

Adherence to certain principles of conduct, which, like mannerisms, is a species of tendency in Ryle's classification of dispositions,[14] is perhaps the most likely contemporary candidate for the analysis of a virtue. Nowell-Smith, for example, holds that virtues and vices are respectively dispositions or tendencies to conform to and to breach standards of behaviour which a moral code seeks to enforce on account of the good consequences that usually attend their observance.[15] Among the virtues that interested Socrates and Plato, holiness (*hosiotes*) and justice (*dikaiosyne*) offer the most obvious fit for a rule-following model. They are closely akin, and holiness can even be regarded as a specialized division of justice.[16] This could issue in a

[13] *Op. cit.*, p. 38.
[14] *Op. cit.*, pp. 132–33.
[15] *Ethics* (Harmondsworth, 1954), pp. 248 ff., pp. 300 ff.; cp. the passage quoted above from Frankena.
[16] Cf. *Euthphr.* 11E–12E, *Cri.* 54B, *La.* 199D, *Prt.* 330C–31E, *Gorg.* 507A–B.

conception of holiness as conformity to religious custom or law, with justice as normally understood left for conformity to rules governing the human sphere. Since conformity to a set of rules can, as such, include no more than the rules prescribe, and what rules can prescribe is restricted by what humans can (logically) decide upon, there would appear to be little room here for the attitudes, feelings, and beliefs which shape the majority of virtues. It would be a question whether holiness and justice, so conceived, should properly be accounted virtues of character at all. But Socrates and Plato, partly for horror of sophistic conventionalism, transformed justice, and with it holiness, into a quality of soul. Such treatment may be implausible for these essentially rule-connected notions but, paradoxically perhaps, it can spotlight difficulties in a reverse assimilation that would make a proper virtue depend on conforming to rules. A case in point is the *Euthyphro's* argument against defining holiness by external standards.

The dialogue starts, predictably, from the assumption that for an action to be holy is for it to be of a certain determinate type (to have a certain *eidos* or *idea*), so that an inquiry into holiness is a search for a feature common to and distinctive of all holy actions (5D). To this end the definitions discussed attempt to specify a standard by which to settle disputes over whether any given action is holy. But they do it by referring the action to some quite external test: is it doing what finds favour with the gods, or with all the gods unanimously, or giving them some kind of service? If these are the questions, Euthyphro should be able to answer them from his authoritative knowledge of religious matters, and he should be able to systematize his answers in rules for pleasing or helping the gods. Behaviour would then be holy or unholy according as it related to these rules, just as, on Peters' account, it is honest, fair, considerate, or ruthless according as it relates to the rules of social appropriateness which govern conduct towards fellow men.

The dialogue's main line of attack on this type of view is against its failure to illuminate what it is about such behaviour that fits it to the standard. Euthyphro's definitions, by explaining holiness as what has some value for the gods, make it unintelligible that the gods should value holiness for what it is. Similarly, if considerateness is explained as (a division of) what is deemed socially appropriate or beneficial, it becomes unintelligible that it should be valued for itself. To paraphrase the central argument: according to Euthyphro, being holy is being something which the gods value, and that is a property which an action acquires by, and only by, the gods coming to value it. Now there are two things this could mean, both true. The first is merely a consequence of the fact that entering into a relation is a change for both gods and men, and it might equivalently be expressed by saying that valuing an action is a property which the gods acquire by, and only by, the action coming to be something they value. The second, which is the one intended, is that the initiative for the change lies entirely with the gods. Next, a corollary of this: For the action, the change is something that befalls it and the result of the change—being something which the gods value—is what Plato at 11A calls a *pathos*, meaning that the responsibility or explanation for it, as for the initial change, resides elsewhere, with the gods. This makes it as absurd that someone should value a thing because it is something he values as that he should carry a thing because it is something he is carrying or see it because it is something he sees. Just as it is only something he is carrying or seeing because he carries it or sees it, as the case may be, so it is only something he values because he values it. Likewise, a thing is holy—if holiness is identified with being something which the gods value—only because the gods value it. How, then, can it be said that the gods value what is holy because it is holy?[17]

[17] Recent exegesis of this argument may be traced through Albert Anderson, "Socratic Reasoning in the *Euthyphro*" (*Review of Metaphysics* 22 [1969]). It has perhaps been overly dominated

Euthyphro does want to say this (10D), and he gets into trouble when Socrates substitutes definiens for definiendum within the "because"-clause—questionable moves on either side, for as a result Euthyphro's position looks to be open to a charge of internal inconsistency and Socrates' refutation of it to one of illegitimate substitution into an opaque context.[18] But the problem remains that if the holiness or considerateness of holy or considerate action (11A: its *ousia*, what it is for it to be holy or considerate) is what has befallen it as the object of a certain attitude, other reasons than its instantiation of these virtues are needed to explain why such conduct elicits the attitude it does; why, in other words, it is found admirable, pleasing, helpful, or socially appropriate.

The argument can be extended to other proposals for assessing conduct by testing something else: for instance, a reformulation of Euthyphro's position as one where a holy action is identified as something prescribed for men by some rules or principles for dealings between man and god. It is not simply that the conduct must have some value to give point or virtue to any rules that may exist to encourage it. For perhaps Euthyphro could explain why it matters that men should behave towards

---

by the passive verb forms with which Plato contrives that his argument should depend only on the nature of the relations discussed, without reference to the parties that might enter into them. In my paraphrase the passive is inessential, and recasting into the active form of Euthyphro's initial position (9E) makes it easier to see the crucial asymmetry in the relation of explanans to explanandum.

18 It is not clear how far the substitutivity problem which surfaces at 10E–11A is due solely to mishandling of a psychological context. For one thing, it might have something to do with explanation as such; for another, the dialogue construes a definition as asserting, not merely the logical equivalence, but the identity of the property signified by the definiens with that signified by the definiendum, and alternative designations of the same universal might be thought interchangeable in contexts where alternative designations for the same particular are not; or at least the interchange should not result in absurdity.

the gods in the manner prescribed; in which case it would be hard to sustain the objection (which underlies much of the dialogue) that the notion of holiness is presupposed in the very idea of right and wrong conduct towards the gods and cannot be defined in terms of it. Rather, the problem is how to specify rules which determine right and wrong conduct towards the gods without (circular) reference to the virtue they are supposed to define.

After ruling out as beside the point a simple injunction "Be holy!" or "Don't be inconsiderate!" the easiest method would be to cite one or more rules and say that conformity to them was the virtue to be defined. Naturally, enumeration would not illuminate the virtue as a Socratic definition should, but the method has other drawbacks than this. *Ex hypothesi,* the existence of rules or principles to discourage ruthlessness and promote considerateness is not due to what ruthlessness and considerateness are, so by what rationale are the rules of social appropriateness to be parcelled out among the many virtues and vices that can be displayed in social intercourse? Again, can 'politeness' be rendered into Greek or French only to the extent that the rules of those societies correspond with ours? And, inherent in any dealings with rules, there is the gap between conformity as such —doing the prescribed thing, whatever the reason—and deliberate obedience.

If the virtue is deliberate obedience, it may still be inspired with evil intent. If it is mere conformity it may also be fortuitous. If, with Peters, we speak of the rules as something to follow or apply in the regulation of one's conduct, we create an internal connection between the virtue and respect for rules and it may be hard to keep the virtue distinct from conscientiousness in general. Nowell-Smith claims that a conscientious man and a brave one display different virtues when they both do the same thing, "the brave thing," the one for duty's sake and the other for that of doing the brave thing itself; but without some further description of what this is that both do, we are back with an injunction to do the brave thing.[19]

Some of these problems also vex the other method of defining a virtue in terms of rules: to characterize a set of rules in general terms and say that the virtue is conformity to rules of that sort. Thus in the *Euthyphro* there lies to hand the suggestion that holiness is that part of justice (approximately, conformity to those rules of conduct) concerned with serving the gods as opposed to men (12E). This may be the closest the dialogue gets to a historically correct view of the concept of *hosiotes,* and the objections brought against it are basically theological: there appears to be no service that could conceivably be of value to a divine being. But perhaps all this shows is that there is no place for *hosiotes* in a rigorous fourth-century theology.

Where men are the beneficiaries, the problem is more one of discriminating finely enough to assign a different kind of rule to each rule-following virtue. It is a substantive question how many virtues one recognizes in rules. As far as Socrates is concerned, it would probably be fair to say that only towards the end of the *Euthyphro* do acts of religious observance take on the appearance of a virtue in action, when discussion of the holy as ministration to the gods leads to a consideration of the *knowledge* involved in right dealings with divine beings. Up to that point the subject is treated in terms which necessarily fail to indicate what holiness in action reveals of the agent's state of mind or soul. But the investigation has no sooner taken a new turn than it founders, before it can show the promise of the Socratic approach or indicate how we are to understand Socrates' pursuit of knowledge as a service to the god who declared that Socrates' knowledge of his own ignorance made him the wisest of men (cf. *Ap.* 20C–23C).

[19] Cf. *op. cit.*, chap. 17, esp. p. 258.

VIRTUES IN POWER—PROTAGORAS 332A–333B,
LACHES 192A–193D

The *Charmides* and the *Euthyphro* witness to a conviction that virtue adverbs express neither the manner
in which an action is executed nor the way it measures
up to some external standard. Such adverbs lead—to put
it crudely—towards the inner side of the action, to "what
makes the agent tick." A rationale for this is formulated
in the *Protagoras* as a general principle for correlating
adverbs and abstract nouns: "Whatever is done in the
same way is done by the same, whatever in the opposite
way, by the opposite" (332C). The principle (though
not, of course, this formulation of it) is fundamental to
the Socratic approach to virtues and vices.

What it amounts to is the following: to describe any action A as done, say, weakly or wisely, slowly or modestly,
is equivalent to describing it as done by weakness or wisdom, slowness or modesty. The adverb in the passive
voice construction is replaced by the corresponding abstract noun in a position where it introduces the subject
of the equivalent active sentence: thus "A is done by
weakness" is the passive version of "Weakness does A."[20]
Plato also illustrates two variant constructions, which he
evidently regards as serving the same purpose: "A is
done with modesty" picks out the factor responsible for
A's being done modestly,[21] and in Greek the dative of an
abstract noun often gives a similar, if somewhat vaguer,

[20] For this equivalence as governing ὑπό ("by") plus abstract
subject, cf. *Euthphr.* 13B7–10, *Chrm.* 171E5–7.
[21] For this use of μετά ("with"), cf. *La.* 192C8–193D1, *Prt.*
324B1, *Men.* 78D4–79C7, 88B5–C3, Xen. *Mem.* 3.5.8. The example here (332B8) is μετὰ τάχους, where μετά might seem to express manner or accompaniment; but the argument is designed to
move from the action to its explanation, and τάχος must (as at
*La.* 192A–B) refer to quickness as an attribute of persons, not
speed.

indication of how an action is to be explained.[22] In other
words, the abstract noun identifies the attribute which
makes the agent perform the kind of action to which the
adverb applies: he does it because he has that attribute.[23]

It is not clear whether Plato seriously supposes this
thesis to hold for all adverbs whatsoever. Despite the
spuriously analytic form in which the principle is cast,
the specific concern of the context is explanation in terms
of a power. The dialogue is exploring a model for the
logical structure of the virtues whereby each is distinct
in nature and function like the separate organs of the
face (cf. 330A–B). Roughly, as seeing is the function
of the eye, so each virtue has as its function some specific
kind of behaviour. The principle is used (in a rather
murky and controversial argument) to insist that the
various applications of a given virtue adverb all imply
the same explanation, and, following from this, that if
two virtue adverbs ever apply together to the same action, the virtues they imply as the explanation of the
action must be identical. That is, accepting the principle
is supposed to commit one to thinking that a coincidence
of two virtue adverbs would refute the model.

Now the principle is in fact a generalization of an
analogy which Socrates introduces into the *Laches* discussion at the point where we left it earlier. Just as what
we call "quickness" (as an attribute of persons) is the
power which gets through much in little time, be the
activity one of speaking, running, learning, playing some
music, or whatever, so, he says, courage is some power
or *dynamis* which is the same throughout all the variety

[22] Cf. *Ap.* 22B9–C3, 26E8–9, 41D7–8, *Prt.* 357D7–E1, *Men.*
90A5, *Mx.* 243D1–7, 244A7–B1. The dative construction is standard in explaining performances by reference to some kind of knowledge or skill, and *Ion* 537C–538A formulates for these cases a principle for correlating performances with their explanations which
parallels the *Prt.* principle.
[23] Cf. also *Hp. Mi.* 365E, *Chrm.* 160D6–E4, 170C1–D9, *Euthd.*
280A6–8, *Men.* 98B7–C10, 99B5, and John Lyons, *Structural
Semantics—an analysis of part of the vocabulary of Plato* (Oxford,
1963), p. 158.

of circumstance and external manifestation (192A–B). This proposal for unifying the list of examples of courage depends on an elementary logical feature which the Greek *dynamis* shares with its English analogues "power" and "capacity": any performance by thing or person implies the possession by the performer of some corresponding power or capacity. So much follows from the principle *ab esse ad posse valet consequentia* plus an assumption from the metaphysics of common sense, that such performances do not happen by fluke or, as Plato would put it, "by divine dispensation" inexplicably. It is plausible to think, also, that in the absence of interfering factors the power will be retained, unimpaired, so as to enable the performer to do again what was done before. This is because powers are differentiated by their manifestations[24]—to know what power is implied by a given performance *is* to know what sort of repeat-performance it is reasonable to expect, in the absence of interference, and under what conditions. Power and performance exhibit the reciprocity asserted by the *Protagoras* principle.

Suppose, then, someone runs quickly down the street. Does it follow that he can run quickly, that he is quick on his feet, that he is quick? We can say either that none of these follow, or that all of them do but with certain implicit qualifications: he can run quickly in some circumstances, he is quick on his feet in some respects, he is quick at something. Either way, only empirical tests to find out what these circumstances and respects are can give determinate content to "what was done before" and to the description of the corresponding power. By itself, the performance implies no more than some kind of quickness, some power satisfying the general formula "gets through much in little time."

It follows that the analogy with quickness fails to secure a single power running through and explaining all the ways *the* brave man might characteristically behave

[24] As Plato recognises at *R.* 447D. I am ignoring, since Plato does, the possibility of complications over differences between the powers of persons and of inanimate things.

in various situations. It implies only a single *kind* of power which could be exemplified as different types of courage, separately by a hoplite soldier like Laches and by the Scythians with their hit-and-run tactics, collectively by Socrates in his many exploits. Accordingly, the principle should read, "Whatever is done in the same way is done by the same *kind* of thing, whatever in the opposite way, by the opposite." In this emended form it no longer has the powers Socrates claimed for it, since it does not assert that a virtue adverb picks out the explanation of the action to which it is applied.

The conclusion to draw seems to be that the qualities of character revealed in an action hint at an explanation rather than actually providing one. Knowledge that a man acted weakly, whether through weakness of character or of limb, is a framework for understanding why he did so, but it does not go far into the workings, as it were, of his mind or body. Consider from this viewpoint Laches' suggestion for living up to Socrates' analogy between courage and quickness, that the power which is courage is a power of endurance or perseverance (192B–C). The examples connected to this definition make it clear that "endurance" (καρτερία) means more than the continuing in or keeping to a course of action (a merely quantitative notion, like quickness). It has to do, rather, with proceeding *despite* certain considerations against the action—a recognition that courage presupposes, if not necessarily fear, then some adverse reaction or attitude to be overcome, rejected, or ignored. But if Laches is proposing (part of) a motivation pattern under which brave action could be subsumed, it is still only a pattern. Even when he adds reasonableness to distinguish courageous from rash risk-taking, the indeterminacy inherent in any pattern of this sort leaves the definition open to Socrates' objection that highly reasonable and professionally calculated risk-taking, by profiteer, doctor, or expert cavalryman, need not count as courage.

This tactic of filling in the pattern with disconcerting

detail can be adapted to other proposals of the same type. For instance, the following:

> It is a necessary and sufficient condition for a man to act generously on any specific occasion that (1) he believes that some other person is in need and would therefore benefit by what he has to give, and (2) he gives to this person because he holds such a belief.[25]

Just expand on the reason for giving: is the belief irrational, or founded on an absurd notion of need? Does the man act on it because he wants to impress, or to live up to a principle? As for the necessity of the reason, must a confectioner who treats customers' children from his own stock, or a teacher generous with his time be activated by a belief that the recipients are in need?

Nevertheless, virtues and vices surely are traits in which thought, feeling, and action combine (as rudeness essentially includes lack of consideration for others, whether through indifference, thoughtlessness, or insensitivity) and combine, moreover, to form connected patterns. Honesty and avarice, for instance, do not merely span acting *and* thinking *and* feeling in certain ways but involve acting thus *because* of what is thought and felt—it is what an honest or avaricious man values and desires and thinks it permissible to do that leads him to act as he does. Socrates is too hasty when he discards Laches' ideas about the brave man's motivation as hitting altogether the wrong note (193D–E). What the discussion has shown to be wrong is not any association between a virtue and a characteristic pattern of motivation, but the attempt to take the behaviour subsumed under the pattern as defining the virtue; that is, to treat the virtue as an attribute which determines a man to action of a specific kind, such as reasonable risk-taking or

[25] Gabriele Taylor and Sybil Wolfram, "The Self-Regarding and Other-Regarding Virtues" (*Phil. Quart.*, [18] 1968), p. 240; cp. Anthony Kenny, *Action, Emotion and Will* (London, 1963), chap. 4.

giving to benefit the needy. So close a tie with a distinctive form of conduct would make possession of a virtue resemble being endowed with a particularly admirable habit, and is to be rejected along with the principle that all instances of acting courageously or generously have the same explanation.

This means, I think, not only that a virtue is not a power or *dynamis,* but that it is not properly a disposition either. For the latter is nothing if not an explanatory notion. It is not enough to follow Ryle's account of dispositions, dividing them into two main types, tendencies (including traits of character like vanity) and capacities, and holding that to ascribe a tendency to something is to say that its state or behaviour is usually or often of a certain sort, or that it is so always or usually or often when certain particular conditions or kinds of conditions are fulfilled, while a capacity is constituted by its not being predictable that a subject will not behave in a certain way under certain conditions.[26] Such things might be predictable or unpredictable on a variety of grounds, whereas a disposition must be some stable aspect of the subject which helps to explain (and is therefore not simply to be equated with) what is or is not to be expected from it. It can be explanatory, moreover, only where its issue is fixed for any recurrence of the conditions of its actualization, which may, of course, be various, with various outcomes, not all of them known. But if none is known with any definiteness, it will be equally vague what disposition is under discussion. Even the accredited dispositional terms of ordinary language, "brittle," "elastic," and the like, are affected to some extent by this sort of imprecision, but the trouble with "vain" is of a different order.

For it is not every form of behaviour which might be considered vain that is to be expected from a man known to be vain. His failing may be restricted to his appearance or his achievements, and may be expressed either by boasting or by preening himself in private. Hence his

[26] *Op. cit.,* chap. 5.

being vain does not explain the prevalence of one rather than another. Presumably there are specific dispositions to be discovered underlying his vanity, but the trait itself does not determine the form of its display. Nor, conversely, is his behaviour, when isolated from the fact of his vanity, of a kind that is necessarily vain; even boasting need not be so, in a Homeric warrior or someone who needs to combat a feeling of inferiority.

In view of all this, the best way of dealing with virtues and vices and other character traits seems to be by analogy with the character of individuals. One may list a number of things as characteristic of a person, but the conjunctive unity of a list is not enough to represent his individuality or to make "acting out of character" as surprising as is compatible with being possible; for that the items listed must be seen as having a certain coherence, as fitting together to make up the "essence" of a person. Similarly, listing actions, motives, emotions, and so on is inadequate to define a trait of character: they must be thought of as characteristic of a type of person before they will cohere into a whole. Then we can say that a man possesses the trait to the extent that he approximates the type it represents.

This gives a sense in which "the notion of a brave, generous, temperate, etc. act is secondary to the notion of a brave, generous, temperate, etc. man."[27] Isolated acts of courage or generosity are not excluded, but it may be hard to pick them out without further consideration of the agent's character in the light of other actions and even other virtues.[28] Correspondingly, a morality cen-

---

[27] Georg Henrik von Wright, *The Varieties of Goodness* (London, 1963), p. 142, who agrees that the virtues are not properly dispositions. The prominence of the character sketch in Greek discussions of virtues and vices, from Plato's *Republic* through Aristotle's *Ethics* to Theophrastus' *Characters,* is no mere literary embellishment.

[28] Cp. Bernard Williams, *Morality and the Emotions* (London, 1965), pp. 17–18. Conrad's novel *Lord Jim* is an extended attempt to assess a putative act of cowardice against the background of a whole life.

tered on being rather than doing will not presume to
map out the path of the good life in individually prescribed steps.

For Socrates and Plato, however, the priority of being
over doing is tied to the explanatory function they assign
to virtue concepts. The favoured Socratic position, that
virtue is knowledge, brings no change in this respect.[29] It
simply enshrines knowledge as the sole factor necessary
and sufficient for the explanation of virtuous conduct. Indeed, the *Hippias Minor* can base a version of the Socratic paradox on the disjunctive proposition that the virtue of justice is a power of the soul or knowledge or both,
arguing from this that *if* anyone does wrong willingly it
can only be the good man, for only he has the knowledge
and/or the capacity requisite for deliberate error in his
sphere of competence (375D–6B). When it comes to
the benefits of virtue, they too are explained by the controlling guidance of knowledge, which is responsible for
all good use of potentially beneficial attributes like
health, strength, beauty, wealth, intelligence, memory,
confidence (cf. *Men.* 87D–89A). It is not that the virtuous life is distinguished from others by benefits, intrinsic
or consequential, which are peculiar to itself: there is
just the good life, dominated and explained by virtue,
the source whence "valuables and *all* other good things
come to men in their private and public affairs."

This, then, is the doctrine which is interpreted and
elaborated by the analogy between virtue and health.
According to dictionary definitions, health is soundness
of body or that condition in which functions are duly
and efficiently discharged, so it is not just a contingent
generalization that the body is "that which is made better by health and is disabled by disease" (*Cri.* 47D–E).
Yet neither is the improvement or injury one that makes

[29] Cf. n. 22 above.

no real difference to the body's well-being, for underlying the conventional connection between the term "health" and a certain bodily condition is a natural connection between that condition, whatever it may be, and the efficient discharge of functions. It is this interplay of nature and convention which is responsible for the statement "health is good or beneficial" appearing to be both non-contingent and non-trivial. Analogously, the concluding argument of the first book of the *Republic*, which attempts to prove that the just man will flourish, specifies functions for the soul in order that justice may be identified as the sound state or condition whereby those functions are well discharged.[30] They include, besides living itself, such things as conducting and controlling and deliberating about the projects and activities which make up a man's life. It is not difficult to agree that these are functions of the mind or soul in the sense given to "function" or *ergon*, namely, that they are things one can only (or best) do with the soul. It is less easy to accept the further thesis that the condition whereby these things are done well is justice, from which it is concluded that the just man lives well in general—but here everything depends on the outcome of an earlier dispute as to whether justice or injustice has the better claim to be distinguished by its judiciousness in practical matters (348D–50D). Judiciousness is a quality everyone can allow is needed if potentially beneficial possessions are to be put to good use.

Even so, a further assumption is required before what amounts to successful exercise of practical reason can be equated with living well in general. We might agree that practical reasoning is a function contributing to one's well-being; even that excellence in it depends on that knowledge and general soundness of mind which is produced by some favoured educational practice, be it Socratic dialectic, drilling in Latin grammar, or the study of

[30] The project is the Socratic one outlined at *Cri.* 47D–E, here given a weightier treatment which may reflect Plato's growing ambition for more positive and permanent results.

literature. But there surely remains a huge gap between this and anything we could recognize as a good life. Conversely, if someone did accord such value to a life based on philosophy, scholarship, or cultivation of the sensibility, his valuation would be an arbitrary singling out of one human function or mode of activity among others, like total dedication to athletic prowess. By contrast, Plato's argument assumes that the notion of what it is for a man to flourish can be treated in the same sort of unitary way as we might consider the thriving of a fine specimen of some kind of plant or animal, or the manifestations of a good physique.

More is involved here than the fact that Socrates and Plato model their moral psychology on notions like health and function, which presuppose a kind or species in the sense that not any and every condition in which functions are efficiently discharged would reasonably count as health, only conditions natural and normal to the organism in question. The root assumption is that virtue explains a good man's way of life, and this could survive replacement of the analogy with health by, for example, an account of virtue as equipment for doing well in human society. So long as virtue is cast as a single principle of explanation, what it explains must be correspondingly limited and invariant.

This consequence is avoided if the priority of being over doing is understood in the terms I have suggested: if, that is, regarding a life as a good one, one that manifests virtue in general or a particular virtue, is less a matter of explaining it than of finding in it the actions, thoughts, and feelings characteristic of a good person. On the other hand, on this view a man has a particular character to the extent that he is "a character" of a certain type, and it may be doubted whether there remains much sense in a Socratic declaration that he benefits if his character is a virtuous rather than a vicious one. That would come close to his benefiting from being himself.

# 11. THE SOCRATIC DENIAL OF AKRASIA

## AKRASIA AND THE MORALITY OF DECISION

The suggestion has been made that akrasia poses a philosophical problem for a moral philosophy in which choice
and decision are assumed to be of fundamental importance in human conduct. Is there evidence that the Socratic tradition exemplifies such a moral philosophy? In
this section we will review such evidence and begin to
trace its bearing on the interpretation of the Socratic
denial of akrasia, especially as that denial is presented by
Xenophon.

This suggestion is a development of the analysis made
by Bruno Snell of one of the themes in the tragedies of
Aeschylus. Snell draws attention to the fact that often the
characters of Aeschylus are faced with a situation in
which they must ponder alternatives and come to a decision. Snell concentrates on the position of King Pelasgus
in the *Suppliants,* but perhaps the position of Orestes in
the *Libation Bearers* is more familiar. Apollo has com-
manded him to avenge his father's death by killing his
mother. Orestes has some intimations of the guilt he will
incur by this act, and at the crucial moment he hesitates
and turns to his companion for advice. The companion
reminds him of Apollo's oracle. Orestes says, "I judge that
you win. Your advice is good."[1] He then goes on with
his deed. This theme of decision runs throughout the
*Oresteia.* In the *Agamemnon,* Agamemnon must choose
whether or not to walk upon the carpet, as he once had
to choose whether or not to sacrifice his daughter. In the

This essay is chapter 1 of *Aristotle's Conception of Moral Weakness* by James J. Walsh (New York: Columbia University Press,
1964). It is reprinted by permission of the author and publisher.

[1] Aeschylus, *Libation Bearers,* trans. R. Lattimore, line 902.

*Eumenides,* the jury of Athenians must decide whether
or not Orestes shall be delivered over to the Furies. Snell
sees in such situations one of the keys to Aeschylean
tragedy:

> Aeschylus presents these pointed situations because he is
> less interested in what happens than in what is done, and
> because he feels that the essence of human action is to be
> found in the act of decision. A chemist combines in his
> test tube several substances which are rarely or never found
> together in nature in order to form a clear and precise idea
> of their reactions. Likewise the dramatist constructs his ac-
> tions with a view to isolating the quintessence of action.[2]

The Greek terms for such a decision are αἵρεσις and
προαίρεσις; Kullmann has collected occurrences of these
terms in Greek literature from Homer through Aristotle,
thus providing evidence that the concept of decision was
in wide use among the Greeks.[3] Of somewhat greater
interest for us are passages in which the concept plays an
important part in determining philosophical doctrine.
Xenophon presents one such passage which relates the
Socratic doctrine regarding akrasia to a philosophical
generalization of the concept of choice:

> When asked further whether he thought that those who
> know what they ought to do and yet do the opposite are at
> once wise and vicious, he answered: "No; not so much that,
> as both unwise and vicious. For I think that all men have a
> choice between various courses, and choose and follow the
> one which they think conduces most to their advantage.

---

[2] Snell, *Discovery,* p. 106. Snell's elaboration of this point occupies pp. 99–108. Snell's further thesis that the theme of decision
is first found in Aeschylus is criticized by Kullmann, in *Beiträge,*
pp. 24 ff. Kullmann argues that the theme is prominent in Homer.

[3] I am assuming that the differences between the Greek terms
αἵρεσις and προαίρεσις, as well as those between the English
terms "choice" and "decision," are not important at this stage of
the inquiry. The differences between the former may have considerable bearing on Aristotle's conception of moral virtue. The
differences between the latter could stand extensive investigation.

Therefore I hold that those who follow the wrong course are neither wise nor prudent."[4]

For Socrates as Xenophon presents him, men choose what they do; and when men choose, they choose what they think best. Therefore, there can be no one who at once knows what is best and does what is worst. We shall return to Xenophon's elaborations on this doctrine.

The ways in which Plato utilizes and interprets the concept of choice are much more complex than this simple doctrine presented by Xenophon, and to explore them all would amount to a major inquiry. We will content ourselves with three passages, spread over the course of Plato's career, to make it clear that the concept of choice, or decision, was never very far from his mind. The first passage is from the *Protagoras*. Socrates is trying to show that a certain art of measurement would be salvation in life, if acting well consisted in choosing large things and rejecting small things. He concludes thus:

> Well then, my friends, since we have found that the salvation of our life depends on making a right choice (αἵρεσις) of pleasure and pain—of the more and the fewer, the greater and the smaller, and the nearer and the remoter—is it not evident, in the first place, that measurement is a study of their excess and defect and equality in relation to each other? (357A–B)

One of the most humorous and dramatic passages in Plato is found in the *Phaedo*, at the point at which Socrates is recounting his intellectual development, and tells

[4] *Mem.* iii.9.4. There is a difficulty in the Greek of this passage. The text has σοφούς τε καὶ ἐγκρατεῖς εἶναι νομίζοι. The sense requires that ἐγκρατεῖς be ἀκρατεῖς. See Gauthier and Jolif, *L'Éthique* II, 591. "Have a choice" translates προαιρουμένους. Gauthier's claim that the word προαίρεσις only appeared a little before Aristotle and that it is not found in Xenophon, and found only once in Plato is a little forced. See *La Morale*, p. 28. The word προαίρεσις may not occur, but other forms of the verb προαίρεσθαι certainly do. See Kullmann, *Beiträge*, pp. 40–41, for a collection of occurrences in Plato.

of his disappointment in the doctrines of Anaxagoras. He explains that if one were to ask for the cause of the conversation they are now conducting, one kind of answer would mention "voice and air and hearing," and another kind would mention the opinions of Socrates and the Athenians as to what is best. He then goes on:

> But it is most absurd to call things of that sort causes. If anyone were to say that I could not have done what I thought proper if I had not bones and sinews and other things that I have, he would be right. But to say that those things are the cause of my doing what I do, and that I act with intelligence but not from the choice (αἴρεσις) of what is best, would be an extremely careless way of talking. (99A–B)

Finally, in the *Laws*, there comes a point at which Plato acknowledges that men will only choose what is pleasant over what is painful, and sets himself the task of showing the superior pleasantness of the temperate life. He begins in this way:

> What, then, and how many are the lives in which a man—when he has chosen (προαίρεσθαι) the desirable and voluntary in preference to the undesirable and the involuntary and has made it into a private law for himself, by choosing what is at once both congenial and pleasant and most good and noble—may live as happily as man can? (733D–E)

It is because men make choices, then, that the art of measurement can constitute their salvation; because they make choices, that purely physical and mechanical conditions are inadequate to the explanation of human action; and because they make choices, that the superior pleasantness of the virtuous life should be set forth by the philosopher. We are assuming that the *Protagoras* is a relatively early dialogue, the *Phaedo* a middle dialogue, and the *Laws* a late dialogue. The theme of choice and decision is thus an important one throughout the development of Plato's reflection on human life.

With Aristotle, there is hardly any need for emphasizing the importance of the concept of decision. In both the *Eudemian Ethics* (1225B18–1227A5) and the *Nicomachean Ethics* (1111B4–1113A14) there is an extensive discussion of προαίρεσις in which the affiliations of this concept with those of appetite and knowledge are worked out. More important, virtue is described in the *Eudemian Ethics* as a ἕξις προαιρετική (1227B8), and in the *Nicomachean Ethics* the virtues are said to be προαιρέσεις τινὲς ἢ οὐκ ἄνευ προαιρέσεως (1106A3–4). That is, virtue is a disposition to choose, a form of choice, or at least not without choice. It is the importance of the concept of choice in his account of the virtues that, in part, makes it so necessary for him to clarify the related concept of the voluntary. We will examine portions of his account of these two concepts below.

As we explore the various efforts of Plato and Aristotle to interpret the phenomena of akrasia in such a way that the effectiveness of reason in action is preserved, we should remember the importance of the concept of choice or decision to them; and we should remember the position which is stated baldly and simply by Xenophon: since men choose what they do and since they choose what they think is best for them, it is impossible that they should really act against what they think is best.

Having gone this far in relating the moral philosophy of the Socratic tradition to the concerns of modern analytic philosophers, it is tempting to go farther and to seek, in this way, a deeper understanding of the meaning of Socrates' doctrine. But, as is widely acknowledged, it is not easy to discover precisely what Socrates' doctrine was, let alone what its deeper meaning might have been. Into the vexed question of the relative value of Xenophon, Plato, and Aristotle as testimony to the doctrines of Socrates we are fortunately not obliged to enter, for all three agree that according to Socrates, one of the con-

sequences of the doctrine that no one does wrong volun-
tarily is that akrasia does not really occur.[5] It has been
argued that what animated Socrates in these doctrines
was the understanding of knowledge as practical knowledge, in some fairly narrow sense of the term "practical."
We should consider this possibility, for it would be of the
greatest value in understanding Plato and Aristotle to
have some sense of the point of departure of the development of the Socratic tradition.

There is a passage in Xenophon and another in the
*Laches* which suggest that the kind of knowledge which
Socrates had in mind in his assertion of the effectiveness
of knowledge in action was practical knowledge of some
sort:

> Between wisdom (σοφία) and prudence (σωφροσύνη) he
> drew no distinction; but if a man knows and practices
> (γιγνώσκοντα χρῆσθαι) what is beautiful and good,
> knows and avoids (εἰδότα εὐλαβεῖσθαι) what is base,
> that man he judged to be both wise and prudent. (*Mem.*
> iii.9.4)

The passage from the *Laches* includes a similar practical
reference, in this case, a reference to the bringing about
of goods:

> Now do you think, my excellent friend, there could be
> anything wanting to the virtue of a man who knew
> (εἰδέναι) all good things, and all about their production
> in the present, the future, and the past (ὡς γίγνεται
> καὶ γενήσεται καὶ γέγονε) and all about evil things
> likewise? (199D)

In both cases the practical reference makes it somewhat
ambiguous whether the knowledge to which Socrates refers is exclusively practical—thus, in the first passage, if
wisdom were itself practical, there would seem to be no

---

[5] See Xenophon, *Mem.* iii.9.4 ff.; Plato, *Prt.* 352A–353A; Aristotle,
*N.E.* 1145B22–27.

need to add that a man should practice and avoid as well as know; and similarly for the second passage. To add the reference to knowledge about production suggests that knowledge *simpliciter* does not include knowledge of production. But the references are quite possibly mere emphatic amplifications of what is already contained in the verbs of knowing.

It has been suggested by several scholars that terms referring to knowledge in earlier Greek writings, and to some extent in nonphilosophical writings from the later period are innocent of the distinction between the practical and the theoretical.[6] We will examine one recent and suggestive attempt to capitalize on this position, and to utilize a distinction prominent in modern analytic philosophy, to reach an understanding of Socratic doctrine. This is the attempt by John Gould to explain the practicality of Socratic wisdom by turning to account the difference between "knowing that" and "knowing how" which has been presented by Professor Gilbert Ryle.[7] Ryle's position is that many of the terms which we use in ascribing intelligence to people refer to their abilities to satisfy criteria in practice, and to regulate their behavior critically in the effort to perform correctly. He is opposed to the "intellectualist" interpretation of this "knowing how," according to which performing critically is actually doing two things, contemplating some proposition and carrying out some physical movement. We can put this position in synoptic form by saying that intelligence is

[6] Snell, *Discovery*, p. 185, says that Socrates' language enforces close relations between knowledge and practical interest. E. R. Dodds expands the scope of verbs of knowing to include moral character and personal feeling; see *The Greeks and the Irrational*, pp. 16–17. R. B. Onions develops the Homeric background and relates this to Socrates and Plato; see *The Origins of European Thought*, pp. 13–22.

[7] Gould, *Development*, especially Chapter I: "The Socratic Theory of Knowledge and Morality." The distinction between "knowing that" and "knowing how" is presented by Ryle in *The Concept of Mind*, especially in chapter II, "Knowing How and Knowing That."

manifested in skill. Gould's utilization of this position is presented in the following remarks:

> Briefly what I wish to suggest is this. In putting forward the thesis that ἀρετή is only to be attained by ἐπιστήμη, Socrates was *not* asserting that ἀρετή necessarily results from a personal apprehension of the nature of good and evil (still less of Good and Evil), but that for the achievement of ἀρετή what is required is a form of moral *ability*, comparable in some respects to the creative or artistic ability of potters, shoemakers and the like; that the ἐπιστήμη which Socrates envisaged was a form of knowing *how*, that is, *how to be moral*.[8]

He emphasizes what is intended by remarking somewhat later that "even for Socrates and Plato, to achieve ἀρετή is not to arrive at a valid ethical theory, but to attain valid moral behaviour."[9]

No doubt for Socrates, or for that matter, for any other Greek, the concept of ἀρετή is in some sense a practical concept. At least he would have rejected a man's claim to have it if the man could not live up to the claim and perform appropriately. It would seem to follow that if ἀρετή is somehow dependent on or identical with ἐπιστήμη, ἐπιστήμη must likewise be practical in character. The idea is presented very simply in Xenophon. At one point he has Socrates answer the challenge of Hippias to give his opinion about justice by saying that he declares his notions by his deeds, which are better evidence than words. This is hardly a philosophical position, but it is the common practice on which a philosophical position might be erected. Again, Xenophon has Socrates develop the idea for courage and cowardice: those who cannot behave well cannot know how they must behave.[10] What this amounts to, however, is a restriction

---

[8] Gould, *Development*, p. 7.

[9] *Ibid.*, p. 13.

[10] For justice, see *Mem.* iv.4.10. For courage, see iv.6.11. To "know how one must behave" (εἰδέναι ὡς δεῖ χρῆσθαι) must have some of the ambiguity in Greek that it has in English. One

on any theory of virtue: since virtue is a disposition to act well, any theory of virtue must include this feature. If we take virtue to be knowledge, we cannot thereby abandon the position that it is a disposition governing action. But this is only to say that whatever knowledge virtue is must have some essential relation to action. It is not to say that that knowledge must be tantamount to skill. That is a further claim, and must be independently supported.

We would do well to take a second look at the potters, shoemakers, and the like. They have τέχνη, craftsmanship, and there is no doubt that this craftsmanship must include the element of skill as Ryle has analyzed it. They must be able to perform critically, and to do so habitually. But they also have lore. The pilot and the doctor, two craftsmen whom the Platonic Socrates, at least, is fond of citing, have their star-lore and casebooks, and in the case of the doctor, may even be in possession of a modicum of theory. As Plato points out on more than one occasion, true craftsmanship is not identical with a mere knack at doing things, but involves as well a (theoretical?) knowledge of the subject matter.[11] And Plato is here but giving expression to a movement of "rationalization" of traditional arts, in which everything from military tactics to household management was being reduced to rules and taught by teachers, including sophists such as Hippias.

If we polarize the elements of craftsmanship into skill and lore, what are we to say about Socrates' interest in craftsmen? If his interest was in the habitual *skill* of the shoemakers, etc., it must seem an odd procedure to put

---

may "know how he must behave" without knowing how to behave as he knows how he must behave. That is, here is a case of "knowing how" which is really a "knowing that." We will not undertake an analysis of this interesting expression for fear of being led too far from Socrates and the Greek.

[11] See the distinction between τέχνη, on the one hand, and ἐμπειρία and τριβή, on the other, at *Grg.* 463B, and the remarks about rhetoric at *Phdr.* 268A ff. See also *Phb.* 55D ff., about the distinction between measurement and practice in the arts.

them to the question and ask for an account of their art,
rather than to ask them for a demonstration of their skill.
But it may be doubted whether Socrates' interest was in
either of these elements as such. It will be worth following rather closely one of Xenophon's anecdotes about
Socrates' relations with craftsmen. He has Socrates discuss the art of the armorer with one Pistias, who is re-
nowned as a maker of breastplates. Socrates wants to
know why he charges more than other armorers. The answer is that Pistias' breastplates fit better than others do.
There is then some examination of the notion of a good
fit: a well-fitting breastplate must be well-proportioned
to the wearer and must not be too tight. It permits movement without chafing. We have, then, a definition of the
characteristic excellence of a breastplate.[12] It is this definition of an excellence which Socrates is after, not an
exhibition of the armorer's sureness with the hammer or
even the knowledge which he has of the properties of
various metals. This kind of interest is in line with such
quotations as the following, which have come to stand
as the essence of Socratism, whether that is the "position" of the historical Socrates or not:

> For just actions and all forms of virtuous activity are beauti-
> ful and good. He who knows the beautiful and good will
> never choose anything else, he who is ignorant of them
> cannot do them, and even if he tries, will fail. Hence the
> wise do what is beautiful and good, the unwise cannot and
> fail if they try.[13]

Indeed, a great deal of clarification would be required
before we could safely turn modern philosophical de-

[12] *Mem.* iii.10.9-15. Of course, Xenophon is out to show how
Socrates' concern for values was useful for one and all alike, even
for armorers. See also iii.10.1.

[13] *Mem.* iii.9.5. It may be objected that Xenophon is hardly the
one to give us the deeper meaning of Socrates' teachings. This may
well be the case. But certainly the Platonic Socrates is even more
concerned for values than for skill or lore. And, dissatisfied as we
may be with what we learn from Xenophon and Plato on this score,
have we anywhere else to turn?

velopments to account in fathoming the doctrines of the Greeks. This is not to say that such an enterprise is impossible, only that it is more difficult than is sometimes supposed. When it is said that the aim of Socrates and Plato was not to arrive at a valid ethical theory, but rather to arrive at valid moral behavior, we have to ask ourselves what might be meant by ethical theory here. If what is sometimes called meta-ethics is meant, that is, a morally neutral study of the logic of moral language, it is perhaps feasible to regard this as foreign to Greek interests—but we should remember that Socrates is said to have learned fine linguistic distinctions from Prodicus, and that Socrates, Plato, and Aristotle were all very interested in definitions. If by ethical theory is meant a coherent and teachable knowledge of good and bad, then surely this is exactly what these philosophers were after, so far as any evidence we have suggests. Furthermore, in Gould's case at least, it is not too clear what is to be conveyed by the term "practical," in the ascription to Socrates of a "practical" conception of wisdom. Gould does not limit himself to the element of skill or know-how that we have been discussing so far. He turns for inspiration from Ryle to Kierkegaard and argues that "ἐπιστήμη now appears as an inward and decisively personal moral conviction (analogous perhaps, though we must beware of being misled by the connotations of the word, to the Christian 'faith'). It is personal, as knowing *how* inevitably is; inward, because it is not the subsuming of the individual into a universal and objective principle."[14] Surely to a Greek a position like this would suggest a

---

[14] Gould, *Development*, p. 24. See also pp. x-xi. In fn. 1, p. 67, he compares Socrates to Kierkegaard, Dostoievsky, and Kafka, again associating technique, certainty, and practice. I wonder how comfortable Kierkegaard would be with the notion of "moral technique." On p. 54 the implication of these associations for akrasia is brought out; the ἀκρατής has never achieved "that sureness about his own best interest which must inevitably direct his actions (since it is only recognizable by this trait) along the right road." Here it is the element of sureness, that is, of conviction, which is stressed.

sophistic emphasis on individualism and perhaps the emotionalism exploited by rhetoricians. But there is little evidence to show that Socrates subscribed to anything like the Protagorean individualism, at least as that is widely interpreted; and certainly Socrates is not to be thought of as a rhetorician producing πίστις.[15] And if these emphases are not intended, we are left only with the suggestion that, since action is personal, wisdom must be personal, too. But in one sense at least, all knowledge is personal, "knowledge that" as well as "knowledge how."

If we lean too heavily on the "practical" aspect of Socratic wisdom, the denial of akrasia in the name of that wisdom can amount to a simple tautology hardly worthy of a master dialectician. That is, if moral knowledge is just skill, then the suggestion that a person can know and not act appropriately is ridiculous. The very fact that there was a problem of akrasia should rule out such a limited interpretation of moral knowledge.[16] Still staying

[15] Gould himself makes this point on p. 24: "Though ἐπιστήμη is conviction, it is conviction based on a genuine presence of intelligent ability." Πίστις can be shaken by the appearance of knowledge, but ἐπιστήμη cannot, for "what is true is never proved false." See p. 25 and *Grg.* 473B. If the emphasis is placed on "what is true," it is knowledge and not conviction which is most important. Indeed, we usually speak of having conviction where we do not have knowledge. See Dirlmeier, *Nikomachische Ethik,* note 143, 3 on p. 478, for a discussion of the "psychologization" of knowledge and belief as "strong" and "weak" in the Old Academy, following indications in the *Ti.*

[16] Much of the appeal of the "practical" in interpreting Socrates comes, not only from the discovery of knowing-how by Ryle, but also from the revolt of moral philosophers against the positions of G. E. Moore and the various Intuitionists. In ethical theory, the rediscovery of the behavioral contexts and functions of moral language led to a host of so-called "non-cognitivist" conceptions of the meaning of moral terms. But with the sobering realization that language can perform many functions at once, some of the importance attaching to the "practical" role of moral language has diminished. See Chapters IX and X of R. B. Brandt, *Ethical Theory,* for a careful and comprehensive discussion of recent tendencies on this question.

with Xenophon, we find Socrates himself presenting a more balanced view. He is asked what the best pursuit for a man is, and replies, consistent with Gould, "doing well" (εὐπραξία). Then the shrewd question of whether good luck is a pursuit is asked. Socrates replies that luck (τύχη) and doing (πρᾶξις) are opposites. "To hit on something right by luck without search I call good luck, to do something well after study and practice I call doing well." (*Mem.* iii.9.14) We can see in this an emphasis on intentional action. In addition to knowing *how* to do something and knowing *that* something is true, there is knowing *what* one is doing. And if one concentrates on what it is that one knows when one knows *what one is doing*, it may seem that what one does depends very closely on what one knows—and then an intellectualist theory of motivation is possible, and the denial of akrasia may not be quite the tautology that it seems to be.

The fact that early Greek is innocent of a developed distinction between practical and theoretical knowledge can be construed in more than one way. It may be that knowledge was taken to be practical, as Gould supposes, or it may be that practical pursuits were taken to be somehow theoretical. Early Greek was apparently not too sure about the difference between knowing and emotion, either, and Dodds has pointed out the consequences of this for the explanation of behavior:

> If character is knowledge, what is not knowledge is not part of the character, but comes to a man from the outside. When he acts in a manner contrary to the system of conscious dispositions which he is said to "know," his action is not properly his own, but has been dictated to him. In other words, unsystematised, nonrational impulses, and the acts resulting from them, tend to be excluded from the self and ascribed to an alien origin.[17]

[17] *The Greeks and the Irrational*, p. 17. In n. 105, p. 26, Dodds goes on to diminish somewhat the "intellectualist" force of this view by describing it as the "inevitable result of the absence of the concept of the will." We will eventually examine what might be meant by this position.

Xenophon shows us Socrates interested in the relations between ignorance and madness, and saying that ignorance of the self with the illusion of knowledge is next to madness.[18] It may be, then, that just as when a fit of madness comes upon a person, he is "out of his mind," so when a person acts in a morally weak way, he is "out of his knowledge." Xenophon presents a passage which points in this direction:

> As for wisdom, the greatest blessing, does not incontinence (ἀκρασία) exclude it and drive men to the opposite? Or don't you think that incontinence prevents them from attending to useful things and understanding them, by drawing them away to things pleasant, and often so stuns their perception of good and evil that they choose the worse instead of the better?[19]

Having come this far with Xenophon, on the supposition that if the Socratic conception of wisdom were narrowly practical we would find this brought out in the practical-minded and unphilosophical soldier rather than in the visionary Plato, let us go on a bit farther and collect what seems to be Xenophon's version of the Socratic doctrine concerning wisdom and akrasia. It is hardly systematic and hardly even consistent. We have seen that "He who knows the beautiful and good will never choose anything else." This suggests that the beautiful and good have some wonderful power to control human choices, and thus that once we see these we will be safe from error and evil. But Xenophon has Socrates disagree with the view that justice, prudence, and learning cannot be lost when once attained. An analogy is drawn between the soul and the body; and just as we must continually

---

[18] *Mem.* iii.9.5. At i.2.50, it is said that Socrates had frequently considered the difference between madness and ignorance; madness calls for confinement, ignorance for instruction.

[19] *Mem.* iv.5.6. Here ἀκρασία is used in a loose sense as "absence of self-control," not necessarily as "having one's knowledge overcome by desire." Plato uses the term this way at times, e.g., R. 461B. See the note on ἔτι ἀκρατεῖς on p. 292 of Burnet, *The Ethics.*

train the body so we must continually train the soul, even to the point of repeating instruction after the truth has been seen. (*Mem.* i.2.19 ff.) So to speak, the soul must be in good condition in order to see the truth. He puts this very straightforwardly in saying that "only the self-controlled have the power to consider the things that matter most and sorting them out after their kind, by word and deed alike to prefer the good and reject the evil." (*Mem.* iv.5.11) This amounts to an extension of virtue beyond wisdom. Far from wisdom leading to self-control (ἐγκράτεια), it is self-control which leads to wisdom. Xenophon avoids this difficulty by calling self-control an "aid to virtue."[20]

It is hard to say, then, whether Xenophon's Socrates has in mind a properly philosophical denial of the possibility of akrasia or not. He does reveal a concern for the importance of choice and for intentional action, but it is not clear whether he goes on from this to an intellectualist theory of motivation. The remarks about ἐγκράτεια suggest otherwise. One position does not come through at all: that the wisdom which Socrates thought of as essential to virtue was tantamount to a combination of skill and conviction, rather than vision. There is a suggestion that some kind of training of the soul is necessary to acquire and maintain wisdom, and a suggestion that the morally weak may no longer have the wisdom that they once possessed. But for the most part, Xenophon's Socrates is hortatory rather than philosophical: for the full realization of the philosophical labors required to make good the denial of akrasia we are left to Plato.

Before turning to Plato, however, we should have a fuller acquaintance with the kind of psychological real-

[20] *Mem.* iv.5.1–2. Ἐγκράτεια is a favorite theme for Xenophon. See i.5.1; ii.1.1. At v.5.10, ἐγκράτεια seems almost to be the sum of the virtues: the self-controlled man has the delights of learning something good and excellent, of studying some of the means to regulate his body well and manage his household successfully, of being useful to friends and city, and of defeating his enemies. Perhaps there is a link between this predilection for ἐγκράτεια and Xenophon's supposed debt to Antisthenes.

ism which would insist on the reality of akrasia. We will find this in the work of Euripides, who almost seems to have written certain of his tragedies with the express intention of demonstrating that human knowledge can be, and is, overcome by passion and desire, and that this occurs without the "driving out" of the knowledge itself.

### EURIPIDES' DRAMATIZATION OF MOTIVATIONAL CONFLICT

In two tragedies by Euripides, the *Medea* and the *Hippolytus,* we find the situation of reason being overcome by passion and desire, which is so directly addressed to the problem of akrasia that it has been speculated that these tragedies form a part of a "dialogue" between Socrates and Euripides on the problem of akrasia.[21] The *Medea* was presented in 431 B.C. and the *Hippolytus* in 428. A comparison of the two tragedies on the themes that are relevant to akrasia will bring out the extent to which their message is anti-Socratic.

Medea has, in her eyes, been deserted by her husband Jason, in order to advance his position in the world. She carries through a plot to kill his newly betrothed replacement for her and she intends to murder her children by Jason as well, in order to complete her revenge. But as the time comes to kill the children, the joys and fulfillments of motherhood come vividly before her and, in great anguish, she vacillates between maternal love and the fury of revenge. Finally she says,

> Go. go! I am no longer able, no longer
> To look upon you. I am overcome by sorrow.

[21] See Snell, "Das frühste Zeugnis über Sokrates," *Philologus* XCVII (1948). Snell sees the *Medea* as starting the topic, Xenophon's *Mem.* iii.9.4 as giving Socrates' first reply, the *Hippolytus* as replying in turn, and Plato's *Prt.* as concluding this "Socratic" phase of discussion. E. R. Dodds discusses the sequence of "replies" critically on p. 187 and in n. 47, p. 199, of *The Greeks and the Irrational.* In n. 50, p. 200, he gives references to the theme of "the moral impotence of reason" in other works by Euripides. Snell gives fragments from the *Antiope* and the *Chrysippus* in n. 1, p. 133.

I know indeed what evil I intend to do,
But stronger than all my afterthoughts is my fury,
Fury that brings upon mortals the greatest evils.[22]

In the *Hippolytus* it is the queen, Phaedra, who under-
goes a similar conflict. She develops an overwhelming
passion for Hippolytus, the religiously chaste son of her
husband by another woman. Phaedra attempts to keep
her passion secret and even resolves to die rather than to
try to consummate it. The secret is discovered by a servant, and Phaedra speaks the following lines in telling of
her struggle:

Many a time in night's long empty spaces
I have pondered on the causes of a life's shipwreck.
I think that our lives are worse than the mind's quality
would warrant. There are many who know virtue.
We know the good, we apprehend it clearly.
But we can't bring it to achievement. Some
are betrayed by their own laziness, and others
value some other pleasure above virtue.
There are many pleasures in a woman's life—
long gossiping talkings and leisure, that sweet curse.
Then there is shame that thwarts us. Shame is of two kinds.
The one is harmless, but the other a plague.
For clarity's sake, we should not talk of "shame,"
a single word for two quite different things.[23]

[22] Ll. 1075–80. Warner translation. Although we shall be primarily concerned for the situation expressed in these lines, the conflict of feeling that leads up to them is not totally irrelevant.
H. D. F. Kitto has remarked that this conflict is "a theatrical struggle rather than a psychologically convincing one." See his *Greek
Tragedy*, p. 202. What "theatricality" there may be here is rather
part of the overriding style of the whole play: Jason is "theatri-
cally" pedantic and obtuse, the poison robe and crown are "theatrical," and what of the dragon-chariot at the end?

[23] Ll. 375–88. Grene translation. Snell sees a Socratic reference in this twofold sense of "shame." See pp. 130–32, *Philologus*,
XCVII (1948). In substantiating this reference, he refers in n. 1,
p. 131, to Xenophon, *Mem.* iv.5.9 ff. for the determination of the
value of an action through the higher value which it serves. The
passage is rather about the paradox of pleasure: those who incon-
tinently seek it get little, whereas those who are continent have
more and superior pleasures.

The first thing to clarify about these two characters is just what kind of a conflict they undergo. Medea's conflict-speech has been called the first decision-monologue, and there is a sense in which this may be true.²⁴ Medea is not torn by conflicting demands of authority as, for instance, the Orestes of Aeschylus is. But for neither Medea nor Phaedra is the moral issue in doubt. That is, neither is seeking a conclusion to a rational deliberation on what she ought to do. There may be some ambiguities as to the moral quality of the protestations of both, which we will discuss presently, but neither is trying to determine what the right thing to do might be. That is already known. Hence, in order to distinguish between these two kinds of conflict, we can call the conflict suffered by Medea and Phaedra a motivational rather than a moral conflict.

In the case of Medea, it is her βουλεύματα, translated by Warner as "afterthoughts," which are overcome by her θυμός, "fury." We should pause a moment over these βουλεύματα. At line 1048, in a moment of relenting in her intention to sacrifice the children, Medea bids farewell to βουλεύματα—in this case the plans for revenge. The βουλεύματα that are overcome by θυμός, then, might possibly be the plans, mentioned at line 1045, to take her children with her when she flees. What is of special interest here is that she might also have said that her maternal feelings were overcome by her fury, for it is certainly these feelings which are most intensely expressed in the preceding lines. But Euripides chooses to stress the βουλεύματα. But it is also possible that the βουλεύματα are neither her plans to take her children with her nor her sobering afterthoughts, but are rather her plans for revenge. In this case, line 1079 should be translated as "It is fury which determines my plans," taking κρείσσων in the sense of "mastery over" rather than "stronger than."²⁵ On this reading, the idea would be that although she knows better, her intentions are gov-

²⁴ See the discussion by Snell on pp. 124–30 of *Discovery*.
²⁵ I owe this suggestion to Professor Morton Smith.

erned by feeling rather than by knowledge. In the first reading she has a plan or intention, and Euripides is saying that an intention can be overcome by fury. In the second, she has knowledge, and Euripides is saying that knowledge is not sufficient for the formation of an intention. It is the second possibility that is most similar to the remarks made in the *Hippolytus*. There it is judgment, γνώμη, which fails to find realization.[26]

It is curious that although Phaedra is the victim of a possibly god-sent passion extreme enough to send her into delirium, she does not mention passion as a reason why judgment goes unfulfilled, but rather speaks of laziness, gossip, leisure, and shame.[27] She is, in effect, saying that women do not come to moral shipwreck because of some failure of their minds, or even because passion is too powerful to be stopped, but because they are simply too weak to carry out what they know to be the right course. This represents an even stronger opposition to the doctrine of the motivational sufficiency of reason than is presented in the *Medea*.

As if to make this emphasis more pointed, Euripides clarifies some of the ambiguity about the moral status of the protestations of his heroines which can be found in the *Medea*. Medea says she is overcome by κακά and that she knows what κακά she intends to do. Warner

[26] Γνώμη is mentioned repeatedly by Phaedra. At l. 240, she has wandered from γνώμης ἀγαθῆς. At l. 247, γνώμη is restored with anguish after her delirium. The crucial ll. 376 and 377 say that men do wrong οὐ κατὰ γνώμης φύσιν. At l. 391, she tells of the path of her γνώμη when her passion first occurred. At l. 1304, Artemis tells of Phaedra's vanquished γνώμη. For γνώμη, see Snell, *Die Ausdrucke für den Begriff des Wissens in der vorplatonischen Philosophie*, "Philologische Untersuchungen," XXIX (1924), especially 31–37. Γνώμη can mean either the intellectual capacity or the result of the exercise of that capacity and often it has a practical rather than a purely theoretical sense, according to Snell. This would make it very close to the English "judgment."

[27] Snell seems to miss this point. On p. 128 of *Discovery*, he has Phaedra say that we do not act on what we know "for we are in the grip of passion." The pleasures of leisured laziness are hardly the grip of passion.

translates the first as "sorrow" and the second as "evil," which presents the ambiguity nicely. At line 1243, she calls her actions δεινά . . . κακά, "fearful wrongs." But she has no conception of the rights of her children, only of how pitiable they are and of the joy they might bring her. It is a question, then, as to whether we should say that her resolutions represent truly moral decisions or not. With Phaedra, the moral element is considerably stronger, even if it is tempered by a certain amount of self-interest. At lines 245–50, she proclaims herself ashamed. At line 323, she calls her passion a "sin" (ἁμαρτεῖν), and at line 331, it is shameful (αἰσχρόν), as it is again at lines 404–5 (αἰσχρά, δυσκλέα). In lines 420 ff. she expresses a genuine concern for the interest of her husband and her children. One could find further evidence, but this should be enough to make clear the increased emphasis on the moral quality of Phaedra's γνώμη. The description of her struggle is all the more pointed for a doctrine of the motivational sufficiency of reason, once it has knowledge of the good.[28]

As a final clarification of the kind of conflict and the kind of failure of reason which are presented in these tragedies, we can compare the two heroines with two other figures who represent another kind of failure of reason. In the *Medea*, this is Jason, and in *Hippolytus*, the servant. Jason and the servant think of themselves as wise in the ways of the world and in what is good for men.[29] As with King Pentheus, the scope of their under-

[28] It is strange that we are not given in the *Hippolytus* any climactic scene of self-surrender by Phaedra. Her betrayal is indirect, through the action of the nurse, to which Phaedra never assents. It may be that Euripides shows us instead that very drifting into shipwreck which she mentions. Instead of taking the action which she once contemplated, namely suicide, she lectures her attendants, and so is caught up in the fatal movement of events.

[29] See Jason's long speech beginning at l. 522, in which he casts up the profit and loss of Medea's situation to show the wisdom of his plans. The servant seems at times to echo sophistic or philosophical themes. At ll. 190–98, she remarks how men "idly . . . drift, on idle stories carried." At l. 433, in which she tries to make Phaedra's resolve out to be impiety, she argues that everyone, in-

standing is revealed as catastrophically limited. But neither Medea nor Phaedra is limited in this way. So to speak, they are not blind to the moral realities which they face. In these two types of characters Euripides seems to be making two types of points about the limitation of reason: reason is insufficient to grasp the full truth about the forces that govern men's lives; and reason is insufficient to control men's behavior when it does grasp some important truth. Whether we are to go on, as has been urged, and attribute to Euripides a theory of the positive function of reason as issuing moral warnings and a theory of the need for moral enthusiasm, is not revealed to us in these two tragedies.[30] And since we are less interested in Euripides' own doctrine than in the challenge which he presents for the Socratic tradition, we will leave the matter there.[31]

Whether or not these characters of Euripides were created in explicit opposition to a position enunciated by Socrates, they pose a challenge to the kind of position we saw presented by Xenophon. If Medea is a possible character, then either knowledge is not sufficient for the formation of an intention, or intentions can be overthrown by anger. It is worth noticing that in the latter case this does not mean that there is some spasmodic outburst of uncoordinated movement, but rather that another set of plans and intentions replaces the first. Either way, the process of reaching a final decision is not ex-

---

cluding the gods, yields to Aphrodite—it is almost nature versus convention. On pp. 187–88 of *The Greeks and the Irrational* Dodds collects other passages from Euripides which suggest the nature-convention controversy. On p. 187, he notes the distinction we are presenting between the motivational and the cosmic limitations of reason.

[30] See Snell, *Discovery*, pp. 129–30.

[31] Nor will we go into the very interesting question as to whether Euripides means to suggest that the source of the actions of these two heroines lies outside themselves. Dodds rejects the view that Medea is possessed; see *The Greeks and the Irrational*, n. 44, p. 199. It is interesting that Phaedra herself thinks of her mother and her sister, relating her passion to a family curse, at l. 343. What we are to make of Aphrodite is, of course, no small question.

hausted by the process of weighing possible courses of action and drawing a conclusion. Euripides might also have made it explicit that some form of reason can as well work for evil as for good, since Medea certainly possesses cunning and art. If Phaedra is a possible character, we must add sexual passion to the number of nonrational forces which are stronger than reason. Furthermore, if what Phaedra says is true, it is not only the melodramatic passions which can frustrate the fulfillment of reason, it is so ordinary a condition as sheer laziness.

Xenophon implies that with the onset of passion or desire, the wisdom of the morally weak deserts them. Euripides shows us persons who give every sign of possessing wisdom of some sort at the time of decision, allowing for the ambiguity of Phaedra's "action." If we followed up the emphasis on the practicality of wisdom suggested by some passages in Xenophon and elaborated by Gould, we would have to deny the title of wisdom to the protestations of these persons, on the sole ground that they do not live up to what they say. This is hardly consistent with the compelling power of the good and the beautiful which further passages in Xenophon imply. Indeed, both in the doctrine that wisdom is narrowly practical and in the doctrine that without self-control the good and the beautiful cannot be known, Xenophon has all but granted everything Euripides would ask. If these positions were the sum total of the Socratic denial of akrasia, it would hardly be worth arguing, for the motivational supremacy of wisdom is maintained only by ensuring in it the conditions of wisdom. It is possible that something like this kind of subterfuge is what Socrates really argued, but it is more likely that the full force of the Socratic position is not to be found in Xenophon's compromises with psychological realism. We shall turn now to a much more uncompromising version of the Socratic position as presented by Plato in the *Protagoras*. It will help us to appreciate the philosophical problem confronted by Plato in certain of his other dialogues if we keep in mind the central contentions of Euripides: intentions, plans, judgment, sound moral belief, can all be overcome by passion and desire, and they can fail to find fulfillment because of laziness and weakness of character. These contentions would seem to imply that virtue cannot be wisdom alone and that reason is not motivationally sufficient.

### THE SOCRATIC DENIAL OF AKRASIA IN THE PROTAGORAS

It may be that the *Protagoras* contains a reply to Euripides' reply to a position Socrates held, and which we have preserved in Xenophon; or it may be that what Xenophon says about akrasia is some kind of garbled interpretation of the *Protagoras* itself. In any case, the Socrates of the *Protagoras* presents a clear and coherent assertion of the motivational supremacy of reason in the form of knowledge, and carries through a closely reasoned investigation of the phenomenon of akrasia, with the aim of showing that things are not what they may appear to be in this situation. The assertion of the supremacy of reason is contained in the following passage:

> Come, my good Protagoras, uncover some more of your thoughts: how are you in regard to knowledge (ἐπιστήμη)? Do you share the view that most people hold of this, or have you some other? The opinion generally held of knowledge is something of this sort—that it is not a strong or guiding or governing thing; it is not regarded as anything of that kind, but people think that, while a man often has knowledge in him, he is not governed by it, but by something else—now by passion, now by pleasure, now by pain, at times by love, and often by fear; their feeling about knowledge is just what they have about a slave, that it may be dragged about by any other force. Now do you agree with this view of it, or do you consider that knowledge is something noble and able to govern men, and that whoever learns what is good and what is bad will never be swayed by anything to act otherwise than as knowledge bids, and that intelligence (φρόνησις) is a sufficient succour for mankind? (352B–C)

Socrates' position is, of course, the latter one, and it is
Protagoras' position as well. After Protagoras agrees with
him, Socrates puts the issue once again:

> Now you know that most people will not listen to you and
> me, but say that many, while knowing what is best, refuse
> to perform it, though they have the power, and do other
> things instead. And whenever I have asked them to tell me
> what can be the reason of this, they say that those who
> act so are acting under the influence of pleasure or pain,
> or under the control of one of the things I have just men-
> tioned.[32]

Before we follow through Socrates' examination of
akrasia, we should pay attention to the version of the
situation which he has presented. Although he speaks of
knowledge being dragged about like a slave, he understands this as people knowing what is best and refusing
to do it. The Greek is οὐκ ἐθέλειν πράττειν, ἐξὸν αὐτοῖς:
"are not willing to do it, though they are able to." The
underlying assumption is that what people do, they
choose to do, and that when they fail to do what they
think is best, it is because they refuse to do so. If the purpose of the Euripidean position were to deny this underlying assumption, then what Socrates will say in the rest
of the *Protagoras* is simply irrelevant.

After presenting the problem and affirming his belief
in the sufficiency of knowledge and intelligence, Socrates
goes ahead to examine the experience called "being overcome by pleasure." In doing this, he utilizes the doctrine
that the good is pleasure, and we will eventually have to
ask what bearing this disconcerting maneuver may have
on the analysis of akrasia itself. The commonest examples of being overcome by pleasure concern food, drink,
and sex; and he argues that the wickedness in these matters lies in their painful consequences, just as the goodness of painful experiences, such as medical treatment,
lies in their pleasurable consequences. But on these

[32] 352D–E. These passages suggest that the intellectualist theory of motivation was far from being simply Greek common sense.

grounds it is obviously absurd to say that a man knowingly does evil because he is "driven and dazed by his
pleasures." This would amount to saying that a man does
evil, knowing it to be evil, because he is overcome by the
good. (355D) Some conception of quantity must be
adopted, and then the only possibility is that for the good
to be overcome by pleasure is for the greater pleasure to
be overcome by the lesser. The problem of akrasia can
now be stated clearly: How is it possible for men to be
such as always to choose the course of action which
yields the greatest total balance of pleasure over pain
and yet sometimes to choose the lesser total?

Put in this way, the answer is equally clear. There is a
systematic temporal illusion in the case of pleasures comparable to illusions of spatial perspective: imminent
pleasures appear greater in anticipation than do those in
the remote future. Akrasia, then, turns out to be ignorance, a special case of the power of appearance to mis-
lead. Such ignorance can only be overcome by an art of
measurement which "by showing us the truth would have
brought our soul into the repose of abiding by the truth
and so would have saved our life." (356D–E) And Socrates concludes his analysis thus:

> Well, the nature of this art or science we shall consider
> some other time; but the mere fact of its being a science
> will suffice for the proof which Protagoras and I are re-
> quired to give in answer to the question you have put to
> us. You asked it, if you remember, when we were agree-
> ing that there is nothing stronger than knowledge, and that
> knowledge, wherever it may be found, has always the up-
> per hand of pleasure or anything else; and then you said
> that pleasure often masters even the man of knowledge,
> and on our refusing to agree with you, you went on to ask
> us: Protagoras and Socrates, if this experience is not "being
> overcome by pleasure," whatever can it be, and what do
> you call it? Tell us. If on the spur of the moment we had
> replied "Ignorance," you would have laughed us to scorn:
> but now if you laugh at us you will be laughing at your-
> selves as well. For you have admitted that it is from defect

of knowledge that men err, when they do err, in their choice of pleasures and pains—that is, in the choice of good and evil; and from defect not merely of knowledge but of the knowledge which you have now admitted also to be that of measurement. And surely you know well enough for yourselves that the erring act committed without knowledge is done through ignorance. Accordingly "to be overcome by pleasure" means just this—ignorance in the highest degree. (357C–E)

One of the persistent questions about the *Protagoras* is whether Plato meant to profess, or whether he meant that Socrates had professed, the hedonism which is so ingeniously utilized in this analysis. Connected with this question is the larger one of whether we should take what is said in the *Protagoras* seriously. Certainly there is no doubt about the seriousness with which the problem of akrasia and the sufficiency of reason is treated in the dialogue itself. By correcting our hedonic perspective we are not only to increase our long-run profits, we are to "bring our soul into the repose of abiding by the truth" and we are to "save our life." Socrates and Protagoras agree that not only is knowledge noble and able to govern, but also that it is able to "come to the rescue" (βοήθειν) of man. These phrases point back to the opening scene of the dialogue, where Socrates reminds the young Hippocrates of the seriousness of trusting his soul to a teacher and absorbing his wares: "but you cannot carry away doctrines in a separate vessel: you are compelled, when you have handed over the price, to take the doctrine in your very soul by learning it, and so depart either an injured or a benefitted man."[33] But there is something odd about expressing a hedonistic morality in this way, at least unless the emphasis is upon escaping from pain rather than upon gaining positive

[33] 314B. For a recent review of the question of the seriousness of the *Protagoras*, concluding that Plato is serious and that he did, for a while at least, profess hedonism, see Tenkku, *The Evaluation of Pleasure in Plato's Ethics*, "Acta Philosophica Fennica," XI (1956), chapter III and especially pp. 44–59.

pleasures, as it does not appear to be here in the *Protagoras;* and what Plato has to say about pleasure elsewhere makes it seem strange that he should ever profess hedonism.

We are not going to settle these questions, but a few observations may be in order. (1) Despite various denunciations of bodily pleasures, Plato never underestimated the importance of pleasure in human life, and especially in the teaching of virtue. His thought culminates in the celebrated passage at *Laws* 653A–B, where pleasure and pain are said to be the forms under which virtue and vice are first present to children. And the teaching of virtue is, after all, the general subject of the *Protagoras.* If one were more concerned for the "unity of Plato's thought" than for "Plato's development," one might see the hedonism of the *Protagoras* as a kind of primer of virtue—much as hedonism is often used by teachers of ethics today. (2) If one looks to the treatment of Gorgias in the *Gorgias,* or the whole of traditional morality in the *Republic,* one can see that Plato discerned as the common presupposition of sophistic and traditional morality nothing other than hedonism. Though Protagoras is reluctant to be as rigorous as Socrates is, has he any other standard of value than hedonism?[34] And it should not be forgotten that it is within the framework of hedonism that the reality of akrasia is asserted. In effect, the claim of the many is that men are not governed by reason, but by pleasure. In effect, the reply of Socrates is that even if men pursue pleasure alone, they are still governed by reason; namely, by their beliefs and calculations as to what pleasures they will obtain.[35] And in effect, Socrates offers Protagoras a philosophical description of his own art: the correction of hedonic perspective. (3) It is true that the *Protagoras* is suffused with comedy; and the ending, especially, so clearly suggests the Protagorean doctrine of double argu-

[34] See what is said about popular temperance at *Phd.* 68E–69A.
[35] See G. M. A. Grube, *Plato's Thought,* pp. 221–23. Grube calls attention to the passage at *Grg.* 500A ff. as well.

ments that the whole thing can easily be read as a wonderful, high-spirited joke on Protagoras. But this would not preclude the teaching of serious doctrine, any more than the humor of the *Lysistrata* precludes a serious plea for peace, or that of the *Symposium* precludes the seriousness of Diotima's mysteries. But the comedy and the caricature suggest a certain critical distance of the writer from the subject, or at least a certain superiority to it. The argument at 359E–360, that war, since honorable, is good, and therefore, pleasant, while it may conduce to the conclusion that courage is wisdom, does not suggest whole-hearted devotion to hedonism.

Perhaps the soundest conclusion to carry away from the *Protagoras* is that whether or not Plato or Socrates ever professed hedonism, we are to take seriously the analysis of akrasia according to which it is equivalent to ignorance, and an ignorance which is explainable by the power of unmeasured appearance to deceive. The theme of hedonic perspective recurs in the *Philebus* at 41D–42C, and again in the *Laws* at 663B, once again in connection with a doctrine of hedonism. In the *Laws*, however, the hedonism is psychological rather than ethical. Whether or not imminent pleasures appear larger than distant pleasures, without the art of moral measurement, they must certainly appear the greater goods.

If we confront this position presented in the *Protagoras* with the one we have crystallized out of the *Medea* and *Hippolytus*, what must we say about the Socratic denial of akrasia? First, that Socrates supposes that even in the situation of akrasia, reason governs men in the sense that they act on their beliefs and calculations. Second, that although Socrates analyzes one situation which might be described as "being overcome by pleasure," he does not analyze the situation which Euripides presents. For Euripides' heroines do not miscalculate. If the Socratic analysis is to be true to them, it must explain how looming pleasures can upset calculations which have once been made, and to all appearances, made correctly. If Socrates assumes that a correct calculation once obtained cannot be shown to be incorrect, the program of construing akrasia as ignorance will become complex indeed. What we find in the thought of Plato (or in the later thought of Plato, if we take the *Protagoras* already to represent a Platonic development of Socratic doctrine) is a progressive coming to terms with these shortcomings of the Socratic analysis as measured against the psychological realism of Euripides.

## 12. PLATO'S *PROTAGORAS* AND EXPLANATIONS OF WEAKNESS

GERASIMOS SANTAS

Understanding the sorts of explanations that can be offered in cases of weakness (weakness of will, weakness of character, and moral weakness) is an important aspect of the philosophical problem of *akrasia*.[1] In a case of weakness a man does something that he knows or believes he should (ought) not do, or fails to do something that he knows or believes he should do, when the occasion and the opportunity for acting or refraining is present, and when it is in his power, in some significant sense, to act in accordance with his knowledge or belief. Because of the first of these characteristics, which are the *given* characteristics of cases of weakness,[2] it always makes sense to raise the question why the man acted in this way—that is, contrary to his knowledge or belief. But, aside from this, it is necessary to find a correct answer to it if we wish to understand the man's behavior and to reach a reasonable evaluative attitude toward the

Reprinted from the *Philosophical Review*, 75 (1966), pp. 3–33, by permission of the editors and the author.

[1] For recent discussions of explanations of weakness, see R. M. Hare, *Freedom and Reason* (Oxford, 1963), pp. 67–85; and Steven Lukes's criticism of Hare in "Moral Weakness," *Philosophical Quarterly*, 15 (1965). Lukes's criticism is perceptive, but neither he nor Hare goes much further than discussing phrases that suggest explanations, whereas what is needed most is an elucidation of the models of explanations that can be offered.

[2] The first and last of these characteristics are explicitly stated by Plato and Aristotle: *Prt.* 352–56, *Nic. Ethics* 1152A. Occasion and opportunity may be associated with circumstances that give rise to temptation and circumstances that make the object of the temptation available, respectively: one may be tempted by the sight or smell of food but the food may not be available, or it may be available but one has no desire for it. Both must be present to have a case of weakness (or strength), and both conditions are usually implicit in Plato's and Aristotle's discussions.

man. Finally, if we discover the sorts of explanations that are (and the sorts that are not) available in cases of weakness, we should be in a better position to understand the relation of knowledge of value (or value beliefs) to conduct.

In this paper I want to examine in some detail a long and elaborate argument that Plato offers in the *Protagoras* (352–56C) to the effect that certain explanations commonly offered in cases of weakness are untenable or absurd. This passage has been discussed often,[3] but the issues and difficulties that it raises about explanations of weakness have not been sufficiently appreciated; I shall try to show that Plato's argument is at the very least a serious challenge to those who think that the phenomenon of human weakness, though perhaps common enough and familiar enough, can be easily understood. In Section I, I set out the context and limitations of Plato's argument, and state the main questions that should be raised about it. In Section II, I try to reconstruct the argument as we find it in the text, and in the next section I indicate briefly how the argument may be freed from the severe limitations set to it and thus generalized. Finally, in Sections IV and V, I try to unravel the main ambiguities in Plato's argument, assess their consequences to the argument, and follow out their implications concerning

[3] Cf., e.g., J. P. Sullivan, "The Hedonism in Plato's *Protagoras*," *Phronesis*, VI (1961), 18–20; A. Sesonske, "Hedonism in the Protagoras," *Journal of the History of Philosophy*, I (1963); G. Vlastos, *Plato's Protagoras* (New York, 1956); D. Gallop, "The Socratic Paradox in the Protagoras," *Phronesis*, IX (1964). The first two papers try to account for the fact that Socrates (and Plato) makes his argument against weakness depend on hedonism which he elsewhere consistently attacks. Too much of the discussion has been centered on this at the expense of more important philosophical questions about the passage which have been raised by Professor Vlastos: the reconstruction, validity, and philosophical significance of Plato's argument against weakness. Although I disagree with Vlastos' interpretation I have learned more from his essay than I can begin to acknowledge. More recently, Gallop has also discussed the issues raised by Vlastos, but his interpretation seems to me wide of the mark.

different kinds of explanations in cases of weakness. Different sorts of explanations employed recently by philosophers and psychologists are discussed.

I

Toward the end of a lengthy discussion about the unity of the virtues, Socrates raises a (relatively) new issue within which the argument against explanations is set: the role of knowledge in action. At 352B he sets out before Protagoras two opposite hypotheses:

> (1) The opinion generally held of knowledge is something of this sort—that it is not a strong or guiding or governing thing; it is not regarded as anything of that kind, but people think that, while a man often has knowledge in him, he is not governed by it, but by something else—now by passion, now by pleasure, now by pain, at times by love, and often by fear.

and

> (2) knowledge is something noble and able to govern man, and that whoever learns what is good and what is bad will never be swayed by anything to act otherwise than as knowledge bids, and . . . intelligence is a sufficient succor of mankind.

Protagoras, asked to reveal his own thoughts on the subject, politely agrees with the second hypothesis, which represents Socrates' own view, but Socrates is set on examining the first hypothesis—the hypothesis of the many —and proceeds to restate it with some additions and distinctions:

> Now you know that most people will not listen to you and me, but say that (a) many, while knowing what is best, refuse to perform it, though they have the power, and do other things instead. And whenever I have asked them to tell me what can be the reason for this, they say that (b)

those who act so are acting under the influence of pleasure or pain, or under the control of one of the things I have just mentioned (352D–E).

In this restatement of the hypothesis of the many, Socrates has distinguished two parts: part (a) states that a certain phenomenon occurs, and part (b) is given as an explanation of the occurrence of that phenomenon. The significant point about this distinction is that Socrates proceeds to give an argument against (b), *not* (directly) against (a).[4] The conclusion of the argument that ends formally at 355B is *not* that no one acts contrary to what he knows to be best, but that (on the premises agreed on) the explanation "overcome by pleasure" has been reduced to absurdity. Of course, Socrates (and Plato) believe that part (a) of the hypothesis is false, and he asserts this at the beginning and the end of the argument (352B, 357D); these assertions indeed provide the wider context within which the argument presented between 352D and 355C is set, but it is not these assertions (the denial of weakness) that the argument attempts to prove, but the absurdity of the explanation of weakness.

Understanding the argument in this way—as an argument against (b)—is very different from understanding it as an argument against (a). Aside from the fact that this interpretation is faithful to the text, it enables us to avoid a general difficulty, noticed by Professor Vlastos in his excellent introduction to the *Protagoras*, a difficulty that would seem to doom the argument to failure from the outset. Commenting on Socrates' statements at 352A–C and 358D—statements which deny part (a) and which on the present interpretation form the wider context of the argument, *not* the conclusion of it—he writes:

The words which are italicized show quite well what kind of statement Socrates is making here: the kind which we would call an empirical one. *K*, like its humbler cousin, *C*,

---

[4] At 352E and again at 354E Socrates says explicitly that the argument is about (b).

purports to tell us a fact of human nature—the kind of matter of fact that can only be found out by observation.
Where then is the reference to such observation? Nowhere
in the whole of this elaborate argument. In the case of C
Socrates at least went through the motions of induction;
here not even this: he is quite content here with a purely
*deductive* proof of it. Now anyone who could excogitate
by pure deduction a fact of human nature would have to
be more than a master of argument—he would have to
be a wizard. And as Socrates is only human, we would not
be risking much if we were to predict that his attempt
will fail.[5]

I agree that it is difficult to see how one can show by a
"purely deductive proof" and no reliance on observations or empirical propositions that (a) is false. But there
is no similar difficulty in showing that, given the description of weakness—as given in part (a)—and the hedonistic hypothesis, then the explanation given in (b) is absurd or untenable; for there is at least a possibility that
the explanation in (b) is incompatible with the description of weakness and hedonism, and this of course could
be shown by a purely deductive proof or by logical analysis alone. In interpreting the argument in this way I am
not denying that Socrates was very much concerned to
convince Protagoras and the *hoi polloi* that (a) or some
version of it is false; indeed his motive perhaps for at-
tacking common explanations of weakness was to convince us that the weakness does not occur at all. But the
falsity of (a) does not follow logically from the absurdity
of the explanation (b); nor does Plato write that it does.
The most we can say is that the absurdity of the common
explanation paves the way to Socrates' own explanation,
and that if we become convinced of the absurdity of the
explanation (b) and of the other common explanations
as well, we may reasonably come to doubt the truth of
(a) or at least come to suspect its apparent innocence.

[5] *Plato's Protagoras,* ed. by G. Vlastos (New York, 1965),
p. xxxix. The italicized words referred to are: "To pursue what one
believes to be evil rather than what is good *is not in human nature.*"
K is the proposition that knowledge is virtue.

In any case, Plato may not succeed here in convincing us that weakness does not occur, but he may succeed in showing that there are some difficulties with the ways we commonly explain weakness.[6]

There are two other points worth noticing about the actual argument that Socrates presents between 352D and 355C, and they are worth noticing because they constitute limitations on the scope and generality of the argument.

The first limitation is that, as Vlastos has pointed out, Socrates argues only against *one* of the five explanations of weakness that he first mentioned; he argues that "overcome by pleasure" reduces to absurdity as an explanation of weakness, but he makes no clear move to show how his argument might be applied against the explanations "overcome by" fear, love, hate, and passion. His argument, then, even if entirely successful, can refute only part of the opinion of the many; they might still be right about people being overcome by fear, love, and so forth.

The second important limitation of the argument is that it depends on the hedonistic hypothesis elaborated by Socrates between 353D and 354E. Not only is Socrates aware of this, but he emphasizes it. At the end of this passage he says that "it is still possible to retract if you can somehow contrive to say that the good is different from pleasure, or the bad from pain." The argument then is not intended to show that "overcome by pleasure" is absurd as an explanation of weakness, but only that it is absurd if one assumes hedonism; that is, it only shows that a hedonist is logically prevented from giving such an explanation. And incidentally, it is quite clear that Plato can argue this without being himself a hedonist.[7]

[6] Here it is worth noting that Aristotle (*Nic. Ethics*, Bk. VII, chs. ii, iii) in a passage that refers us to the present argument in the *Prt.*, dismisses the question whether *akrasia* occurs, and concentrates on providing explanations that make its occurrence possible.

[7] This seems to me to settle the question whether "the hedonism of the *Protagoras*" is compatible with the antihedonism of the *Grg.* and other dialogues. As for the question why did Socrates use hedonistic premises in his argument, I see no mystery here at all, for

The point of setting out the context and limitations of Socrates' argument, aside from faithfulness to the text, is that we must, first, try to reconstruct and assess the soundness of the argument within its context and limitations. If the argument fails within these narrow bounds, we need go no further, aside from determining the mistakes it contains. But if it has some measure of success, as I shall try to show, then we can, and must, raise the question whether it can be freed from those limitations, whether it can be freed from the hedonistic hypothesis, and whether it can be brought to bear against the other explanations of weakness. This is the strategy I follow in this paper.

II

The argument that Socrates offers between 352B and 356C divides into three stages: (1) descriptions of cases of weakness and statements of the explanations commonly offered for the occurrence of weakness so described (352B–353D); (2) elaboration of the hedonistic hypothesis on which Socrates' argument depends (353D–355A); (3) substitution of "good" for "pleasure" in the explanation "overcome by pleasure," "painful" for "evil" in the description of the case, and argument that on either substitution the resulting explanation has been reduced to absurdity (355A–356C). (From 356C to 358E Socrates, apparently assuming that he has disposed of the explanations of the many, proceeds to elaborate his own familiar explanation, that what is called weakness is due to misestimation of the values, of the alternatives due to their nearness or remoteness in time.) I shall discuss each stage of the argument in turn, concentrating on stage (3), which is the source of all the important difficulties that arise in trying to understand and assess the success of

---

the argument is in fact a perfect example of Socrates' favorite mode of argument; it attempts to show that one belief of the many, that in certain cases men are "overcome by pleasure," is incompatible with another belief of theirs, the belief in hedonism.

Socrates' argument. In doing this, I shall stay close to the text, but at the same time I shall give Plato the benefit of the doubt in cases of ambiguity and incompleteness of expression. My aim in this section of the paper is to reconstruct the argument so that any success that it may have, however limited, can be brought out, the only limitations in this being the text and the nature of the case.

In stage (1) Socrates offers four different descriptions of cases of weakness, and lists five possible explanations of cases so described,[8] but at the beginning of stage (3) of the argument Socrates picks out one of these descriptions and matches it with the explanation "overcome by pleasure," and his subsequent argument about the absurdity of the explanation concerns this pair:

> It is often the case that a man, knowing the evil to be evil [knowing bad things to be bad things], nevertheless commits it [does them], when he might avoid it [them], because he is driven and dazed[9] by his pleasures (355B).

The sorts of cases that the many have in mind when they give this sort of explanation, according to Socrates, are those in which a man is overcome by the pleasures of "food or drink or sexual acts" (353C).[10] There are obvious ambiguities in Socrates' description of the case just quoted. In one sort of case a man may know (believe) that what he does (A) is bad, but he may also know that the alternatives to A open to him (B or C) are worse. This clearly is a case of doing the lesser of several evils, not a case of weakness. To get the latter we must suppose that the man thinks that either B or C is a good or at least a lesser evil than A; in short, we must suppose that he thinks that what he does is *bad in comparison to*

---

[8] Cf. 352B for the explanations, and 352D, 353C, 355B for the descriptions.

[9] One of the alternative phrases to "overcome" that Socrates uses. For a discussion of these, cf. final section of this article.

[10] The pleasures of food, drink, and sex are the proper objects of weakness according to Aristotle (*Nic. Ethics*, Bk. III, ch. x, and Bk. VII, ch. iv).

*the alternatives*. In a second sort of case a man may think
of the alternatives of what he is doing (*A*) as simply not
doing or avoiding *A* (rather than doing something else),
and he may think of the value of not doing *A* as simply
the absence of the value contained in doing *A* (nothing
lost and nothing gained). Here of course the man may
think that *A* contains only good, or only evil, or both
good and evil. In the last (mixed type) case, he may
think that the good outweighs the evil (so that *A* is *good
on the whole*) or the converse (*bad on the whole*), or
that neither outweighs the other. It is in fact this mixed
type of case that Socrates seems to be discussing, since
throughout the passage he finds it necessary to compare
with each other only the values contained in what the
agent does, not the value of what he does with the value
of the alternatives open to him. And here quite clearly
we must suppose that the case Socrates is considering is
one in which the man knows that what he does is *bad on
the whole*.[11]

In stage (2) of the argument we are invited to suppose that the people who give the explanation "overcome by pleasure," the *hoi polloi*, are hedonists. What
kind of hedonists? We do not have to classify them.[12]
It is sufficient to notice that the following points about
them are agreed to by Socrates and Protagoras. (1)
When the *hoi polloi* assert that something which they
say is pleasant is also bad, the only reason they can give
is that it results in pain which outweighs the pleasure (so
that it is painful on the whole); and when they judge

[11] Within the second sort of case, if what a man does is bad
on the whole, then it is also bad in comparison to the alternatives
since the latter are thought of as nothing lost and nothing gained.

[12] J. P. Sullivan (*op. cit.*) makes out a good case that both ethical and psychological hedonism are involved. We can add the following linguistic evidence for Sullivan's view. In eliciting hedonism
from the many (353D–354E) Socrates introduces his questions
with two sorts of verbs: (a) "call," "say," "assert," in questions
such as "Why do you . . . such and such good (bad)?"; (b) "pursue" and "avoid" in "Do you . . . pleasure (pain)?" The answers
he gives to the questions introduced by verbs in (a) clearly suggest
ethical hedonism, those in (b) psychological.

something which they say is painful to be good the only
reason they can give is that it results in pleasure which
outweighs the pain (so that it is pleasant on the whole)
(354C–E). (2) The *hoi polloi* pursue pleasure as a good,
and avoid pain as an evil (354C). (3) The *hoi polloi*
cannot contrive to say that the good is different from
pleasure and the bad from pain (if they could the argument would not go through) (355A). (4) According to
the hedonism of the *hoi polloi* we have two things and
four names: the names "good," "bad," "pain," and "pleasure" (the point being that "good" and "pleasure" are
names for one and the same thing, and similarly with the
other pair). In the next stage of the argument Socrates
indeed proceeds to *substitute* "good" for "pleasure" and
"painful" for "evil."[13]

We come now to the final stage (3) of the argument
(355C–356C), by far the most difficult. Plato's text here
seems full of obscurities and ambiguities, but there are a
few signposts in it, which have not been sufficiently noticed and which will help us to a sound interpretation of
the passage and an appreciation of Plato's argument. The
first of these is that at the beginning of this stage of the
argument, having already said that without assuming
hedonism his argument does not go through, Socrates
says:

> I tell you that if this is so [that is, if we assume the hedon-
> ism described above], the argument becomes absurd, when
> you say that it is often the case that a man, knowing the
> evil to be evil, nevertheless commits it, when he might
> avoid it, because he is driven and dazed by his pleasures.

The complete dependence on hedonism in which Socrates places his argument against the explanation "overcome (or driven and dazed by) pleasure" indicates

---

[13] It looks as if we must suppose that the agent, as well as the
*hoi polloi*, is a hedonist since some of Socrates' substitutions are
within intensional or referentially opaque contexts; thus at 355E, in
the sentence "He knows it to be bad" he substitutes "painful" for
"bad."

clearly not only that this explanation is to be reconstructed along hedonistic lines but also that the alleged
absurdity is to be found in a conjunction of the explanation and hedonism, not simply in the explanation. Second, shortly after the above passage, Socrates begins the
long paragraph which contains stage (3) of the argument by announcing:

> The absurdity of all this will be manifest if we refrain from
> using a number of terms at once, such as pleasant, painful,
> good, and bad; and as there appeared to be two things let
> us call them by two names—first good and evil, and then
> later on, pleasant and painful.

Socrates completes both of these substitutions by the end
of this long paragraph, and after that (356C) the absurdity of the explanation "overcome by pleasure" is not
even mentioned once. This suggests quite clearly that the
absurdity that Socrates has in mind must be sought in
the text of this paragraph, not in later text (when Socrates elaborates his own explanation) as some writers have
supposed.[14] Finally, though in several places the expressions that Socrates uses that have been translated by "because he is overcome by pleasure" are ambiguous and
could be rendered by "being overcome by pleasure," in
two passages (352D–E and 355C) Socrates makes it perfectly clear that being overcome by pleasure is given by
the many as the reason or cause (*aition, to dia ti*) of the
behavior of acting contrary to one's knowledge; and
hence "*because* he is overcome by pleasure" is the correct translation of the expressions that Socrates uses, suggesting as it does that "overcome by pleasure" is given as
an explanation of the behavior of acting contrary to one's

---

[14] Gallop (*op. cit.*, pp. 119–21) suggests that in order to see the
absurdity that Socrates has in mind, we must go all the way to
357D–E, but this does not account for what Socrates does and
what he says he does in 355B–356C. The two entailments that Gallop gives (p. 121) are not in the text, and do not hold unless we
add psychological hedonism in the premises; but once we do that
we obtain the absurdity and need not bother to go beyond 356C.

knowledge. The upshot is that—though Socrates does not *always* say this during stage (3) of his argument—it is the statement "Sometimes men do what they know (or believe) is bad, when they can avoid it, *because* they are overcome by pleasure" that Socrates argues is absurd; not the statement "Sometimes men do what they know (or believe) is bad, when they can avoid it, *and* (yet) they are overcome by pleasure."[15] These two statements are of course of different logical form; in conjunction with hedonism the former may turn out upon analysis to contain an absurdity, while the latter may not. Moreover, the former directs our attention to the fact that Socrates is arguing against an explanation, not simply against a statement of fact—an explanation that needs reconstruction.

These preliminaries out of the way, we come now to the difficult matter of locating the absurdity that Socrates has in mind; it is worth giving in full here Socrates' argumentation (following the last quotation) during the first substitution:

Let us then lay it down as our statement, that a man does evil in spite of knowing the evil of it. Now if someone asks us: Why? we shall answer: Because he is overcome. By what? the questioner will ask us; and this time we shall be unable to reply: By pleasure—for this has exchanged its name for "the good." So we must answer only with the words: Because he is overcome. By what? says the questioner. The good—must surely be our reply. Now if our questioner chance to be an arrogant person he will laugh and exclaim: What a ridiculous statement, that a man does evil, knowing it to be evil, and not having to do it, because he is overcome by the good! Is this, he will ask, because the good is not worthy of conquering the evil in you, or because it is worthy? Clearly we must reply: Because it is not worthy; otherwise he whom we speak of as overcome by pleasures would not have offended. But in what sense, he might ask us, is the good unworthy of the bad, or the

[15] Without realizing it, Gallop slips from the first to the second statement (*ibid.*, pp. 118, 120) and argues that there is nothing absurd about the second; this of course does not show that there is nothing absurd about the first.

bad of the good? This can only be when the one is greater and the other smaller, or when there are more on the one side and fewer on the other. We shall not find any other reason to give. So it is clear, he will say, that by "being overcome" you mean getting the greater evil in exchange for the lesser good. That must be agreed.

Socrates is here discussing a case of doing something or avoiding it (say, eating another serving of Athenian pastries or refusing to do so) where doing the thing in question contains both good and bad (harm and benefit) or both pleasure and pain (say, the pleasure of eating the pastries and the subsequent indigestion). Socrates is trying to give an analysis of "overcome by good" so that it becomes absurd, on the hedonistic premises already agreed on, as a reason or cause of weakness. Vlastos has correctly pointed out that "worthy" (*axion*) is used by Socrates here as a value term, so that the good (benefit, pleasure) contained in a course of action is "worthy of conquering" the evil (harm, pain) also contained in it if and only if the good exceeds the evil in quantity so that the course of action is good on the whole.[16] Once we see this, it becomes clear from the two questions that Socrates raises and himself answers in this passage that he is taking "overcome by good" in *one of two possible senses* —and this indeed is the most important ambiguity of the whole argument. In one sense (1) a man who does something that contains both good (benefit) and bad (harm) may be said to be "overcome by the good" if the good is worthy of conquering the bad; that is, if the good outweighs the bad. In another sense (2) a man in similar circumstances may be said to be overcome by the good (pleasure) if his desire for the good (pleasure) that the course of action contains is *stronger* than his fear of (desire to avoid) the bad (pain) it contains. Socrates ignores the possibility of taking "overcomes" in sense (2), and this is a serious fault in the argument. We must not be

[16] Cf. also H. Sauppe and J. A. Towle, *Plato's Protagoras* (Boston, 1892), p. 152.

satisfied with this criticism, however; we need to follow out the argument with *each* of (1) and (2) if we are to appreciate the issues involved, and for the moment we must follow Socrates. Now once we grant Socrates' interpretation of "overcome by . . . ," the explanation of the *hoi polloi* can be interpreted in three different ways, all untenable:

$D_1$. Sometimes a man does something which is bad, knowing it to be bad, when he can avoid doing it

because

$E_1$. the good contained in what he does is worthy of conquering—that is, outweighs—the bad contained in what he does.

$E_2$. the good contained in what he does is worthy of conquering—that is, outweighs—the bad contained in what he does and the man knows this.

$E_3$. the man takes (chooses, prefers, decides to take) the (known) greater harm (evil) contained in what he does in return for securing (as the price of) the (known) lesser good contained in what he does.

Socrates does not explicitly separate the first two interpretations but this does not damage his argument, for both $E_1$ and $E_2$ contradict the description of the case; this is what Socrates is pointing out when he says that we must suppose that the harm contained in what the man does outweighs the benefit, otherwise the man would not have erred or (in our terms) he would not have done something which was *bad on the whole;* by hypothesis our man does something that contains good and bad where the bad outweighs the good and by hypothesis again he knows this. Once we rephrase the description so as to make this clear, the conjunction of the description with either $E_1$ or $E_2$ is self-contradictory:

$D_2$. Sometimes a man does something which contains good and bad where the bad outweighs the good, knowing

that this is so, when he can avoid doing it, because
$E_1$ and/or $E_2$.

There is one way in which $E_1$ can be saved, and that is
by adding "the man thinks or believes" in front of it, and
deleting "knowing it to be bad on the whole" from the
description; but this way out is Socrates' own, and impossible for the many, for it amounts to a denial of weakness, since the man is now acting in accordance, and indeed on the basis of, his value beliefs (though mistaken
ones, of course). We may notice that $E_1$ and $E_2$ would
not contradict $D_2$ if "good" had not been substituted for
"pleasure" in $E_1$ and $E_2$. Similarly with the second set of
substitutions. Here we see clearly what exactly ethical
hedonism contributes to Socrates' argument.

Explanation $E_3$ does not contradict the description.
The absurdity it involves consists in $E_3$ (considered as
an explanation of the case described in $D_2$) contradicting one of the principles of the hedonism of the *hoi
polloi;* but before we go into this we must consider more
carefully the line in Plato's text of which $E_3$ is a translation.[17] This line is obscure mainly because of two difficulties, only the first of which has been resolved by writers on the passage. Gallop points out correctly that the
preposition *anti,* normally rendered "instead of" or "in
exchange of," cannot be so rendered here because both
these expressions suggest that the agent does not "take"
the good or benefit contained in the case, whereas quite
clearly Socrates is discussing a mixed case where the
course of action the agent follows contains both harm
and benefit (this is made quite explicit at 353C among
other places). Following J. L. Stocks, Gallop correctly
suggests that we take *anti* in the sense of "as the price of"
or "in return for securing," and I follow this rendering
which enhances our understanding of the argument.

The second and more serious difficulty is how to understand the crucial verb *lambanein* in this line (this is the

[17] δῆλον, ἄρα, φήσει, ὅτι τὸ ἡττᾶσθαι τοῦτο λέγετε, ἀντὶ
ἐλαττόνων ἀγαθῶν μείζω κακά λαμβάνειν.

verb that replaces "overcome" in the whole sentence; this replacement I shall discuss later); it has been translated as "gets," "takes," "chooses."[18] Now *lambanein,* and its literal translation "take," in the present context, may be understood in either one (or both) of two different ways: to refer to (1) what the agent in fact does, the actual execution of the action which contains more harm than benefit (say, the man's actual reaching for, taking hold of, and eating the pastries), or (2) to what the agent seeks, chooses, or possibly decides or prefers to do. In the latter case the use of the verb would introduce a referentially opaque or intensional context; in the former case it would not.[19] There are several excellent reasons for rejecting (1) and adopting *lambanein* in sense (2) as the correct interpretation of the text. The major reason against (1) is that if we were to understand *lambanein* in the sense of (1), then E3 would not be an explanation at all, for it would simply (do nothing more than) *repeat* part of what we already have in the description of the case, namely that the man does what (he knows) is bad on the whole. It is not that E3 so interpreted involves absurdity or contradicts hedonism; it is not an explanation at all. This is not what Plato is talking about.[20] The major reason in favor of understanding *lambanein* in the sense "seeks to" or "chooses" is that it enables us to see the relevance of what Socrates proceeds to do immediately after this line when he takes up the second substi-

[18] *Lambanein* can also mean "to receive," "to accept," and possibly even "to prefer."

[19] At 356D *lambanein* is coupled with *prattein* (καὶ πράττειν καὶ λαμβάνειν); unless we take this to be mere repetition, the addition of *lambanein* suggests an intensional aspect. E. G. Sihler, in *The Protagoras of Plato* (New York, 1881), p. 127, has noticed that this pair is parallel to another pair five lines later: καὶ ἐν ταῖς πράξεσιν καὶ ἐν ταῖς αἱρέσεσιν, the last term corresponding to *lambanein,* again suggesting that *lambanein* is to be taken in an intensional sense.

[20] A second reason against the interpretation of E3 with *lambanein* in sense (1) is that the preposition *anti* cannot with good sense be taken with a verb that refers only to the execution of an action (behavior divorced from any intensional element).

tution, and to bring out the absurdity that Socrates is talking about. On the second substitution we obtain:

> D3. Sometimes a man does something which is painful on the whole, knowing that this is so, when he can avoid doing it,

because

> E4. he takes (chooses, prefers, decides to have) the (known) greater pain contained in what he does in return for securing the (known) lesser pleasure.

Socrates repeats once more interpretation (1) of "overcome," and immediately after that proceeds to elaborate a principle which is implied by the hedonism of the *hoi polloi* (which we may remember is a premise of the whole argument) and which contradicts the explanation *E3* once we take *lambanein* in the sense of "seeks," "chooses," or "prefers":

> For if you weigh pleasant things against pleasant, the greater and the more are always to be preferred [*leptea*]: if painful against painful, then always the fewer and the smaller. If you weigh pleasant against painful, and find that the painful are outbalanced (outweighted) by the pleasant—whether the near by the remote or the remote by the near—that action must be (is to be) done to which the pleasant are attached; but if the pleasant are outweighed by the painful, that action is not (must not) be done (356B–C).[21]

[21] Ληπτέα and πρακτέα "are to (or must) be preferred" and "are to (or must) be done"—need not be taken in a sense in which they entail "*will* be preferred" and "will be done." They should be taken in the sense of "will be preferred *if* psychological hedonism is true (all men desire or seek to maximize [their] pleasures and/or minimize [their] pains)," and in the sense of "will be done *if* psychological hedonism is true and the agent knows, has the opportunity and ability, and is not prevented." Gallop's supposition that Socrates needs (for his argument) the first sense of ληπτέα and πρακτέα is quite unfounded (*op. cit.*, pp. 128–29). People have failed to appreciate that Socrates takes (quite correctly once we grant his sense of "overcome") the explanation "overcome by

The very last part of this hedonistic principle contradicts directly the explanation of the *hoi polloi* in its last substitution; and a similar principle, obtained by substituting "good" for "pleasant" and "bad" for "painful" in the above principle, contradicts directly the explanation of the *hoi polloi* that is obtained by the first substitution (that is, $E_3$). This indeed is the absurdity that Socrates is talking about. But in order to appreciate this we must see at once that the hedonistic principle elaborated by Socrates does *not* assert a connection between a man's evaluations or ranking of the alternatives before him (the immediate results of the "weighing" that Socrates is talking about) and his behavior (the execution of a particular action), but rather a connection between his evaluations and what (presumably as a result of the evaluations) he seeks or chooses to do. If Socrates' hedonistic principle were interpreted as asserting the former connection, Socrates would indeed at this point be begging the wider issue at stake within which the argument against explanations is set: the relation of knowledge to action. But Socrates need not rely on this. All that he needs at this stage is the latter connection, between a man's evaluations or rankings of the alternatives and what he seeks or chooses (decides, prefers) to do.

This interpretation of the hedonistic principle on which Socrates relies to obtain the absurdity, is perfectly consistent with—indeed it is suggested by—the psychological hedonism that Socrates and Protagoras earlier attribute to the masses: people "pursue pleasure as being a good and avoid pain as being an evil" (354C). "Pursue" and "avoid" (*diokein* and *pheugein*) must be understood to refer to one's seeking to obtain pleasures and seeking to avoid pains, not to one's actually obtaining pleasures

---

pleasure" to be an explanation of behavior in terms of what men seek or desire to do, not in terms of what they actually do (cf. n. 23); and consequently, in order to obtain contradictions, all that he needs is a principle only as to what men seek or desire to do, not what they in fact do.

and successfully avoiding pains.[22] The principle asserted
is *not* that (1) people always act in a way that maximizes
their pleasures and/or minimizes their pains, but that
(2) people always seek to act in such a way as to maximize pleasure and/or to minimize pain, where "seek" is
clearly opaque. Principle (1) is clearly and obviously
false, since people often make mistakes, or lack the opportunity or the ability, or are prevented from maximiz-
ing and/or minimizing their pleasures. And it is clear
that the psychological hedonism on which Socrates is
relying here would employ (2), not (1), as a principle
of explanation of human behavior. A typical explanation
along these lines would include (2) as the operative
principle, statements about the agent's knowledge or estimate of the amounts of pleasures and pains involved in
the alternatives before him, and possibly statements
about opportunity and ability to do or avoid the behavior
at issue.[23] What Socrates has shown is that on the as-

[22] At 356 φεύγειν (*pheugein*) is coupled with μὴ πράττειν and
contrasted with *lambanein* (not πράττειν) of the pair in the previous line, thus suggesting that *pheugein* introduces an intensional
element. Cf. also n. 19.

[23] A model explanation along the lines suggested by the hedonism that Socrates attributes to the masses:

Why did S do A at $t_1$?
(1) S did A at $t_1$.
because
(2) All men seek to maximize their pleasures and/or minimize their
pains.
and
(3) S knew (believed) at $t_1$ that A would maximize his pleasures
and not-A (avoiding A) would not (or A is pleasant on the whole
and not-A is not).
This model (Model I) may be the model that Plato has in mind
and it may properly be called a teleological model. It is to be noticed that (2) and (3) do *not* logically entail (1); this model does
not satisfy Hempel's requirements for a scientific explanation.
  Now this may happen: one may argue that only a limited number of factors can account for the possibility of (2) and (3) being
true and (1) being false—say, lack of physical ability to carry out
the action (e.g., the man does not swim or ride a bike or is blind),

sumption of hedonism (ethical and psychological), one explanation of weakness commonly given by the masses, "overcome by pleasure," reduces to absurdity in the sense that (once we make the substitutions allowed by ethical hedonism and interpret "overcome" in the sense indicated) it contradicts the very principle of psychological hedonism which is universally employed by hedonists in the explanation of behavior.

In summarizing this section of the paper, we may say that Socrates is indeed successful in reducing the explanation of weakness commonly given by the masses, "overcome by pleasure," to absurdity provided (1) that we allow him as premises the combination of ethical and psychological hedonism that he attributes to the masses, (2) that we grant him his interpretation of "overcome," and (3) that we understand the main verbs used in the various statements of psychological hedonism ("take," "pursue," "avoid") in an opaque sense. But the success of Socrates' argument is clearly very limited. To begin with, as an argument against non-Socratic (and non-

---

lack of opportunity, or, finally, external, physical coercion. Now on the basis of *this* one might argue that (2) implies a stronger generalization: (2′) Whenever a man is faced with two or more alternatives and he has the physical ability and the opportunity to do either and is not physically coerced to do any, he will do the one which he knows or believes at the time will maximize his pleasures and/or minimize his pains.

(2′) together with appropriate factual premises entails (1), and makes it possible to have, in logical form, a deductive type explanation of a certain sort (II). Whether Socrates would go on to attribute (2′) as well as (2) to hedonists is not clear; what is clear from the text is, first, that he does not in fact do so, and second that he does not need to for his argument. For his argument all that he needs to suppose is that hedonists hold (2) and that their model of explanation of behavior is (I). For once "overcome by . . ." is interpreted in Socrates' way, the explanation contradicts (2), and that is enough. For a recent discussion of attempts to reduce teleological explanation (I) to those of type II, cf. I. Scheffler, *The Anatomy of Inquiry* (New York, 1963), pp. 88–110. Several variants of teleological explanations are implicit in the patterns of practical inference that G. H. von Wright discusses in "Practical Inference," *Philosophical Review* LXXII (1963), 159–79.

early-Platonic) explanations of weakness, Socrates' argument is limited *to* "overcome by pleasure" and *by* its hedonistic premises; what about the other explanations Socrates mentioned at the outset, and what about any of these explanations offered by nonhedonists? In the second place, what happens to Socrates' argument and, more generally, to the explanations commonly given by the masses, when we interpret "overcome" in the sense Socrates has ignored—that is, the sense in which "overcome" refers to the relative *strength* of the desires (feelings, passions) for or against the alternatives before the agent (rather than to the relative values of the alternatives)? Finally, why should Socrates (and Plato) have ignored this important, and indeed more plausible, sense of "overcome"? In the remaining sections of this paper I take up each of these questions in turn.

### III

Can Socrates' argument against "overcome by pleasure," as reconstructed above, be generalized so as to apply to the other explanations originally mentioned by Socrates—"overcome by" passion, love, pain, fear? And can Socrates' argument be "freed" from its hedonistic premises, in the sense that some other plausible Platonic non-question-begging premises can be found which can be successfully substituted for the hedonistic premises? If we can show that the answers to these questions are affirmative, we thereby show that the success of Socrates' argument is not so limited after all, and that his argument is of some general significance.

I shall try to show in *one move* that the answers to both questions are affirmative by constructing an argument, parallel to Socrates', against the explanation "overcome by fear" without relying on hedonistic premises. The case of weakness and its explanation before us now is as follows:

Sometimes a man fails to do something which is good, and

> which he knows to be good, when it is in his power to
> do it,

because

he is overcome by fear.

The main reason I have selected the explanation "overcome by fear" is that Socrates later on in the *Protagoras*,
when he begins a discussion of courage at 358D, provides
us with a definition of fear:

> Well, I said, is there something you call dread or fear?
> And is it—I address myself to you, Prodicus—the same as
> I have in mind—something I describe as an expectation of
> evil, whether you call it fear or dread?

In the argument we are about to construct, this definition of fear can take the place that ethical hedonism had
in Socrates' argument: that is, if granted as a premise in
the new argument, it allows us to substitute "expectation
of evil" for "fear" in the explanation:

> Sometimes a man fails to do something which is good, and
>     which he knows to be good, when it is in his power to
>     do it,
>
> because
>
> he is overcome by the evil he expects.

Socrates can now argue that this explanation is absurd for
reasons similar to the ones we attributed to him for arguing that the explanation obtained after the first substitution in his own argument is absurd; that was, it may be
remembered:

> Sometimes a man does something which is bad, knowing
>     that it is bad, when it is in his power to avoid it
>
> because
>
> he is overcome by the good.

To see the parallel absurdity of the explanation "over-come by the evil he expects" we need do only two things: eliminate the ambiguities of the statement, and indicate what principle is to take the place and perform the function of psychological hedonism. Eliminating the ambiguities (that is, eliminating interpretations analogous to $E_1$ and $E_2$ for analogous reasons) we obtain:

> Sometimes a man fails to do something which is good on the whole, knowing that it is good on the whole—that is, knowing that the good that it contains outweighs the evil (bad) that it contains—when it is in his power to do it

because

> he seeks to (chooses, prefers, decides to) avoid the greater good in return for (as the price of) avoiding the lesser evil.

Well, what principle can take the place of psychological hedonism here? A principle, which Socrates (and Plato) argues for in many early dialogues,[24] and which can be assumed here without begging any of the questions at issue: that every man desires or seeks (pursues) to get good things and seeks or desires to avoid getting bad or evil things; and the consequent principle that everyone pursues (or desires to do) things which are good on the whole or good in comparison to the alternatives, and seeks to avoid things that are bad in comparison to the alternatives and/or bad on the whole. It is this last part of the principle that contradicts the explanation "over-come by fear" as reduced above.

IV

What happens to Socrates' argument against explanations of weakness and, more important, what happens to

[24] Cf., e.g., *Men.* 77B–78B, *Grg.* 468C, and G. Santas, "The Socratic Paradoxes," *Philosophical Review*, LXXIII (1964), 147–64.

these explanations themselves when we take "overcome by . . ." to refer to the relative *strengths* of the agent's desires for and against the course of action before him?

Let us begin by noticing a point in the argument that we have so far ignored. At 356A, during the second substitution at the last stage of the argument, Socrates briefly raises and answers an objection to his argument:

> For if you should say: But, Socrates, the *immediately* pleasant differs widely from the *subsequently* pleasant or painful, I should reply: Do they differ in anything but pleasure and pain? That is the only distinction. Like a practice weigher, put pleasant things and painful on the scales, and with them the *nearness* and *remoteness*, and tell me which count for more [italics mine].

On the basis of Socrates' answer here, the immediately subsequent passage, and the analogy of size at 356D, we can confidently interpret Socrates' answer as follows. This feature of the case, the pleasure being near in time and the pain remote in the future, does indeed make a difference in the explanation, it is not an irrelevant feature; but the only difference this feature can make is a difference in pain or pleasure or rather in the quantities of pleasure and pain. It is not, however, a difference in the *actual* quantities of pleasure and pain involved in the case (we are not to suppose that the further the pain is in the future the smaller it will be!), but in the *estimated* or *believed* (by the agent) quantities of pleasure and pain. This answer leads Socrates to *his own* explanation of the case, elaborated after the last stage of the argument we have examined: that just as in the case of size and variation of distance, so here also—because the pleasure is near the agent in time and the pain far he misestimates the quantities and supposes that the pleasure outweighs the pain; so that he was acting in accordance with, indeed on the basis of, his hedonistic principle, even though he made a mistaken application of it. Socrates' answer to the objection and his own explanation are of course once more predicated on the assumption that "overcome by pleasure" must refer to the pleasure outweighing the pain (in the agent's estimate).

But it is possible to give quite a different answer to Socrates' question—not an answer that Plato rejects, but one which he seems to ignore. We may suppose, without contradicting anything that Plato says: (a) that the agent, Agathon, knowing or believing what he did, had a desire for the pleasure he expected from eating the pastries and a desire to avoid (or a fear of) the pain he also expected afterward; (b) that these two desires (or the desire and the fear) may be considered as conflicting desires, and conceived as causes; (c) that these desires, considered as causes of behavior, can be supposed to have degrees of causal strength. Making the common additional assumption which is usually treated as a kind of law, that the behavior that issues from conflicting desires is that in accordance with the stronger desire (or the subject always acts in accordance with the stronger desire), we can now construct a causal explanation of our case as follows:

(1) Agathon was faced with the alternatives of eating or not eating Athenian pastries.

(2) Agathon had a desire to eat the pastries and a desire to avoid eating (or a fear of eating) the pastries.

(3) Agathon's desire to eat and desire not to eat the pastries (or the fear of eating) are conflicting desires.

(4) No other (interfering) desires or motives were present that were connected with the two alternatives.

(5) In every case of conflicting desires (and no interfering motives or external forces) the subject satisfies (acts in accordance with) the stronger desire.

(6) Agathon's desire to eat the pastries was stronger than his desire not to eat them.[25]

(7) Agathon ate the pastries.

[25] This premise could be inferred from the fact that the pleasure of eating is near and the pain far, if it could be established that, in general, strength of desire varies (in some consistent way) with distance (space and/or time) of the object of the desire from the agent.

The phrase "overcome by pleasure" is now understood as a shorthand for this explanation, and in particular as referring to (6) and (5).

Explanations of this kind—that is, those that use (5) or some version of it as the main explanatory principle —are always logically relevant to cases of weakness (even though we may sometimes prefer other kinds of explanations) since conflicting motivations are characteristic of such cases, whether the conflicting motives be practical beliefs (or knowledge) and desires, as in Plato, or calm and violent passions, as in Hume.[26]

It should be noticed at once that an explanation of this kind can be perfectly respectable provided that we have ways of determining the relative strength of the conflicting desires independently of knowledge or information as to what action ensues from the conflict.[27] This condition (let us call it A) *must* be satisfied; otherwise, if our only way of telling which desire is stronger were to wait and see what action ensues, the main principle of the explanation (5) would be empty of empirical content, and the explanation would be trivial. Applied to our example, condition A requires that we be able to determine whether (6) is true independently of knowledge or information that (7) is true.

Now so far as explanations of weakness are concerned, it is important to realize that condition A may be satisfied in at least two significantly different ways.

[26] What appears as a violent disagreement between Plato (*R.,* Bk. IV) and Hume (*Treatise,* Bk. II, Pt. III, sec. iii) as to whether "reason" and the "passions" can conflict may not be so violent. Plato holds that if a man believes that something is good (for him) then he wants (to have, to get, to possess) it (cf. Santas, "The Socratic Paradoxes," *loc. cit.,* for the evidence). If it happens, say, that the man also fears the object, then the conflict between the belief and the fear can be "reduced" to the conflict between the want and the fear.

[27] With minor modifications this kind of explanation can satisfy the Hempel-Oppenheim requirements of a scientific explanation provided that condition A is satisfied. The similar type of explanation that I cite below, employed by Neal Miller, does satisfy these requirements.

(I) One way is to suppose that there is some consistent correlation between the agent's evaluation or rankings of the alternatives before him and the strength of the conflicting desires that attach to these alternatives. This supposition would satisfy condition *A* since it is certainly possible to ascertain the agent's rankings (for example, by asking him) of the alternatives independently of knowing what alternative he actually takes (and, in addition, it is of course possible to rank alternatives without actually acting on the rankings because, say, one is prevented from doing so). Applied to our case, the supposition that would satisfy condition *A* is that if Agathon believes that the pleasure of eating the pastries outweighs the subsequent pain, then his desire to eat the pastries is stronger than his desire not to eat (or his fear of eating). It is conceivable that some such supposition is true, given some appropriate restriction of its scope; but whether or not this is so, it is certainly plausible, and its plausibility is perhaps enhanced by the difficulty of finding some *other* way to satisfy condition *A*. We may notice further that if we satisfy condition *A* in the way just indicated, the ground or evidence for (6) will usually be a belief statement such as (6′) Agathon believes that the pleasure of eating the pastries outweighs the subsequent pain. The success of such an explanation depends on (6′) being true, but not on what Agathon believes being true (Agathon may indeed be mistaken in his ranking and the reason for this may be that the pleasure was near and the pain much later—all this is consistent with the success of the explanation in question).

Before proceeding to the second way of satisfying condition *A* I wish to point out an important consequence of the first way of satisfying condition *A*. If one assumed or supposed (whether explicitly or implicitly) that (5) or some version of it is the relevant explanatory principle in cases of conflicting motives or desires or drives, and further that the first way (I) is the *only* way to satisfy condition *A*, then clearly the occurrence of *akrasia* or weakness will appear an impossibility to him (or, at least, *akrasia* will appear inexplicable). For in cases of *akrasia* the agent is supposed to be acting contrary to his knowledge or belief of which alternative is best (or better)—that is, contrary to *his own* ranking of the alternative; but, given our present supposition, this implies that he acts in accordance with the weaker, not the stronger, of the conflicting motives! At the same time, the present suppositions are quite consistent with the agent's acting against *the correct* ranking (correct even according, for example, to the agent's hedonistic principles); and this will be the case precisely when the belief in (6'), not (6') itself, is false. The explanation will work equally well here; and the inclination will be to say that what occur are cases where the agent acts against the correct (even by his own value principle) ranking, not his own ranking. There is some evidence in the argument in the *Protagoras*, not that Plato thought of the matter explicitly in this way, but that he was thinking of it in this kind of context. For he begins the whole argument by asking which is stronger or more powerful in directing human conduct, knowledge of good and evil or such things as pleasure, pain, fear, love and so forth; and this language suggests (5) or some version of it as the relevant explanatory principle. And when, as we have seen, he comes to interpreting "overcome by pleasure," he does so by referring us to the hedonistic values of the alternatives, and this suggests that the strength of the motive is to be inferred from the value ranking of the alternatives.

(II) A significantly different manner of satisfying condition A would obtain if we had ways of determining the relative strength of the conflicting motives independently of any knowledge (or information) of the agent's evaluations or rankings of the alternatives to which the conflicting motives refer and of course independently of information of what behavior in fact ensues. If condition A can be satisfied in this manner, this allows, at the very least, for the possibility that the stronger (strongest) desire is not always the desire referring to the alternative that has the agent's higher (highest) ranking. Indeed, on the present supposition, there would be no a priori reason to expect that "stronger motive" correlates consistently with "higher ranking"; we might well find out that under certain conditions (for example, when the agent is in some state of emotional excitement), there is no correlation at all between "stronger motive" and agent's "higher ranking." Now the supposition that sometimes, even quite often, people act against their own rankings or evaluations of the alternatives before them (even though they are not externally forced or compelled to, and have the opportunity to act in accordance with their own evaluations) will not be puzzling at all; for such behavior will no longer appear inexplicable.

Can condition A be satisfied in the second way? It seems that it has been satisfied in cases of explanations of animal behavior resulting from conflicting motives or drives, where the model of explanation used is similar to the one I have outlined, and the explanatory principle (5) or some variant of it is explicitly used.[28] Roughly speaking, it has been possible to show that the strength of two conflicting drives or motives—say, the desire for certain food (approach drive) and the fear of the electric shock that accompanies the obtaining of the food (avoidance drive)—increases as the animal approaches the goal, and that in fact the rate of increase of the avoidance drive is always greater than that of the approach drive (and it has been possible to measure the rate of increase of strength by measuring pull or speed at

[28] Neal E. Miller, "Comments on Theoretical Models Illustrated by the Development of a Theory of Conflict," *Journal of Personality*, XX (1951–52), 82–100. This is a careful and philosophically sophisticated account of experiments in verification of a theory that could be used to explain behavior in cases of conflicting "tendencies," "responses," or "drives," or "motives." One of the hypotheses verified by the experiments is: "when two incompatible responses are in conflict, the stronger one will occur." This article, and the related literature cited below, is worth reading by all those who talk of human beings being "overcome," "seduced," etc., by their passions, feelings, etc.

different points). In addition it has been possible to determine the initial strength (under controlled conditions) of the approach and avoidance drives (by vary-
ing such things as the time of deprivation of food or the
intensity of the electric shock). In consequence, it has
been possible (under controlled conditions) to plot and
predict the relative strengths of the approach and avoidance drives or motives at any given distance from the
goal, and to predict what behavior will result (reaching
the goal or not) in accordance with the principle that the
animal's behavior at any given point (and at the end)
will be in accordance with the stronger motive. More
recently, exactly the same explanatory model has been
used, perhaps without enough caution, in cases of human behavior resulting from conflicting motives; but it
is not clear to me in this case (of human behavior) that
condition A has been satisfied.[29] In any case, the success
of the explanatory model in the case of animal behavior
seems to point to the possibility that explanations of the
same kind, satisfying condition A in the second (II)
way, can be given of human behavior in cases of conflicting motives.

v

We have seen that Plato uses the language of
strength[30] and yet overlooks the possibility of interpret-

[29] Jesse E. Gordon, *Personality and Behavior* (New York, 1963),
pp. 389–426. Gordon applies the Miller models to human behavior,
but Miller's care and clarity are nowhere to be found, and Gordon
leaves us in the dark as to how strength is to be measured in the
case of humans. Gordon does not display the caution and safe-
guards that are necessary when models, successful in the case of
lower animals, are applied to humans. General applications of the
Miller models are summarized in B. Berelson and G. A. Steiner,
*Human Behavior: An Inventory of Scientific Findings* (New York,
1964), pp. 271–76. Cf. especially C6 and C6.1.

[30] E.g., ἰσχυρόν, κράτιστον, ἡττᾶσθαι, νικᾶν. In the *Phdr.*
(237D–238A) we have the following passage: "We must observe
that in each one of us there are two ruling and leading principles,
which we follow whithersoever they lead; one is the innate desire

ing the various explanations of weakness, "overcome
by . . . ," in terms of the strength of the conflicting desires. How can we account for this? One possibility of
course is that Plato did not distinguish the concepts of
strength and value or value estimate. It is difficult
enough to find a way of determining the strengths of
conflicting desires (passions, feelings) independently of
knowledge of ensuing behavior (condition $A$) and independently of knowledge of the agent's rankings or value
estimates of the objects of his desires—the second way
(II) of satisfying $A$ (pp. 291–92 above). The very possibility of doing either or both of these might not occur to
one unless he encounters certain difficulties (of which
the denial of weakness may be one). William McDougall's discussion is a good illustration of this point.[31] Or
the necessity to satisfy condition $A$ may be forced on one
but he may not see further any need to satisfy condition
$A$ in any way other than (I) (p. 290 above), as
Mill's discussion illustrates.[32] I know of no explicit evidence that Plato saw any necessity to satisfy condition $A$
at all, certainly none that condition $A$ is to be satisfied in
any other way than (I). He seems to run together

---

for pleasures, the other an acquired opinion which strives for the
best. These two sometimes agree within us and are sometimes in
strife (στασιάζετον); and sometimes one, and sometimes the
other has the greater power." Aside from the fact that the language of strength is also used here, it is illuminating to compare the
doctrine of this passage with the hedonism assumed in the *Prt.* and
the explanation "overcome by pleasure."

[31] *Social Psychology* (New York, 1960), 23rd ed., ch. ix. Mc-
Dougall quotes with approval William James's conception of the
problem in cases of "moral conflict": "*I* (ideal impulse) in itself
weaker than *P* (the native propensity). *I* + *E* (effort of the will)
stronger than *P*." McDougall thinks that the occurrence of weakness exemplifies the first proposition, which he treats as a law of
psychology, and thus can easily be accounted for; it is the occurrence of the opposite of weakness that is difficult to account for,
and here the problem is the analysis of *E*. He uses the language of
strength constantly but he does not seem to see that there is a problem about giving a sense to the notion of "stronger than."

[32] *An Examination of Sir William Hamilton's Philosophy* (London, 1867), ch. xxvi.

strength and value estimate; when, for instance, he considers an objection that might be understood to imply that strength of desire varies with variation of distance from the object of the desire, he understands it rather to imply that the agent's estimate of the value of the object varies with distance. The whole confusion is made easier to fall into by the fact that strength is not entirely independent of value estimate.[33]

A second possible line of explanation relates to two hitherto unnoticed features of the passage we have examined. One of these is a shift in Plato's language, from the language of strength to the language of value estimates, of which the turning point is at 355D where the passive "overcome by" is replaced by "to take" or "to choose." A list of the relevant phrases in the order in which they occur is sufficient to confirm this: "dragged about" (352B–C), "under the control," "being overcome by" (repeated five times before 355D), "being overpowered by," "being driven and dazed"; "take," "choose," "weigh," "choose," "choice of odd and even," "right choice of pleasure and pain" (357B). This shift from the language of strength (all in the passive voice) to the language of value estimate (all in the active voice) suggests the possibility of another shift during the passage, a shift in the sorts of cases being considered: from cases where the agent is acting in the heat of passion, "driven out of his senses" (as Wayte says),[34] where he has lost control of himself, to cases of calm and cool choice and action. Indeed the radical shift in the language cannot but remind one of Austin's charge.[35] The second unno-

---

[33] Berelson and Steiner, *op. cit.*, p. 271, C5.

[34] ". . . harried along and driven out of his senses" (W. Wayte, *The Protagoras of Plato* [Cambridge, 1871], p. 147).

[35] "Or we collapse succumbing to temptation into losing control of ourselves—a bad patch, this, for telescoping. . . . Plato, I suppose, and after him Aristotle, fastened this confusion upon us, as bad in its day and way as the later, grotesque, confusion of moral weakness and weakness of will. I am very partial to ice cream, and a bombe is served divided into segments corresponding one to one with the persons at High Table: I am tempted to help myself to

ticed feature of the passage is that Plato repeats three times (up to 355D), as part of the description of cases of weakness, that the agent "could avoid" what he did or "did not have to do" what he did.[86] Plato does not say what he means by this; he could be referring to physical ability, lack of physical coercion, or opportunity. It is also possible, I suggest, that he is referring to psychological ability to do or refrain from doing or to lack of psychological compulsion. This concept is of course difficult and in need of analysis; but if for the moment we suppose that this suggestion is near the mark, a new and interesting line of conjecture opens up that makes more intelligible Plato's treatment of weakness in the *Protagoras*, and perhaps even gives new life to his argument. The conjecture is that when a man acts contrary to his knowledge or belief of what is best (for him), *and* the true explanation of his action is in terms of the strength of his conflicting desires (passions, feelings)—an explanation of the sort outlined above (p. 288)—*and* condition A is satisfied in manner (II), then the agent acted under psychological compulsion or was not psychologically able to refrain from doing what he did. Thus, if a man, say, knows or believes that eating another serving of Athenian pastries would give him pleasure but would also harm him, and also believes that the harm outweighs the pleasure (so that he believes the pleasure is not worth the harm), but he eats nevertheless, and the true explanation of his eating is that his desire for the pleasure was stronger than his fear of the harm, and we can determine this independently of knowledge of his action and knowledge of his value estimate, then

two segments and do so, thus succumbing to temptation and even conceivably (but why necessarily?) going against my principles. But do I lose control of myself? Do I rave, do I snatch the morsels from the dish and wolf them down, impervious to the consternation of my colleagues? Not a bit of it. We often succumb to temptation with calm and even with finesse" ("A Plea for Excuses" in *Philosophical Papers* [Oxford, 1961], p. 146).

[86] ἐξὸν αὐτοῖς, ἐξὸν μὴ πράττειν, οὐ δέον αὐτὸν πράττειν (352D, 355A, 355D).

he was not psychologically able to refrain from eating. The plausibility of connecting this type of explanation with psychological compulsion is enhanced by two considerations. First, when all these conditions are (accepted as) satisfied we have the feeling that our man is no longer an agent; he is not *doing* anything, something is happening to him—the very point suggested by Plato's passive language of strength (overcome, overpowered, dazed, and driven). The second point is that if we accept the explanation and still say that the man *could* (psychologically) have refrained from eating, it seems that the only thing we can mean is that he *would* have refrained *if* his *fear* had been stronger instead. Now we are faced with the question whether the man had control, in any clear sense, over the *strength* of his feelings (and whether in general one can be said to have any such control). Until a clear affirmative answer can be given to this question, the verdict that the man was not (psychologically) able to refrain will have to stand. Until such an answer is given, we can say, tentatively, that this sort of explanation in terms of strength can be used to give *one* clear sense to the notion of psychological ability or at least psychological compulsion.[87]

Finally, if this conjecture is accepted, it constitutes a defense of Plato's argument. For it follows from it that if we interpret the explanations of the masses, "overcome by . . . ," in terms of strength (the interpretation that Plato ignores or overlooks thus weakening his argument), then one of the conditions included in the description of the case explained is contradicted, namely, the condition that the man could or was able (psychologically) to refrain from acting contrary to his knowledge of what is best (for him). The "wider" issue in the whole passage in the *Protagoras* was whether it is possible for

[87] It is worth noticing that what I have said here does not necessarily hold of explanations in terms of strength where condition A is satisfied in the first way (I). Socrates' remark at 357C, when he reverts to the language of strength, is no objection to what I am saying here.

men to act contrary to their knowledge of what is best
when they can refrain. The "narrower" issue, what the
argument was all about, was whether, assuming that this
is possible, the explanation can be that men are overcome by their passions, pleasure, pain, fear, love, and
so forth. By interpreting "overcome by" as referring to
the value estimates or rankings of the agent, Socrates
succeeded in showing that one such explanation leads
to contradiction (taking hedonism as a premise). This
paved the way to his own explanation (ignorance is what
is best) which in effect answers the wider issue negatively, since the explanation cancels out one of the conditions in the description of weakness. It now results
that if we remedy the most serious weakness in Socrates'
argument, and construe "overcome by . . ." on the
model of explanations in terms of strength, the wider
issue is answered negatively once more since we now
cancel out another condition, namely that the agent
could (psychologically) have refrained from acting contrary to his knowledge. That this condition is included
in descriptions of weakness is fair enough. For the philosophically puzzling cases of (prudential and moral)
weakness, in so far as their occurrence reflects on the notion of having or holding (or "assenting to") a practical
principle, rule, or belief, are the cases where the man
was *not* under (psychological as well as physical) compulsion. The cases where he was are, after all, under-
standable enough—at least if our concept of compulsion
is clear enough.[38]

[38] I am indebted to Professor Rosalind Ekman Ladd and to Mr.
Jonathan Malino for many helpful comments.

# 13.  SOCRATES ON DISOBEYING THE LAW

I

Socrates is commonly characterised, and indeed on occasion characterised himself (or is so represented by
Plato), as a negative thinker: one who provoked a member of his circle to propose a confident opinion on, say,
the nature of virtue, or of one of the virtues, and who
then proceeded, by unrelenting use of the *elenchus*
method, to destroy first the opinion offered, and then
the successive amendments and substitutions advanced
to meet his earlier objections. The result of a philosophical conversation would be that half a dozen or so suggestions had been eliminated, but not even a tentative
positive conclusion reached; the *Euthyphro* is a typical
example. Although the method was liable to exasperate
his victims, Socrates insisted that it was not eristic, but
reflected his own genuine perplexity on the subject under discussion (cf. *Men.* 80C). His unremitting scrutiny
of received opinions, deflating them but confessing himself ignorant of what the true answer was, must have
done much to create the establishment's antipathy to
him, resulting in his trial and conviction on a charge of
corrupting youth.

A noteworthy feature of Socrates' discussion of a
man's duty or obligation to obey the law is that it does
not follow the usual would-be eliminative method. In
the *Crito* he does not play the part of the interrogator,
asking Crito whether and why we should obey the law,
and wearing him down with counterquestions; he comes
out forthrightly himself with his own answers and with
his reasons for them. And the *Apology*, which also raises

This is a previously unpublished essay, written especially for this
volume.

the question of obedience to the law, is not a dialogue
at all; throughout, Socrates is represented as speaking
in his own person, first defending himself at his trial,
then, after his conviction, proposing a suitable sentence,
and finally, after sentence of death had been passed by
the court, making his final address.

While the detailed ordering and dating of Plato's dialogues are likely to remain beyond any definitive settle-
ment, there is nowadays little disagreement among scholars about the general sequence. While both the *Apology*
and the *Crito* cannot have been composed before Socrates' trial in 399 B.C., they were almost certainly written
shortly afterwards and belong to the early group of dialogues in which the character "Socrates" may be taken
fairly to represent the views of the actual Socrates. Furthermore, whatever use Plato later made of "Socrates"
to expound and discuss Plato's own philosophical views,
it is impossible to believe that, when writing about something on which he felt so strongly as the McCarthyite
trial and execution of his revered teacher, he would have
done anything other than present the beliefs and arguments of the historical Socrates as accurately as he could;
both works are by way of being obituary memoirs. We
can, therefore, confidently rely on them as a source of
Socrates' views on one's duty to obey the law.

That in itself generates a problem, for there appears
to be a flat contradiction between the two works. In the
*Apology* Socrates says (29D) that if the court were to
discharge him conditionally on his giving up engaging in
philosophical enquiry and debate, he would unhesitat-
ingly disobey the order. In the *Crito* he suggests (50B)
that a city cannot survive if its court's verdicts and orders do not prevail; furthermore, if it is his general principle that any law must be obeyed, that, taken together
with the statement (50C) that there is a law of Athens
laying down that the judgement of a court is legally
binding, entails the conclusion that one must not try to
evade the court's judgement, including the prescribed
sentence. The *Crito* proceeds to develop arguments, not

merely for obeying the laws in general, but also for abiding by court decisions in particular, even if, in a particular case, the decision was unjust or wrongly given (50C). The underlying thesis here is that a court's judgement or order is verdictive (in this respect analogous to the ruling of an umpire or referee in a game), and that, even if the legal system provides for appeals, a series of appeals has to be finite, and where it stops it stops; if an error in justice persists right to the end, then, even so, the sentence must be carried out; and where the sentence is, as in the case of Socrates, execution by suicide, the sentenced man owes it to the laws to carry it out himself.

How are we to relate the views in the *Apology* with those in the *Crito*? In terms of Socrates' biography, the end of the trial and the conversation in his prison cell are separated by little, if any, more than four weeks. In terms of composition, the two works were probably more widely separated, by how much we cannot tell; but, for reasons already given, we can hardly doubt that they are substantially accurate in their report of Socrates at that time; that rules out misrepresentation by Plato.

One writer indeed has taken the step of supposing that the inconsistency was deliberate, and is to be attributed to Plato, not to Socrates. Grote (*Plato*, Vol. 1) maintains that in composing the *Crito* Plato quite deliberately presented Socrates as an out-and-out defender of the law, complete with highly emotional appeals to patriotism, in order to counteract the bad impression which he had made at his trial (correctly reported in the *Apology*) of being an intellectually arrogant person, who regarded himself as being a privileged exception who was above the law. One of the accusations levelled against him at his trial, according to Xenophon, was that of "inducing his associates to disregard the established laws . . ."; if he had such a reputation, his performance at his trial would have done nothing but confirm it. And people who claim for themselves the right to break the law with impunity do madden their fellows, both by their arro-

gance, and by the fact of their not being amenable to
rational consideration of the possibility of their being
wrong. It is not difficult to believe that, whether deserv-
edly or not, Socrates had that reputation, and that for it
he was widely hated. Plato then, according to Grote,
deliberately set out in the *Crito* to do whatever he could
to correct the unfortunate public impression which Socrates had made, and to restore his reputation; the dialogue, in consequence, is meant not as a serious philosophical discussion, but as a rhetorical performance
designed solely to change people's attitude to Socrates;
and that is why Plato has Socrates rest all the emphasis
on two themes: first, the paramount necessity of obeying
the law and a legal decision, however unjust it may be;
and second, his own personal devotion to his native city
of Athens.

The trouble with this interpretation of the *Crito* is that
the only thing tolerably certain about it is the public
reputation of Socrates from which it starts. The rest is
pure conjecture; we have no evidence, external or internal, that the *Crito* was not a genuinely Socratic dialogue.
If we could independently establish that it was not, then
we could use that to explain the difference in Socrates'
attitude towards disobedience to the law in it and in the
*Apology* respectively. But, as we cannot independently
establish that it was not a genuinely Socratic dialogue,
we cannot just *say* that it was not, and then *conclude*
that that accounts for the difference; this is simply to
beg the question at issue. We have no positive reason to
read the *Crito* as a job of rhetorical whitewashing by
Plato. And, in view of Plato's known opinion of rhetoric,
as expounded in the *Gorgias,* we should in any case only
be patching up one inconsistency at the price of disclos-
ing another.

In default of other evidence we have, then, to take
it that, as presented by Plato, Socrates was speaking sin-
cerely both in the *Apology* and in the *Crito;* which rules
out *knowing* inconsistency. Similarly, we can rule out a
change of mind within the last month of his life, for in

the *Crito* he insists that there has been none; he cannot abandon his old principles unless confronted by arguments better than anything so far produced (46B–C). We are left, then, with two alternatives: (a) that there was an inconsistency, but he was unaware of it; (b) that there is an interpretation of the passages involved which does not render them incompatible. (a) is so implausible that it is very hard to accept. How could a man with any pretensions to being reasonable and high principled, let alone a Socrates, declare at his trial that he would not obey a particular court order, and then less than a month later refuse to disobey a court order because such orders must always be obeyed—and *not* notice the contradiction? Such an inconsistency cannot be rationally explained; it will have just to be accepted, but only if no alternative under (b) can be found.

Various possibilities offer themselves. (1) Is the court at *Apology* 29C being imagined to be offering Socrates a conditional discharge, the condition being that he will no longer spend his time in philosophical enquiry and discussion? Socrates, in his reply that he must obey God rather than them, and that he would not change his way of life, even if he had to die many deaths (30C), would be rejecting the offer. This would not be inconsistent with his line in the *Crito*, for he would be saying that he could not accept an offer, the terms of which were such that he could neither abide by them (this would be to disobey his God), nor violate them (this would be to disobey the law). But this interpretation will not do, because it depends on the notions of an offer and its acceptance or rejection; and they are not there in the text. We must not blur the distinction between a court offering an accused man a conditional discharge on the one hand, and a court discharging an accused man conditionally on the other. In the first case, the discharge is not made, unless and until the conditional offer is accepted; in the second case the discharge is made, but it holds good for only as long as the man meets the condition. It is like the difference between binding a man over in his own recognisances to keep the peace, and releasing him on probation, subject to his keeping the peace. There is no doubt that what we have in the *Apology* is the notion of the court discharging Socrates conditionally, not its offering him a conditional discharge. The court says (as imagined by Socrates): "This time we shall not be persuaded by Anytus; instead, we are discharging you—however, subject to this condition, that you no longer spend your time in this pursuit or in doing philosophy; and, if you are caught still doing it, you will die" (29C). And Socrates' reply begins: "If you were to discharge me on these terms . . ." (29D). There is nothing about offering to discharge, only about discharging.

(2) Could Socrates be making use of the distinction between a law, which must (as a matter of logic) be legally correct, and a legal decision of a court, which might not be? He would be announcing that he would not meet the condition laid down by the court, because it was itself in some way illegal; it might be unconstitutional, or the court might be acting *ultra vires*—that court might not have the authority to impose *that* condition. This situation is real enough. Leaving aside cases in which there is a problem of legal interpretation, it does happen from time to time that a trial court gets the law wrong or exceeds its jurisdiction; and one of the prime reasons for the existence of appeal courts is to provide an opportunity for reversing such errors. So Socrates would be maintaining throughout that we must obey the law, and consistently with that claiming the right, or even the duty, to ignore a court's judgement if it was illegal.

Nevertheless, this interpretation of Socrates' attitude in the *Apology* cannot be accepted either, and for two reasons. First, he nowhere does suggest that such a decision by the court would be illegal, let alone that its illegality would be his reason for refusing to comply with the condition which it imposed. The nearest he comes to giving his reason is in his references to God: "I will obey God rather than you" (29D); "for know well, this is what God commands, and I think no greater good has yet befallen you in the city than my service to God" (30A). Second, this interpretation would repair one inconsistency between the *Apology* and the *Crito*, but only by opening another; for, as previously mentioned, Socrates in the latter insists that requirement to obey the law carries with it requirement to abide by the judgement of a court, however unjust it may be (50B). It cannot be said that such a judgement is illegal, for there is a law on the books specifically excluding that. And if, for reasons yet to be considered, we are morally obligated to do whatever we are legally required to do, we cannot justify disobedience to a court along the lines of the present interpretation.

(3) Can Socrates in the *Apology* passage be advancing a doctrine of natural law—that no putative law or legal requirement which is not in accordance with the commands of God is legally valid? Socrates clearly is in a position in which he finds a conflict between a supposedly valid requirement of law and the commands of God, and he clearly is saying that the commands of God are to be preferred to the commands of man. But he cannot be saying that putative legal requirements are not actually legal requirements if they are in conflict with the commands of God; for, if he were, he would be involving himself in the same inconsistency as under the previous interpretation, allowing in the *Apology* and disallowing in the *Crito* that a court order could fail to be legally valid. Socrates may have been a natural law theorist of *a* sort, but he was not one of *that* sort. We have to distinguish between appealing to the will of God in justification of disobedience to a law or legal order, and appealing to the will of God in justification of a denial that they are a law or legal order. Correspondingly, while few of us were distressed by the fate of men like Goering or Eichmann, some had misgivings about the legality of the trials.

(4) It is certain that Socrates *is* appealing to the will of God in justification of his preparedness to disobey the

court, if it puts a ban on his philosophical activities. In
declaring that he will undergo anything, even death,
rather than submit to what is morally wrong (32A), he is
adhering to the principle of the conscientious objector.
What is wrong and what is illegal may coincide; and they
did in the case of the decision to try *collectively* the ten
admirals after the battle of Arginusae, which Socrates
was the only member of the executive of the time to
oppose. But they may not coincide; Socrates does not
suggest that the Thirty, in instructing him to go with
others to arrest Leon of Salamis, were giving an order
that was illegal. But, because he was not prepared to be
terrified by a powerful government into doing anything
that was either *adikon* or *anhosion* (i.e., either wrong
in relation to men or wrong in relation to God), he disobeyed the order (32D). This is in line with one theme
in the *Crito*, viz. that, regardless of what popular opinion
may say, there are no circumstances in which one should
willingly do wrong; if that is so, a man should not willingly do wrong, even when he receives an order from
his government to do something which in fact is wrong
(49A). It perhaps does not appear to be in line with
another theme in the *Crito*, viz. that a man must either
do whatever his city orders him to do or must persuade
her where the rightness of the matter lies (51C); and he
specifically mentions a law court as an instance where
this rule must hold. It is true that Socrates distinguishes
between a state and the politicians who act in its name,
so that he was able with a clear conscience to disobey
the wicked orders of the Thirty; and again he distinguishes between the laws and the men who supposedly
implement them (54C). A convicted man may (if he is
able to) console himself that it was human error or evil
in the application of law that brought about his conviction; the law itself was not at fault. But this does not
help us, because of Socrates' insistence that it is not for
a private citizen to render a court's judgement ineffective; the rule that the judgement of a court is to be effective is itself a rule of law (50B).

(5) Nevertheless, the permitted alternative to obedience, viz. persuading the laws that their order is wrong, suggests a solution to the difficulty. What in the *Apology* Socrates is prepared to do against the court is not the same as what in the *Crito* he is not prepared to do against the court. Generically, it is in both cases a question of obedience or disobedience, but at the specific level there is a difference. In the *Apology* Socrates is not taking the line which he had the reputation of taking, namely that being divinely directed he was altogether above the law, and consequently would ignore the court's judgement, no matter what it was. It is only one possible judgement that he is prepared to disobey, namely one banning him from further philosophizing in Athens. And his disobedience will take the single form of *openly* continuing to practise philosophy the way he always has; there is no suggestion of concealment, of trying to evade the law by holding clandestine philosophical meetings. He will conduct himself exactly as he always has, pursuing the truth with anybody he meets, foreigners or citizens of Athens alike (30A). On the other hand, the disobedience to a lawful command which he is not prepared to countenance in the *Crito* is of the kind which would do violence and injury to the law, and which would be exemplified by the course of action which Crito is urging on him, viz. escape. And all disobedience to lawful commands *is* of this kind, with the single exception of attempting to *convince* the state that it is wrong in the law or command concerned. But this permitted exception to the rule of obedience is precisely what he had proposed to follow in the *Apology*. There, while insisting that he must obey God rather than the court, he made it clear that obedience to God not merely coincided with trying to convince Athens that he was right, it actually consisted in that: "I shall obey God rather than you, and, as long as I breathe and have the ability, I shall never give up philosophizing, and both exhorting you and demonstrating the truth to you" (29D).

This is civil disobedience indeed, but of the kind that

stays and attempts to change minds by reason, and does not try to escape the legal consequences of doing it; not of the kind that uses violence, or tries to dodge the law by escaping. Socrates' kind of civil disobedience may be quixotic; that will depend on how ineffective in the particular circumstances the lone voice of the protester is. But such obedience is not dishonourable: as long as the protester stays within the reach of the law, no harm is done to it, and it does not suffer any disrepute—as might be the case, if a successful escape were to show its ineffectiveness. The one course other than obedience to the law and its commands which Socrates' argument in the *Crito* (51–52) permits is the one course which he had said in the *Apology* (29–30) he would, if banned from philosophy, take. Once we see that it is not the doctrine of the *Crito* that a man must always, and no matter what, obey the laws of his state, the supposed conflict between that dialogue and the *Apology* disappears.

II

Socrates' arguments in the *Crito* why he should not make a last minute escape fall into two parts: first a negative section (44B–48D) in which he convinces Crito of the inadequacy, indeed the irrelevance (48C), of the reasons which he had given why Socrates should allow his friends to organize an escape; and then a positive section (49B–54D) in which he himself gives the reasons why he should not. The two points to notice about the first section are the nature of Crito's plea, and the unsatisfactoriness of Socrates' reply to it. Although it has not always been appreciated, the reasons which Crito advances are moral ones, reasons why Socrates *ought* to agree to the escape; appeals to Socrates' sense of prudence or personal advantage would, no doubt, have been useless, and Crito sensibly makes none. (It has to be acknowledged, however, that here, as in the *Republic*, Socrates does in the end rest the case for doing what is right on its being the best policy, i.e., to the advantage of the agent [54B–C].) Crito claims (1) that Socrates owes it to his friends to escape, (a) because, if he does not, he will be depriving them of his irreplaceable friendship (44B); (b) because, if he does not, they will thereby acquire a poor public reputation: it will be generally (although incorrectly) believed that, when they could have saved him, they failed either through meanness or from fear of the risk to themselves (44C–E). (That a man should, at such a time, be concerned with his own reputation may not be morally creditable. But that does not have the consequence that the claim that a second man should consider the effect of his conduct on the first man's reputation is not a moral claim.)

(2) Crito claims that it would not be right for Socrates to throw his life away when rescue is possible, (c) because he will be allowing his enemies to achieve the very result they wanted (45C); (d) because he will be betraying his children: either people should not have children at all, or they should discharge their responsibility of bringing them up and educating them. Socrates professes to have cared for goodness all his life, yet, when given a chance to play the part of a good and courageous man, he is just taking the easiest way out (45D–E).

Of those four arguments, Socrates makes no reference at all to (a) and (c), summarily dismisses (d) as irrelevant (48C), and concentrates only on (b), his reply to which is, in fact, not a refutation of Crito's claim, but at crosspurposes with it. Summarily, his line is not to disagree with the factual element of Crito's argument, viz. that Crito and Socrates' other friends, who could have helped him escape but did not, would be condemned by popular opinion for meanness or cowardice, but to maintain that on such difficult questions as those of right and wrong one should attend not to all opinions, but only to some, namely the sound opinions of those who really know about right and wrong (46D–48A). This does not answer Crito's point, which had been that one has to pay regard to public opinion,

just because of the harm it can do, regardless of whether
the opinion is correct or incorrect. If the question had
been, not whether a certain popular opinion was held,
but whether it was either correctly or justifiably held,
Socrates' objection would have been to the point. The
only assertion that he makes directly counter to Crito's
claim is that public opinion is so fickle that it is incapable of doing either great harm or great good (44D).
This, if it were true, would be a serious objection to
Crito, but Socrates does not pursue it. Instead he
switches to his theme that one cannot expect to get a
well-informed or intelligent opinion from the man in the
street. But, as any politician knows who takes seriously
his public responsibility, there can be circumstances in
which it is more important that a certain opinion is held
than that it is incorrect. That such a recognition can easily degenerate into the most sycophantic form of dema-
goguery is a good reason for being cautious how much
weight should be given to it in a particular situation,
but is not a good reason for denying it. Erroneous public
opinion has to be lived with, until it can be corrected. If
living with it can take the form of ignoring it, so much
the better; but, as the effect of public opinion is a function, not only of what the opinion is, but also of the
strength with which it is held, it cannot be right to say,
with Socrates, that the *only* question is that about the
correctness or justifiability of the opinion concerned. If
there is a reason why public opinion ought to be ignored
in the particular situation of Socrates and his friends who
wish to rescue him, it must be a reason more specific to
the situation, or type of situation, than that which Socrates produces himself. Injury to Crito's reputation may
not be a good, let alone a good enough, reason for Socrates to agree that he *ought* to escape, but it is not totally
irrelevant to it.

In the only place where Socrates even mentions Crito's
argument (d), he does so to lump it together with (b)
as irrelevant to the question of whether or not it would
be right to make an escape (48C). Why he should have

been so casual in his attitude towards parental responsibility we cannot tell. He cannot have been reflecting a general attitude of the day: there is plenty of evidence in literature to the contrary, and Crito himself had just expressed the orthodox view. One would all the more like to know what Socrates really believed here, because of the great emphasis which he was shortly going to place on the responsibility of children to their parents: a generalised form of that was one of the two grounds on which he rested the proposition that we ought to obey the law.

He has two positive arguments about why we should obey the law, both stemming from the general principle that it can never be right to do what is wrong, even in requital for wrong treatment that one has suffered (49B); and, as there is no difference between ill treatment and doing wrong, one should not give ill treatment in return for ill treatment which he has suffered (49B–C).

It appears that in talking of giving ill treatment in return for ill treatment one has received, Socrates is thinking in terms of revenge or retaliation, of the injured party getting his own back. Whether he would have thought it was also wrong in the case of retribution, or of institutionalised punishment in general, we have no means of telling. But they do need distinguishing, for it does not follow from the fact that a certain action would be wrong if performed in retaliation that an otherwise identical action would be wrong if performed in retribution. Further, conduct which would be wrong, if it were not the execution of punishment, might not be wrong, if it were. One cannot answer the question whether to deprive a man of freedom by shutting him up in a cell is wrong, without a further description of the situation, in particular of the reasons for and the purpose of shutting him up, together with the rules, if any, which applied to the situation. Descriptions can be correct or incorrect; but, because even when correct they cannot be complete, i.e., such that it would be logically impossible for anything further to be added, selection of the specific description to be used determines the moral assessment to be given. The principle that it is always wrong to give out ill treatment, even in return for ill treatment received, needs more refinement before it can be accepted as the truth which Socrates took it to be.

In order to demonstrate that one should not disobey the law, Socrates develops two arguments showing how disobedience is wrong. Neither of them is the familiar straightforward utilitarian argument that the regulation of conduct by laws provides social benefits not otherwise (as readily, at least) obtainable; but underlying both is the utilitarian consideration of the social harm produced by disobedience, that disobedience destroys laws and state (50B): the appeal is an appeal to the *consequences* of disobedience. (Producing a utilitarian justification for having a system of laws at all is not necessary to a utilitarian justification, given that we have a system of laws, of the need for obedience to them.)

In view of the fact that concepts like duty and obligation do not fit happily into the framework of Socratic or Platonic thought, it may sound paradoxical to say that Socrates' two arguments foreshadow a distinction between duty and obligation, but nevertheless it seems to be true. The first argument is that a man ought to obey the laws of his country because he owes them the kind of regard he owes to his parents (50D); the second is that he ought to obey the laws because he has undertaken to do so (51E). (Although Socrates actually formulates the arguments in the singular form, as giving the reasons why *he*, Socrates, ought to obey the laws of *Athens*, he would have to allow that, being reasons, they must be general in their application.)

Given the personification of the laws which Socrates imagines for the purposes of the discussion, the representation of them as oversized parents is not too farfetched to be illuminating. By making it possible for people to marry, and to secure the means of rearing and educating their children, the state (which, for these purposes, is not to be distinguished from its laws) has the same kind of rights, only more so, against an individual as his human parents have. The idea that is being foreshadowed here is of something being what we ought to do because it is a duty, where duties are things a man can find himself having without having incurred them. "Duty" is characteristically a role-word, "duty as a . . . ," e.g., duty as a citizen, subject, visitor, parent, child, etc.; and more widely, when used in the plural, it refers to the tasks or jobs that go with the role. The reason why a child ought to obey and respect those who gave him life and saw him through the insecure period before he could fend for himself can have nothing to do with his having taken on a role, for it is not true that he did; they took on theirs, but he did not take on his. A citizen has the role in his native state, although he did not take it on, and with the role go certain duties. In the end, the reason why a man has certain duties towards his parents, or ought to treat them in a certain way, has to come down to some form of gratitude or return for what they have done for him. Provided that the parents/laws have performed their function satisfactorily, they have rights, Socrates thinks, over the children/subjects which the latter do not have over them (51A). Socrates' parent-laws analogy is not perfect. Although the morality of some societies may require a man to obey his parents even after he has reached adulthood and maybe become a parent himself, this is neither common nor reasonable. And he will have other duties towards them besides; indeed the duty to obey is the first, and perhaps the only one, to lapse. In the case of the law, the only duty is to obey, and it does not lapse. Nevertheless, the analogy goes far enough. By being a citizen of a country which through its laws provides him with certain advantages of security and stability a man has duties which he has in no way undertaken. And his having them does not depend on his being free to leave; he may not be, and the duties do not vanish if he is not; this is indeed part of the reason why duty and obligation need to be distinguished.

Socrates' second argument is the argument later employed in the Social Contract theory of political obligation, that a man ought to obey the law to the extent that he has given an undertaking that he will. A man ought to do whatever he has undertaken to do, provided that what he has undertaken to do is right (49E), and that the undertaking has been freely given, i.e., not extracted by either duress or fraud (52E). Undertakings can be given by actions, as well as by formal written or spoken promises (52D). A man continuing to live in a state when he is free to leave it, as Athenians were (51D), thereby gives an undertaking to obey the law, which is nonetheless a real undertaking for being silent. Here again the basis of Socrates' argument is perfectly sound. However much the notion of tacit agreement or consent may have been overworked and overstretched by later political theorists, and by politicians trying to put rebellious youth in its place, the natural citizen of a state does not fail to have, or avoid having, the obligations which the naturalized citizen of it has, merely because it is false of the former, although true of the latter, that there was a time $t$ at which he formally undertook the obligations, and that he undertook them by declaring that he did. It is tempting to add that Socrates, in juxtaposing but not treating as synonyms *syntheke* and *homologia* (52D–E), was recognising the difference between mutual promises (those for which a consideration is received) and gratuitous promises (those without consideration). Some legal systems (e.g., England) recognize only the first as promises and as eligible for legal enforcement, other systems (e.g., Scotland) recognize both; in morality we recognize both. Unfortunately, so little indication is given in the *Crito* of the difference supposed between *syntheke* and *homologia*, and Plato was always, as an author, so far from being a precise technician in his choice of words, that we run the risk of ascribing to Socrates a distinction which he had never thought of.

While Socrates in effect maintained that a man ought always to perform his duty as a citizen, and always to fulfil his obligation as a contracting party, to obey the law (subject to the qualification, previously discussed, of his right to attempt to convince the law that it was in some area and in some respect wrong), that was not, for him, the end of the line. While it appears that he would have regarded the propositions that a man ought to perform his duties, and that he ought to fulfil his obligations, as necessary (thereby excluding exceptions) and as non-tautologous, he did not think that no reason could be given in support of them. What he would be doing, if he allowed the escape plan to go on and render the court's verdict and sentence ineffective, would be for his part to destroy the laws and the whole city (50B). A man ought to obey the law: he has both a duty and an obligation to do so; and a challenge to either is to be met by pointing out the socially destructive consequences of disobedience.

It may be questioned whether either of Socrates' theses is tenable: (1) that a man should always obey the law; (2) that he should always obey *because* the consequences of disobedience are, or would be, socially destructive. The weakness in (2) has to be shown first, because, although, even if (2) is false, (1) might still be true, the possibility of (1) being false is thereby opened up. As long as it is accepted as true that the consequences of any disobedience to law are socially destructive, it provides a strong inducement to retain (1).

First, it should be noticed that Socrates is using a "What would happen if . . . ?" argument. And we have to distinguish more clearly than he appears to do the question what would happen if he, as a single private individual, flouted the court's decision in his particular case, from the question what would happen if court decisions were always flouted by private individuals. We can allow that universal flouting of court decisions would sooner or later destroy the whole legal system; this is to justify the requirement of wholesale obedience by appeal to the socially destructive consequences of wholesale disobedience. But the harmful consequences of a single act of disobedience by a single individual would, unless his example triggered off wider disobedience, be negligible. So, the answer to the question "What would happen if . . . ?", more specifically "What would happen by way of harm to the state and its laws if . . . ?", asked of a single act of disobedience, as asked of a single broken promise, would almost always be "Nothing." For the "What would happen if . . . ?" question to have the effect of showing that conduct, which would be wrong in the wholesale case (because it would be socially destructive), would be wrong in the single case (although it would not be socially destructive), it has to be combined with a principle of fairness or justice; if a practice of everyone behaving in a certain way is justified by the social need for it, then it is not fair to the rest for anyone to gain an advantage for himself by making an exception of himself when his doing so will not imperil the practice. Disutility is the argument against destroying the practice, or against exceptions to it which will imperil it; the argument against exceptions which will not imperil the practice has to be the unfairness of exempting oneself from a practice which is socially useful or even indispensable.

If the only argument against general disobedience were of the kind produced by Socrates, namely that it has socially destructive effects, we have to ask how far it is true that it does. There are six possibilities of some or all people disobeying some or all of the laws:

    i. Some people disobey some laws.
   ii. All people disobey some laws.
  iii. Some laws are disobeyed by all people.
  iv. All laws are disobeyed by some people.
   v. Some people disobey all laws.
  vi. All people disobey all laws.

(The other mathematically possible cases are, in fact, identical with i. and vi. respectively.) i. almost certainly is true of every society, and probably ii. (there is nobody of whom it is true that there is no law which he ever disobeys) is also, but neither by itself has been enough to ruin any society. In the case of iii. (there are some laws of which it is true that nobody obeys them), if the laws in question are bad ones, the consequences of universal disobedience could be, although they are not necessarily, good; the same consideration, in a weaker form, applies to i. and ii. Similarly with iv.: although it may not be a good thing if it is the case that there is no law which is not disobeyed by someone, it is not in itself disastrous. v. could be true without its being much more than a nuisance, if the number of consistent violators were small enough for the officers of the law to be able to cope with them easily. Indeed, over all the cases i.–v., whether the disobedience imperilled the law and the state would depend on the extensiveness of the "some." This is not to say that in all these cases disobedience is right, or even all right, but it is to say that in plenty of instances falling under them it could not be maintained that disobedience was wrong for Socrates' reason, viz., that such disobedience threatened the survival of the state. And it is not cynical to say that, even if it were never right for anyone to disobey any of the laws to which he was subject, it might nevertheless be a good thing if somebody occasionally did, so that the example of his conviction and sentence might discourage other potential lawbreakers.

In fact, the only case to which the argument of social disaster clearly applies is vi. Some would regard even that as questionable, asking us to imagine a through-and-through evil legal system, the destruction of which we ought to hasten as fast as we can by systematic disobedience. But against that it can be objected that a 100 per cent pernicious legal system could not exist, for it could not meet one of the necessary conditions of being a legal system, viz., that of actually regulating men's conduct. Individual laws, even wide areas of a body of law, can be pernicious, but a whole system could not be.

It might be suggested that in 50B Socrates is using a

quite different line of argument from the one here criticised, and be maintaining that a state cannot survive in
which anyone is free to take the law into his own hands,
i.e., to decide for himself when to obey or to disobey a
law, and to decide with impunity. It is far from clear
that that is what he does mean; but, even if it is, it is
again incomplete without the fairness principle. Granted
that it is true that a state could hardly survive the practice of everybody pleasing himself when to disobey the
law, this has no bearing on the individual case (given
that there is no risk of its generating the practice) except through the principle of fairness.

When Socrates' thesis (1), that a man should always
obey the law, is separated from thesis (2), which gave
the final reason for it, and which has been shown to be
untenable, it itself appears less plausible. There are, of
course, reasons both of utility and of fairness both why a
man should obey the law, and why he should obey a
particular law. But it follows from that that it cannot be
true that a man should always, and in whatever circumstances, obey the law, or a particular law. If the case
for obedience rests on fairness and utility, it must be
conceivable that fairness and utility would, in certain
circumstances be served by disobedience. Not only is
it conceivable, it is actual: the American Revolution
against English colonial rule will do as an example. And,
if fairness and utility can lie at all on the side of disobedience, it is conceivable that they should outweigh
the claims of obedience. We may be thankful to live in
a society in which duty to disobey the law appears very
rarely and in very extreme circumstances, but we should
remember that we live in a society which owes its origin
precisely to some men seeing that as their duty and
following it.

# 14. PLATO'S EARLIER THEORY OF FORMS

R. E. ALLEN

The subject here is the theory of Forms which Plato puts into the mouth of Socrates in the earlier dialogues. The primary text is the *Euthyphro*, an early dialogue.[1]

You will recall the circumstances under which the *Euthyphro* begins. Socrates has come to the Porch of the King Archon to answer an indictment for impiety, an indictment which will lead to his conviction and death. Euthyphro, an Athenian *mantis* or seer, has come to prosecute his aged father for murder, lodging his prosecution in behalf of a man who was himself a murderer taken in the act. It is, he thinks, the pious or holy thing to do, and the gods demand it.

The story of Euthyphro's prosecution is generally thought to have a basis in fact, on the ground, often excellent in history, that it is too good not to be true. Plato tells the story with a delicate irony all his own; but he

This paper was originally read at Princeton University, March 14, 1967.

[1] The degree to which the discussion of the *Euthphr.* also represents the mind of the historical Socrates is, in my view, impossible to determine. There is good reason to think that Plato's portrait of Socrates in the early dialogues is meant to be accurate; for one thing, Plato's purpose in writing must surely in part have been to defend Socrates' memory, and that purpose could not have been served by presenting to men who had known him a picture which was in any obvious way false. On the issue of Forms, there is evidence in Xenophon as well as Plato that the historical Socrates asked the "What is it?" question (*Mem.* I. i., cf. I. iv., IV. vi.); and there is a suggestion in the *Clouds* of Aristophanes, v. 194 (not amounting to proof) that Socrates used the formula αὐτὸ καθ' αὐτό, and therefore presumably the thought that lay behind it. But whether the historical Socrates intended the "What is it?" question to be circumscribed in precisely the way the *Euthphr.* suggests cannot at this point be determined on the basis of evidence. Plato himself might have been hard put to distinguish between what, as an artist, he had invented, and what he had found.

uses it to point a philosophical moral. Euthyphro is prosecuting his father because he is convinced that it is right and fitting to do so, and piety or holiness requires it. But his father, his relatives, and most ordinary Athenians would have regarded such a prosecution as a thing most monstrously impious. In this conflict of moral opinion, each side holding incompatible views with equal confidence, where is there a sufficient basis for decision to be found?

Plato's introduction to the *Euthyphro* is meant to exhibit a need which will later be explicitly stated: the need to find a standard by which to determine what things are holy and what are not.

Socrates begins the dialectic of the dialogue with a modest request. Euthyphro, in undertaking the thing he is doing, must surely know accurately how things stand respecting divine law and matters of holiness and unholiness. So Socrates would like to become his pupil; after all, he has himself an indictment for impiety to meet. Just what is holiness?

The question is a highly ambiguous one. Socrates might have been asking for a synonym of holiness, or an example of holiness, or a distinguishing mark by which to set off holy things from other things. But he is in fact asking for a definition of the essential nature of holiness, and he works to make his meaning clear (*Euthphr.* 5C–D).

> What sort of thing is the pious and impious, both with respect to murder and other things as well? Or is not the holy, the same in itself, the same in every action? And the unholy, in turn, the utter opposite of the holy—is it not like itself, and does not everything which is to be unholy have a certain single character (ἰδέα) with respect to unholiness?

Euthyphro misses the point of the question. He replies with an example: holiness, he thinks, is doing just what he is doing now, prosecuting murderers and temple thieves; and not prosecuting them is unholy. In the same way, Laches, a soldier, thinks that courage is sticking to your post and not running away in the face of the enemy (*La.* 190E). Charmides, a sought-after youth, thinks that temperance is keeping quiet and being modest (*Chrm.* 159B). Cephalus, an elderly business man, will say that justice is telling the truth and paying your debts (*R.* I, 331C). And Hippias, a Sophist who apparently had wider interests, thinks that the beautiful is a beautiful maiden, though he later hazards the guess that it is gold (*Hp. Ma.* 287E, 289E).

Socrates repeats his question. Other things are holy besides prosecuting murderers and temple thieves, and what he wants is an account of the character all holy things have (6D–E):

> You will recall, Euthyphro, that I did not ask you to give me an account of one or two of the many things which are holy, but of that characteristic itself (αὐτὸ τὸ εἶδος) by which all holy things are holy. For you agreed, I think, that it is by one character (ἰδέα) that unholy things are unholy and holy things holy. . . . Give me an account of what this same character (ἰδέα) is, so that I may look to it and use it as a standard (παράδειγμα), which, should those things which you or someone else may do be of that sort, I may affirm that they are holy, but should it not be of that sort, deny it.

The words εἶδος and ἰδέα, here translated neutrally as "characteristic" and "character," have a range of ordinary meanings: sort or kind, figure, including the human figure, the nature of a thing, or the look of a thing, its *species* or outward appearance. But the words are here used in a special way. The εἶδος or ἰδέα of holiness is a universal, the same in all its instances, and something its instances have; it appears to be a condition for the existence of holy things, that *by which*—the dative is instrumental—holy things are holy; and it is a standard or παράδειγμα for determining what things are holy and what are not. In short, the words εἶδος and ἰδέα here carry freight they do not ordinarily bear, and for that reason, commentators have often translated them as "Idea" or "Form." "Form" is preferable, since it escapes the subjective and psychological connotations that hover around the word "idea" in English.

Socrates wishes to know what is the same, ταὐτόν, in every holy action, and will not take an example in reply. For many things are holy, and what Socrates wishes to know is the nature of the Form they all share.

This pattern of argument is found in other dialogues. In the *Laches* (191E–192B), when courage is defined by the example of courage in battle, Socrates argues that this is not enough. Courage is found, not only in war, but in perils at sea, in disease, poverty, and politics, and what he wishes to be told is what is the same (ταὐτόν) in all these instances. In the *Hippias Major* (300A–B), Socrates claims that if two different things are beautiful, they must have something identical (τι τὸ αὐτό) which makes them beautiful, and that this common thing (τὸ κοινὸν τοῦτο) must be present to them. When Meno, in an early middle dialogue, undertakes to define virtue with a list of examples, Socrates corrects him with an analogy. Suppose you are asked what a bee is. There are many different kinds of bees, but it does no good to name them; bees do not differ as bees, and the question demanded some account of the character all bees share. So it is with virtue: "However diverse and multitudinous the virtues may be, they have all a common characteristic (εἶδος) through which they are virtues, and it is on this that anyone who would say what virtue is must fix his gaze" (*Men.* 72C).

The claim that the εἶδος or ἰδέα of holiness is the same in all holy things, and that it is something they all have (ἔχον, 5D3), may be abbreviated as the claim that Forms are universals. As universals, they play a regulative role in dialectic. They are the antecedents of "it" in Socrates' question, "What is it?" and they therefore specify the peculiar nature of that question, and so restrict the range of answers which may sensibly be given to it. Because holiness is a universal, Euthyphro cannot answer the question, "What is holiness?" by offering examples of things which are holy.

Socrates wishes to be told the nature of holiness in order to use it as a standard by which to tell what things are holy and what are not.[2] This demand for a standard is of the essence of Plato's dialectic, which is directed not merely toward abstract understanding, but toward the right ordering of life. The aim is to grasp the principles of that order, and to be able to identify them in concrete cases. In the *Republic* (I, 344D–E) it is claimed that it is important to know what is holy and what is just and what is virtuous, because on that knowledge depends the conduct of a life. In the *Charmides* (175E), the young Charmides is said to be most temperate; but without knowing what temperance is, he will have no advantage from its presence in his life—this to a man who later became one of the Thirty. If the aim of dialectic is to define a Form, the practical aim is the discernment of Form in things. Forms are in moral matters what scales are to weight and yardsticks to length, a basis for sufficient decision (cf. *Euthphr.* 7B–D).

As with the assumption that Forms are universals, the assumption that they are standards plays a regulative role in dialectic, ruling out all those answers to the "What is it?" question which imply that the Form is in some way qualified by its opposite.[3] This is where Euthyphro's next attempt at definition goes wrong, "holiness is what is loved by the gods." The formula escapes a principal defect of his first attempt: it provides, not an example, but a distinguishing mark, setting off, at least in intention, all those and only those things which are to be holy. The requirement of universality has now been met. But the definition still proceeds in a sense by example: it specifies a group of individuals—things, actions, persons (7A)—marked off from the rest by being loved by the gods. And it is the individuals, not their distinguishing mark, which are identified with holiness.

Euthyphro's theology, however, is, so to speak, vulgarly Olympian. The gods quarrel among themselves,

---

[2] *Euthphr.* 6E; cf. *Ly.* 223B, *Hp. Ma.* 286C–D.
[3] *Euthphr.* 6E–8B; cf. *Hp. Ma.* 289C, *R.* I, 331B–D, 339C–D.

loving and hating the same things. So some holy things, by his account, are unholy, and Socrates has still not found out what holiness is.

This refutation seems worthless. A definition of animal which applied to non-animals would clearly be too broad; no animal is a non-animal. Neither is any odd number even. But some tall things are short—tall pygmies, for example—and Hippias' maiden, though beautiful, was ugly compared to a goddess. It is not self-evidently false that some holy things are unholy, and if Euthyphro's theology is sound, his definition implies that it is true.

But this neglects the peculiar character of Socrates' question. Euthyphro's definition specifies, not a universal, but a group of things set off from others by a distinguishing mark, that of being loved by the gods. But Socrates had requested, not an account of things which are holy, but an account of a Form of holiness which should serve as a standard for judging what things are holy and what are not. A set of things which are examples of holiness, but also in some part examples of unholiness, is hardly fitted to serve as a standard. We can scarcely identify a thing as holy by comparing it to things some of which are also unholy. The difficulty, indeed, lies even deeper. We cannot determine that that to which we compare it is itself either holy or unholy, without knowledge of holiness and unholiness in and of themselves.[4]

This is directly connected with the self-identity of Forms. Socrates earlier on had suggested that holiness is αὐτὸ αὑτῷ, the same in itself, and that its opposite, unholiness, is αὐτῷ ὅμοιον, like itself (5D). This suggestion is expanded at 7A to mean that holiness is not identical with unholiness, but its utter opposite, and the refutation of Euthyphro's definition is so stated as to imply that it violates this principle: you cannot say what holiness is by stating ὃ τυγχάνει ταὐτὸν ὂν ὅσιόν τε

[4] Cf. H. F. Cherniss, "The Philosophical Economy of the Theory of Ideas," *Studies in Plato's Metaphysics*, ed. Allen (London, 1965), 2-3.

καὶ ἀνόσιον (8A). The assumption here is that if holiness were in any way unholy, it would not be the opposite of unholiness. The intuitive principle underlying this inference is plain: that by which or in virtue of which things are holy cannot be itself in any way unholy.[5] The self-identity of Forms implies the radical exclusion of their opposites, and that exclusion is directly connected with the use of the Form as a standard. It can never be a true answer to the question, "What is holiness?" to name something which is in any way unholy. Thus, holiness cannot be identified with the group of things which are holy, if some of those things are also unholy too.

But the root of the difficulty underlying Euthyphro's definition is exposed by his attempt to amend it. He had offered a definition by distinguishing mark. The flaw in this shows up when he tries to avoid the problem of qualification by opposites, and defines holiness as what is loved by *all* the gods.

Socrates begins by asking whether the group of things which are holy are loved because they are holy, or holy because they are loved. Euthyphro gives the common-sense answer, they are loved because they are holy. He had already granted without question that the gods love what they believe noble, good, and right, and hate what they think opposite (7E); the goodness in things is, for him as for most plain men, a reason for loving and not a consequence of it. But this leads to the collapse of his definition. Socrates, by a beautiful and ingenious argument, demonstrates that if this is so, being loved by all the gods is not the οὐσία, the nature and reality, or essence, of holiness, but merely a πάθος of it, a property which happens to be connected with it[6] (10E–11A).

Just as with the assumption that Forms are universals and standards, so the assumption that an account of them must state essence plays a regulative role in dialectic: an answer to the question, "What is holiness?" cannot merely provide a distinguishing mark which happens to characterize holy things; it must provide an analysis of

[5] Cf. *Prt.* 330C–E.
[6] Cf. *Prt.* 349B, *Hp. Ma.* 301B, C, E, 302C.

the nature of holiness, that by which holy things are holy.[7]

The request to know the essence of holiness, as opposed to a distinguishing mark, involves a peculiar priority. Just as one cannot know what things are holy without knowing what holiness is, so one must know what holiness is before one can know what properties—or distinguishing marks—happen to be connected with it. This point is not explicitly made in the *Euthyphro*. But in the *Laches* (190B–C), one cannot know how virtue can be acquired without knowing what it is; in the *Republic* (I, 354B–C) one cannot know whether justice is profitable, or makes its possessors happy, without knowing what it is; in the *Protagoras* (359E–361D), Socrates and Protagoras cannot agree on whether virtue is teachable, or whether it is knowledge, because they do not know what it is. In the *Meno* (71B), Socrates cannot say whether virtue is taught or acquired by practice or present by nature, because he does not know what it is; how, indeed, could one say ποῖόν τί ἐστιν without knowing ὅ τι ἔστιν? (86E). The results of trying are shown in the failure of the dialectic at 100B.

The priority of οὐσία to πάθος, τί to ποῖόν τι, is directly implicated with the fact that Forms are standards. The ground of connection between holiness and other properties must lie either in the nature of holiness itself or in the things which are holy; that holiness is teachable, for example, is either a claim about the Form of holiness, or about those things which have the Form. In either case, one cannot estimate its truth without knowing what holiness is, since one must know what holiness is before one can determine what things are holy.

Aristotle defines an essence as, "what a thing is καθ᾽ αὐτό, in itself, the account of which is a definition."[8] Socrates,

---

[7] It is perhaps worth pointing out that the relation involved in providing a distinguishing mark is implication, whereas that involved in a statement of essence is some sort of identity. Cf. *Euthphr.* 10D, 15B, 15C.

[8] *Metaphysics* VII.iv.

having demanded of Euthyphro an account of what holiness is in itself, next proceeds to give him a lesson in how to define (*Euthphr.* 11E–12A). Euthyphro must begin by saying what holiness is a part of, as reverence is a part of fear. He must then say what part it is, as even number is that part of number divisible by two. Euthyphro's remaining attempts at definition in the dialogue conform to this plan. He next defines holiness as that part of justice concerned with service to the gods, and then, when that is refuted, as an art of (i.e., that part of art concerned with) prayer and sacrifice.

It is not, I think, misrepresenting Socrates' plan to say that he is here after definition *per genus et differentiam*, though this is surely not beyond dispute, and though the immediate rider must be added that such definition will involve, not division into simpler elements from which the species may be constructed, but a kind of mapping within genera. But for present purposes, the important thing is that the definition in view is real and not nominal. It is analysis of essence, rather than stipulation as to how words shall be used or a report as to how they are in fact used.

Mill thought that real definition is simply nominal definition plus an existence claim. Thus the real definition of triangularity would be: "'Triangle' means 'plane rectilinear figure with three angles,' and there are triangles." This view is probably at least as old as Euclid, and by some accounts, it is Aristotle's own. Aristotle certainly thought that, "What is meant by a unit and the fact that a unit exists are different things" (Post. Anal. I 72A24); and in Euclid's *Elements*, existence is not deduced from definitions, but demonstrated by construction. All of this may have its roots in the *Phaedo*, where Socrates recommends the use of a method of hypothesis as a δεύτερος πλοῦς, after failing to grasp the nature of things directly (99D; cf. 100A–E, 101C–D). And, of course, it is closely similar to the account of the connection between existence and analyticity offered in much modern logical theory.

But it is not what real definition involves in the *Euthyphro*. The dialectical procedure there cannot be described as an attempt to define the word "holy," coupled with an attempt to find out whether it applies to anything. In the first place, the requirements for answering the "What is it?" question are not those of nominal definition; nominal definitions are definitions of words, not of standards or essences,[9] and there is no good reason why they should be required always to be *per genus et differentiam*. And, in the second place, existential import is taken for granted, not demonstrated, in the early dialogues; Euthyphro and Socrates assume without question that there are holy things, and ask only what their nature is. This assumption of existence is made in every early dialogue in which the "What is it?" question is initially answered by appeal to examples—which is to say in every early dialogue in which it is asked. The reason is not far to seek. An essence is not a "possibility," or a "hypostatized meaning"; it is the nature of something which is.[10] And real definition, in the early dialogues, is analysis of essence.

Now, what does all this imply? It seems to imply something which is properly called a theory of Forms. That theory is, in the first place, a technical theory, a body of rules governing the practice of a useful art, that of dialectic. Thus, the question, "What is holiness?" cannot be answered by examples, nor by specifying a group of things some of which are unholy, nor by providing a distinguishing mark. It must be answered by an analysis of the essence of holiness, because holiness is a Form.

So it is a technical theory—a logical theory, if you will, in some sense of that much used and much abused term. But it is also a metaphysical theory. It assumes the existence of Forms, as universals, standards, and essences.

[9] Unless, of course, one wishes to say that the meaning of the word "holiness" is holiness, and that in order to understand what "holiness" means one must understand what holiness is. But nominal definition, so construed, becomes essential definition: one is not then defining the *word* "holy."

[10] Cf. Aristotle, *Post. Anal.* II.92B3–12, *Metaphysics* VII.1031A 12 ff.

That assumption is stated or implied throughout the early dialogues.[11]

It is to be remembered that one mark of being is power. As essences, Forms do not, so to speak, just sit there. They do honest work. They affect the career of the world, being that by which things are what they are.[12] There is an argument in the *Hippias Major* which makes this point explicitly. Socrates leads Hippias to agree that justice *is* something (ἔστι τι τοῦτο) and that this is true of wisdom too, for "things which are just and wise and so on would not be such *by* them, if they were not something." Because beautiful things are beautiful by beauty, Hippias is compelled to agree that beauty *is* something too. Socrates then goes on to ask, What is it? (287C–D).

The argument is an excellent one. If beauty is that by which beautiful things are beautiful, and beautiful things exist, beauty exists. Beauty is not a word, not a thought, not a concept. It is an existing thing, for the things it makes beautiful are existing things, and they are not made beautiful by our words or thoughts or concepts.

This conflicts with the commonly held view that there is no commitment to the existence of Forms in the early dialogues, and that talk of them there is "merely a matter of language." That seems to me to confuse language with what language is used to affirm. The Muses may inspire a poet, made drunk by their presence, to compare the redness of a rare sunset to the redness of a rare beefsteak; they do not, or do not thereby, inspire him with the belief that he has added redness along with sunsets and beefsteaks to his ontology. But if that same poet, in more sober mood, were to ask what redness is, explaining that he wished to be told the nature of a characteristic common not only to sunsets and beefsteaks, but to barns, fire engines, Russians, and all such similar things; and if he went on to add that when he learned what it is, he

[11] *Euthphr.* 5C–D, 6D–E, 11A, 15C–D; *Men.* 71A–B, 86C–D; *Prt.* 329C, 330C, 349B–C, 352E; *Euthd.* 290B–C; *La.* 189E–190B, 191E, 192A–B, C; *Hp. Ma.* 287C–D.

[12] *Euthphr.* 5D; *Hp. Ma.* 287C–D, 288A, 300A; *Men.* 72C; cf. *Prt.* 332B, E.

expected to use it as a standard for distinguishing what is really red from what isn't; and that he expected a proper account of it to state its οὐσία, its nature and reality, and be formulated *per genus et differentiam*—if, in short, he laid down rules for real definition and followed them in his inquiry, we should begin to suspect that the inspiration the Muses had visited upon him was metaphysical, rather than poetical, and that he now came equipped with a view of the way the world is, and what it contains, which goes considerably beyond anything which ordinary language or common sense can show.

If this is true, if Socrates' questions involve a metaphysical assumption about existence, how is it that his respondents are able to reply to them? Surely it is significant, it may be argued, that a man like Euthyphro, who, whatever he is, is no dialectician, should accept without demur the suggestion that there is an εἶδος of holiness. Surely it is significant that Protagoras, whom Plato himself portrayed as a conventionalist in morals, agrees without hesitation that justice "is something." Protagoras can hardly have meant to embrace an ontology of abstract entities; his agreement is more likely to be prompted by the uses of language: all of us who are not cynics or otherwise disreputable believe, after all, that there is such a thing as justice.

Socrates, armed with a metaphysical theory, is able to apply it—and, indeed, take it for granted—in conversation with ordinary men. The reason, I think, is that though the Socratic theory of Forms is a metaphysical theory, it is also essentially continuous with common sense, being, in one sense of that overworked word, a theory of meaning. "What do you say temperance is?" Socrates asks Charmides. "Since you know how to speak Greek, you no doubt can say what it seems to you to be" (*Chrm.* 159A; cf. *La.* 197E; *Prt.* 329D; *Alc.* I, 111C, 112A–D). When Critias charges Socrates with arguing only to refute him, Socrates replies (*Chrm.* 166C–D):

> How can you believe, if I try my best to refute you, that I do so from any other motive than to examine what my own

words mean, for fear that it may at some point escape my notice that I think I know something I do not.

Plain men had talked of holiness long before Socrates came to ask them what it was exactly that they meant. His inquiry is distinguished by the precision of it. He does not want synonyms of holiness, or examples of it, or distinguishing marks of it, but an analysis of the nature of it. His question is hardly one which common sense, left to its own devices, will ask. But it is a question to which common sense may certainly be led, and the dialectic of the *Euthyphro* is in fact a record of such leading; Socrates works throughout to make Euthyphro see the real nature of his question. The progress of dialectic involves passage from the naïve existence claim that "there is such a thing as holiness" to the highly sophisticated existence claim that there is an essence of holiness, and that it can be defined. But if we are willing to admit this last, the passage is continuous; for the commitment to essence is then latent in the common sense use of words. The essence of holiness is what we mean by the word "holiness"—when we fully understand our meaning.

Not all philosophers, of course, would admit this. It implies that questions of meaning are in the final analysis ontological questions, questions about the nature and structure of the world; they are not merely "second-order" questions, questions about the language in which we talk about the world. And since we understand the nature and structure of the world imperfectly, it also implies that we often do not know what we mean by what we say—witness Euthyphro. If meaning implies essence, it is simply not true of ordinary language that, "Everything is in order as it is."

The solution, it may be, is to deny essences. "One thinks that one is tracing the outline of the thing's nature over and over again, and one is merely tracing round the frame through which we look at it. A picture held us captive. And we could not get outside it, for it lay in our language and language seemed to repeat it to us inexorably. When philosophers use a word . . . and try to

grasp the *essence* of the thing, one must ask oneself: is
the word ever actually used this way in the language-
game which is its original home?—What *we* do is to
bring words back from their metaphysical to their every-
day use."[18] So Wittgenstein. If this view is true, the assumptions on which Socratic dialectic rest are false. So
are the typical Socratic claims that virtue is knowledge,
that courage is wisdom, that holiness is just. These words
are not used that way every day—no more in ordinary
ancient Greek than in ordinary modern English. Socrates' identification, or connection, of things which are lin-
guistically distinct is unintelligible apart from the notion
of essence—unless we are to explain his claim about the
unity of the virtues as mere tyrannical legislation over
language.

I have suggested that there is a theory of Forms in the
early dialogues, and that it involves a metaphysical claim.
I have not suggested that it is *the* theory of Forms—that
theory of the choir of heaven and the furniture of earth
found in the *Phaedo, Republic,* and other middle dialogues. Burke once remarked, "though no man can draw
a stroke between the confines of night and day, yet light
and darkness are upon the whole tolerably distinguishable." So it is with the early and the middle dialogues.
The difference between the *Euthyphro* on one hand, and
the *Phaedo* and *Republic* on the other, is perhaps not the
difference of light and darkness. But it is tolerably plain.
The philosophy of the middle dialogues is a nest of coupled contrasts: Being and Becoming, Appearance and
Reality, Permanence and Flux, Reason and Sense, Body
and Soul, Flesh and the Spirit. Those contrasts are rooted
in an ontology of two Worlds, separated by a gulf of deficiency. The World of Knowledge, whose contents are
the eternal Forms, stands to the World of Opinion,
whose contents are sensible and changing, as the more
real stands to the less real, as originals stand to shadows

[18] *Philosophical Investigations* (Oxford, 1953), para. 114–16.
The position directly under criticism is Wittgenstein's own in the
*Tractatus,* but I suppose the comment to be relevant to the present
context.

and reflections. The visible world is an image, unknowable in its deficiency, of an intelligible world apprehended by reason alone.

This is "separation," and it is possible to fix with some precision the kind of separation it is. It assumes both that sensible instances of Forms are deficient resemblances of Forms, and that they are less real than Forms. There is no trace of either of these claims in early dialogues such as the *Euthyphro*, nor of the characteristic doctrines of the middle dialogues with which those claims are implicated—Recollection, and the radical distinction between Knowledge and Opinion. The Theory of Forms in the middle dialogues is meant to answer questions, especially questions arising out of problems of knowledge, which the early dialogues have not yet raised.

Let me now summarize. W. A. Heidel once remarked of the *Euthyphro* that, "none of the briefer Platonic dialogues can be compared with it for the value of its suggestions towards philosophical theory."[14] This is surely true. The philosophical interest of the dialogue does not lie in the product of its dialectic—no product is announced—but in the rules by which that dialectic proceeds. Those rules, and the assumptions on which they rest, constitute *a* (not *the*) theory of Forms. It is a theory which operates much more at the level of assumption than of explicit statement, but a theory nonetheless, and one whose elements may be put with some precision.

Socrates' aim, in the *Euthyphro*, is to obtain an answer to the question, "What is holiness?" He assumes, in pursuing his inquiry, that there is an εἶδος or ἰδέα, or Form, of holiness, and that this Form is the same in all holy things. He further assumes that the Form of holiness may be used as a standard by which to judge what things are holy and what are not; that it is an essence, by which or in virtue of which holy things are holy; that it is capable of essential definition, and (apparently) that that definition will be *per genus et differentiam*. These assumptions constitute a theory of Forms.

That theory is both logical and metaphysical. Logically,

---

[14] W. A. Heidel, *Plato's Euthyphro* (New York, 1902), 27.

Forms play a regulative role in dialectic; as antecedents of "it" in questions of "What is it?" they determine the kinds of answer which are acceptable, and perhaps more importantly, unacceptable, in Socrates' search for definition. Metaphysically, Forms exist and affect the career of the world; they are the real natures of things, and the world is what it is because they are what they are.

These two sides of Plato's theory, logical and metaphysical, meet in the notion of real definition. Dialectic is governed by rule, and directed toward discovering the nature of things. Its rules are determined by its aim. To say that Forms exist is to say that real definition is possible; to say that real definition is possible is to say that Forms exist. The theory of Forms in the *Euthyphro* is not a superstructure gracelessly added on to dialectic; it is the foundation of dialectic. Without it, dialectic would not proceed by the rules it uses, or work toward the goal at which it aims. Socratic moral inquiry is inquiry about reality.

This is metaphysics, but not the metaphysics of the middle dialogues. The middle dialogues do not abandon the "What is it?" question. They pursue it in the light of a new ontology. That ontology rests on two principles, the immortality and divinity of the rational soul, and the complete reality and eternity of the objects of knowledge. Those principles, in F. M. Cornford's phrase,[15] are the pillars of Platonism, and their architrave is the doctrine of Recollection, the doctrine that the truth of things is always in the soul. The foundation on which this lofty structure rests is a theory of Forms which implies the diminished reality and deficiency of resemblance of sensible objects. None of this is found in the early dialogues.

The theory of Forms in the middle dialogues, then, is neither the same theory as that of the early dialogues, nor a different one. Not different, because it contains the earlier theory as a part. Not the same, because it is directed toward issues which the early dialogues do not raise.

---

[15] *Plato's Theory of Knowledge* (London, 1950), 2.

# NOTES ON CONTRIBUTORS

REGINALD E. ALLEN is Professor of Philosophy at the University of Toronto.

M. F. BURNYEAT is Lecturer in Philosophy, University College, London.

S. MARC COHEN is Assistant Professor of Philosophy, Rutgers University.

KENNETH J. DOVER is Professor of Greek in the University of St. Andrews.

A. R. LACEY is Lecturer in Philosophy, Bedford College, University of London.

GEORGE NAKHNIKIAN is Professor and Chairman of the Department of Philosophy, Indiana University.

RICHARD ROBINSON was formerly Associate Professor of Philosophy at Cornell University. He was a Tutor of Oriel College and a University Lecturer at Oxford University from 1946 to 1969, and has been a Fellow of Oriel College from 1946 to the present.

GERASIMOS SANTAS is Professor of Philosophy, University of California at Irvine.

JAMES J. WALSH is Professor and Chairman of the Department of Philosophy, Columbia University.

A. D. WOOZLEY, formerly Professor of Moral Philosophy in the University of St. Andrews, is now Professor of Philosophy in the Corcoran Department of Philosophy, University of Virginia. He has served as editor of the *Philosophical Quarterly*.

GREGORY VLASTOS is Stuart Professor of Philosophy at Princeton University. He had previously taught philosophy at Queen's University in Kingston, Ontario, and at Cornell University.

# SELECTED BIBLIOGRAPHY OF BOOKS
# AND ARTICLES IN ENGLISH
# ON SOCRATES' PHILOSOPHY

I. BOOKS AND ARTICLES BY
CONTRIBUTORS TO THIS VOLUME

Allen, R. E., *The Euthyphro and Plato's Earlier Theory of Forms* (London, 1970).

———, "The Socratic Paradox," *Journal of the History of Ideas* 21 (1960), 256–65.

Robinson, Richard, *Plato's Earlier Dialectic*, Second Edition (Oxford, 1953).

Santas, Gerasimos, "The Socratic Paradoxes," *Philosophical Review* 73 (1964), 147–64.

Vlastos, Gregory, *Plato's Protagoras*, B. Jowett's translation revised by M. Ostwald, edited with Introduction by G. Vlastos (New York, 1956), xxiv–lvi.

———, "Socratic Knowledge and Platonic 'Pessimism'," *Philosophical Review* 66 (1957), 226–38, at 226–32.

———, "Was Polus Refuted?" *American Journal of Philology* 88 (1967), 454–60.

———, "Socrates on Acrasia," *Phoenix* 23 (1969), 71–88.


II. BOOKS BY OTHER AUTHORS

(a) Commentaries or Translations with Notes of Philosophical Interest

On the *Apology*: Riddell, J., *The Apology of Plato* (Oxford, 1865).

On the *Apology, Crito,* and *Euthyphro*: Burnet, J., *Plato's Euthyphro, Apology of Socrates, and Crito* (Oxford, 1924).

On the *Charmides*: Tuckey, T. G., *Plato's "Charmides"* (Cambridge, 1951).

On the *Euthydemus*: Sprague, Rosamond K., *Plato: Euthydemus* (New York, 1965).

On the *Gorgias*: Thompson, W. H., *The Gorgias of Plato* (London, 1871).

———, Dodds, E. R., *Plato: Gorgias* (Oxford, 1959).

On the *Protagoras*: Guthrie, W. K. C., Plato's *Protagoras and Meno* (London, 1956).


(b) Books

Adkins, A. W. H., *Merit and Responsibility: A Study in Greek Values* (Oxford, 1960), Chapter 13, "Plato: Logic and Elenchus."

Barker, E., *Greek Political Theory* (London, 1918), Chapter 5, "Socrates and the Minor Socratics."

Chroust, A. H., *Socrates, Man and Myth* (London, 1957).

Cornford, F. M., *Before and After Socrates* (Cambridge, 1932).

Crombie, I. M., *An Examination of Plato's Doctrines*, Vol. I: *Plato on Man and Society* (London, 1962), 204–45.

Field, G. C., *Plato and his Contemporaries* (London, 1930), Chapters 10 and 11 on "The Socratic Literature," and 12 on "The Socratic Philosophers."

Friedländer, P., *Plato*, Vol. II: *The Dialogues, First Period*, English translation by H. Meyerhoff (New York, 1964).

Grote, G., *Plato and the Other Companions of Socrates* (London, 1888), discussion of the earlier dialogues in Vols. I and II.

Gould, J., *The Development of Plato's Ethics* (Cambridge, 1955), Part One, "The Personal Ideal" (Socrates' moral philosophy and character).

Gulley, N., *The Philosophy of Socrates* (London, 1968).

Guthrie, W. K. C., *History of Greek Philosophy*, Vol. III: *The Fifth-Century Enlightenment* (Cambridge, 1969).

Hackforth, R., *The Composition of Plato's Apology* (Cambridge, 1933).

Huby, Pamela, *Greek Ethics* (London, 1967), Chapter 3, "Socrates."

Jaeger, W., *Paideia*, II, translation by G. Highet (Oxford, 1941).

Levinson, R. B., *In Defense of Plato* (Cambridge, Mass., 1953), on Socrates, 233–307 *et passim*.

North, Helen, *Sophrosyne* (Ithaca, N.Y., 1966), 155–65, on the Socratic conception.

O'Brien, M. J., *The Socratic Paradoxes and the Greek Mind* (Chapel Hill, 1967).

Owens, J., *A History of Ancient Western Philosophy* (New York, 1959), 165–75, on Socrates.

Popper, Karl, *The Open Society and its Enemies*, Fourth Edition (Princeton, 1962), on Socrates, 189–201 *et passim*.

Shorey, P., *What Plato Said* (Chicago, 1933), on Socrates, 74–155 *et passim*.

Sinclair, T. A., *A History of Greek Political Thought* (London, 1951), Chapter 5, "Socrates and his Opponents."

Sprague, Rosamond, *Plato's Use of Fallacy* (London, 1962), Chapters 1 and 4, on the *Euthydemus* and the *Hippias Minor*.

Strauss, L., *Socrates and Aristophanes* (New York, 1966).

Taylor, A. E., *Varia Socratica* (Oxford, 1911).

——, *Plato, the Man and his Work* (London, 1926), Chapters 3 to 7 on "Socratic Dialogues" and Chapter 10 on "Protagoras."

——, *Socrates* (London, 1932).

Versenyi, L., *Socratic Humanism* (New Haven, 1963).

Winspear, A. D. and Silverberg, T., *Who Was Socrates?* (New York, 1939).

(c) Articles and Essays

Anderson, A., "Socratic Reasoning in the *Euthyphro*," *Review of Metaphysics* 22 (1969), 461–81.

Bambrough, J., "The Socratic Paradox," *Philosophical Quarterly* 10 (1960), 229–300.

Brown, J. H., "The Logic in *Euthyphro* 10A–11B," *Philosophical Quarterly* 14 (1964), 1–14.

Burnet, J., "The Socratic Doctrine of the Soul," *Proc. of the British Academy* 7 (1915–16). Reprinted in *Essays and Addresses* (London, 1929).

Clapp, J. G., "Some Notes on Plato's *Protagoras*," *Philosophy and Phenomenological Research* 10 (1949–50), 486–99.

Ehnmark, E., "Socrates and the Immortality of the Soul," *Eranos* 44 (1946), 105–22.

Ferguson, A. S., "The Impiety of Socrates," *Classical Quarterly* 7 (1913), 157–75.

Fox, M., "The Trials of Socrates," *Archiv für Philosophie* 6 (1956), 226 ff.

Gallop, G., "Justice and Holiness in *Prot.* 330–331," *Phronesis* 6 (1961), 86–93.

——, "The Socratic Paradox in the *Protagoras*," *Phronesis* 9 (1964), 117–29.

Gauthier, David P., "The Unity of Wisdom and Temperance" (Critique of D. Savan, "Socrates' Logic and the Unity of Wisdom and Temperance"), *Journal of the History of Philosophy* 6 (1968), 157–59.

Geach, P., "Plato's *Euthyphro*: An Analysis and Commentary," *Monist* 50 (1966), 369–82.

Gordon, R. M., "Socratic Definitions and Moral Neutrality," *Journal of Philosophy* 61 (1964), 433–50.

Gould, Th., "Socrates as an Existentialist," *Arion* 3 (1964), 112–15.

Greenberg, N. A., "Socrates' Choice in the *Crito*," *Harvard Studies in Classic Philosophy* 70 (1965), 45–82.

Grube, G., "The Structural Unity of the *Protagoras*," *Classical Quarterly* 27 (1933), 203–7.

Gulley, N., "The Interpretation of 'No one does wrong willingly' in Plato's Dialogues," *Phronesis* 10 (1965), 82–96.

Hackforth, R., "Socrates," *Philosophy* 11 (1933), 259–72.

——, "Hedonism in Plato's *Protagoras*," *Classical Quarterly* 22 (1928), 39 ff.

Hall, J. C., "Plato: *Euth.* 10A1–11A10," *Philosophical Quarterly* 18 (1968), 1–11.

Havelock, E., "The Evidence for the Teaching of Socrates," *Trans. of the American Philological Association* 65 (1934), 282–95.

——, "Why was Socrates tried?" *Phoenix* Supplement 1 (Studies in honor of Gilbert Norwood), 1952, 95–108.

Hoerber, R. G., "Plato's *Euthyphro*," "Plato's *Lysis*," "Plato's *Lesser Hippias*," "Plato's *Greater Hippias*," *Phronesis* 3 (1958), 95 ff.; 4 (1959), 15 ff.; 7 (1962), 121 ff.; 9 (1964), 143 ff.

Jackson, H., "Socrates," *Encyclopaedia Britannica,* Eleventh Edition, Vol. XXIX (London, 1911), 331–38.

Kidd, I. G., "Socrates," *Encyclopedia of Philosophy,* Vol. IX (New York, 1967), 480–86.

Laguna, Th. de, "The Interpretation of the *Apology*," *Philosophical Review* 18 (1909), 23–27.

Mulhern, J. J., "*Tropos* and *polytropia* in Plato's *Hippias Minor*," *Phoenix* 22 (1968), 283–88.

O'Brien, M. J., "The 'Fallacy' in *Prot.* 349D–350C," *Trans. of the American Philological Association* 92 (1961), 408–17.

Savan, D., "Self-predication in Protagoras 330–31," *Phronesis* 9 (1964), 130–35.

——, "Socrates' Logic and the Unity of Wisdom and Temperance," in R. J. Butler, ed., *Analytical Philosophy,* Vol. II (Oxford, 1965), 20–26.

Sparshott, F. E., "Socrates and Thrasymachus," *Monist* 50 (1966), 421–59.

Stocks, J. L., "The Argument of Plato, *Prot.* 351A–356C," *Classical Quarterly* 7 (1913), 100 ff.

Strycker, E. de, "The Unity of Knowledge and Love in Socrates' Conception of Virtue," *International Philosophical Quarterly* 6 (1966), 428–44.

Sullivan, J. P., "The Hedonism in Plato's *Protagoras*," *Phronesis* 6 (1961), 9–28.

Vogel, C. de, "Who was Socrates?" *Journal of the History of Philosophy* 1 (1963), 143–61.

Woodbury, L., "Simonides on Arete," *Trans. of the American Philological Association* 84 (1953), 135–63.

# INDEX LOCORUM

(Passages in Aristophanes, Aristotle, Plato and Xenophon)

Plato (*cont'd*)

| Apology | 41D | 7, 210 |
|---|---|---|
| Apology | 41D7–8 | 226 |
| Charmides | 159A | 124, 331 |
| Charmides | 159B | 321 |
| Charmides | 159B–160D | 215 |
| Charmides | 159C | 202 |
| Charmides | 160D | 95 |
| Charmides | 160D6–E4 | 226 |
| Charmides | 160E | 131, 138, 141 |
| Charmides | 160E–161B | 131 |
| Charmides | 164D ff. | 213 |
| Charmides | 165B | 79 |
| Charmides | 165D | 10 |
| Charmides | 166C–D | 9, 331 |
| Charmides | 167C | 101 |
| Charmides | 170 | 100 |
| Charmides | 170C1–D9 | 226 |
| Charmides | 171E5–7 | 225 |
| Charmides | 175E | 323 |
| Cratylus | 291B | 57 |
| Cratylus | 384B | 57 |
| Cratylus | 391B | 57 |
| Cratylus | 391C | 56 |
| Crito | 44B | 309 |
| Crito | 44B–48D | 308 |
| Crito | 44C–E | 309 |
| Crito | 44D | 310 |
| Crito | 45C | 309 |
| Crito | 46B–C | 303 |
| Crito | 46D–48A | 309 |
| Crito | 47D–E | 211, 233 |
| Crito | 48C | 211, 309, 310 |
| Crito | 49A | 306 |
| Crito | 49B | 311 |
| Crito | 49B–C | 311 |
| Crito | 49B–54D | 308 |
| Crito | 49D | 11 |
| Crito | 49E | 11, 314 |
| Crito | 50B | 300, 305, 306, 312, 315, 317 |
| Crito | 50C | 39, 300, 301 |
| Crito | 50D | 312 |
| Crito | 51–52 | 308 |
| Crito | 51A | 313 |
| Crito | 51C | 306 |
| Crito | 51D | 314 |
| Crito | 51E | 312 |